Baseball Research Journal

Volume 49, Number 2
Fall 2020

Published by the Society for American Baseball Research

BASEBALL RESEARCH JOURNAL, Volume 49, Number 2

Editor: Cecilia M. Tan
Design and Production: Lisa Hochstein
Cover Illustration and Design: Gary Joseph Cieradkowski, StudioGaryC.Com
Copyediting assistance: Allison Schaum, Patrick Murray
Proofreader: Norman L. Macht
Fact Checker: Clifford Blau

Published by:
Society for American Baseball Research, Inc.
Cronkite School at ASU
555 N. Central Ave. #416
Phoenix, AZ 85004

Phone: (602) 496–1460
Web: www.sabr.org
Twitter: @sabr
Facebook: Society for American Baseball Research

Contents

Note from the Editor

Historians start your engines. The events of the year 2020 cry out for documentation. While living through it, some of us may have struggled to make sense of it all, but perhaps in hindsight it will become clear. If the accounts we leave behind are accurate, a hundred years from now folks like us will look back and be able to understand the otherwise surreal-seeming snapshots that will be archived from this past month alone: the people sitting at restaurant tables next to parking meters, the surgical masks around the necks of the World Series champions during their on-field celebration, the presidential legal team setting up a podium in a landscaper's parking lot.

Write it down. Take screencaps. Photograph it. Make clippings from the newspapers. Archive PDFs. You may think we have such a plethora of information sources these days that these steps are hardly necessary. But look how much about the 1918 pandemic was forgotten, despite that being the heyday of American newspapers, when many Americans read several a day and every city had numerous papers competing.

And there will be many who will want to "forget" the strain and darkness of baseball in 2020—what I've been calling The Irregular Season. The truncated spring training, the bitter labor tussle between owners and players that resulted in a mere 60-game season, the outbreaks of COVID-19 among Miami Marlins and then other teams—with Justin Turner of the Dodgers even receiving a positive test result during the clinching game of the World Series. Teams and MLB were forced to improvise, with rules and procedures, and even schedules and travel itineraries, changing on the fly. Alternate sites, taxi squads, the Blue Jays playing in upstate New York, broadcasters working from their home parks while the teams were away, the press scrum happening via Zoom, The Irregular Season really happened. Maybe the super-short season was a blessing, sandwiched between the spring and winter COVID-19 infection surges. Hindsight will tell. Write it all down now because piecing it together later is going to be a bear.

We're going to be analyzing the effects of 2020 for years to come. How many players will find their careers affected by it? The minor leagues were shut down and so were (most) college sports. The major leagues saw an off-the-charts number of players sidelined with injuries. Some big leaguers opted out of playing entirely; a few decided to have surgery during the interregnum. I expect many SABR members out there, as well as decision-makers in front offices around the league, are already starting to analyze and predict the effects.

Baseball's economics have been affected, too. Large numbers of front-office employees have been laid off in the wake of the lost 2020 revenue. This will surely reverberate through the upcoming negotiation of the Collective Bargaining Agreement. What changes might be wrought in the way teams do things or the way the league operates, born in reaction to 2020 but having repercussions for decades? The article that anchors this issue of the journal, appearing last, is Richard Hershberger's account of the "First Baseball War," in which the nineteenth-century clash between leagues contributed to the creation of the reserve system that suppressed free agency until the late twentieth.

In 2020 we also saw massive, nationwide protests against police brutality and racial injustice, and we saw baseball players and the league itself take unprecedented steps to acknowledge racial injustice in the United States. The commissioner's office already has a department that has been actively addressing issues relating to diversity and inclusion in ways that would have been unheard of even two decades ago. Will the pandemic-driven layoffs from front offices hurt the initiatives toward more hiring of women and underrepresented racial and ethnic minorities that the league has been promoting? (Probably.) But 2020 also gave us two other unprecedented firsts: Kim Ng has been hired as the first woman general manager of an MLB team as well as the first Asian American GM, and Alyssa Nakken is the first woman in uniform to take the field as part of the coaching staff of a major league team, the San Francisco Giants. She is joined by a bevy of women coaching and instructing in the minors—Rachel Balkovec for the Yankees, Rachel Folden for the Cubs, Christina Whitlock for the Cardinals… except that in 2020 there were no minor league seasons.

History is always being made; that is SABR's stock in trade. But in a watershed year, the changes come fast and thick. I haven't even mentioned the fact that during the year 2020 the minor leagues as we knew them didn't merely miss this season: they ceased to exist. On September 30, the agreement between MLB and the affiliated minor leagues expired, and MLB has unilaterally imposed control, eliminating 40 of 160 teams with one fell swoop. At the same time, MLB has been courting partnerships with the independent leagues, using the Atlantic League in 2019 as a testing ground for rules changes that were put into practice in MLB in 2020.

And I haven't even mentioned all the rules changes! Are 2020's universal DH and extra-innings procedures a harbinger of things to come? But this introduction is already twice as long as usual. To sum up: we're going to be writing about, talking about, and researching 2020 for a very long time, and not "just" about baseball. Every one of these changes in baseball can be tied to a parallel in American life or society, from adapting to the pandemic to advances for women's equality, from the fight for racial justice to the fight for raising the minimum wage. Even the consolidation of control of the minor leagues is in line with late-stage capitalist corporate practices, including vertical integration and end-to-end lifecycle production. The World Series may have been played in a "bubble" but baseball doesn't exist in a vacuum.

Which isn't to say that one can't write about "just" baseball. Plenty of articles in this issue are compelling and intriguing without invoking geopolitics. I would be captivated by Theo Tobel's breakdown of brushback pitches even without knowing that he is a high-school student taking part in remote learning due to the pandemic. Randy Robbins noticed a statistical quirk in the record of Warren Spahn and it prompted an examination of one of the game's pitching greats. Will Melville and Brinley Zabriskie undertake the task of trying to determine how much benefit, if any, the 2017 Astros derived from their cheating efforts, while Irwin Nahinsky analyzes the effects of luck and skill on team success.

But so many pieces of baseball history and analysis can't help but be tied to a bigger world, and I find many of them to be bittersweet this time around: Ron Backer looks at Lou Gehrig in a new light—klieg lights, in fact—in his article on Gehrig's Hollywood career, which like his life and playing career was cut short by ALS. Mary Hums and her team document MLB's decision to change the name of the "disabled list" to "injured list," including the advocacy and rationale behind the change, and an analysis of fan reactions to it. Charlie Pavitt delves into the fact that a player's ethnicity can be a predictor for what position he plays in MLB. Howard M. Wasserman examines Jewish players through the lens of their performances on Yom Kippur, while Alan Cohen examines one of the great hitters of all time, Josh Gibson. Because of racial segregation, Gibson never had the opportunity to play in the major leagues, but because many Negro League teams did play games in major league ballparks, we can look at those performances to prove how prodigious he truly was.

I don't know what the 2021 season holds in store. Whether the season starts on time, or happens at all, may depend on medical science (vaccines) and on geopolitical and logistical issues (how quickly vaccine doses can be distributed to the populace). I just know that as I write this, 2020 isn't quite over yet, and we won't be "closing the book" on it for a long time.

— Cecilia Tan
Publications Director
November 2020

Josh Gibson Blazes a Trail

Homering in Big League Ballparks, 1930–1946

Alan Cohen

> Josh missed immortality and a chance to endorse breakfast food by being born on the wrong side of the social structure.[1]
>
> —Jimmy Powers, *New York Daily News*, 1937

Josh Gibson was the most dominant power hitter in the Negro Leagues from 1930 through 1946. His production was so prodigious that his Hall of Fame plaque reads he had almost 800 home runs. Unfortunately, documentation is limited. Teams barnstormed across the country, playing wherever the bus stopped. Black newspapers, for the most part, appeared weekly and had details of relatively few games. White newspapers sometimes took notice, but the articles about games in rural areas were not particularly detailed. However, when the Negro League teams were given the opportunity to play in big league ballparks, the coverage in the media was more significant, and fans—both Black and White—saw that Josh Gibson was capable of homering anywhere and everywhere. Writers in mainstream newspapers from New York in the East to Chicago in the Midwest joined with Black mainstays such as the *Pittsburgh Courier* and *Chicago Defender* in lauding Gibson's power.

Josh Gibson first set foot in a big league park as an 18-year-old in 1930, as a member of the Homestead Grays. He played at Forbes Field and Yankee Stadium that year. Legend has it that one of his homers sailed out of Yankee Stadium in 1934 (or was it 1930?) and that two of his homers cleared the back left field bleacher wall at Griffith Stadium. It was also asserted in the *Philadelphia Inquirer* and reported in an Associated Press release that, after he homered in Philadelphia's Shibe Park on July 18, 1944, he had hit at least one home run in each of the ten big league ballparks in which he played up to that point in his career.[2] Later, newspapers including the *Washington Post* and *Philadelphia Inquirer* would claim that he had homered in every big league ballpark in which he played.

How true are these legends? What is the real story? Gibson's records are incomplete as he played most of his games beyond the spotlight of the big league arenas, and there was not a premium on keeping score beyond the tally of runs. In this article, Josh Gibson's feats at big league ballparks will be documented and establish that he *did* homer at every big league park in which he played—all 15.

In the early years of his career, most games played in big league cities were not contested in major league parks. Black owners staged games in other venues, whether because of the high rental fees or racism on the part of owners of the big league ballparks. Also, during the early part of Gibson's career, most big league ballparks did not have lights, while Negro League games were often played at night. In New York, Dexter Park and Dyckman Oval were used for most Negro League games. In Pittsburgh, games were held at Greenlee Field. In Philadelphia, games were held at the 44th and Parkside Ballpark (also known as the Bolden Bowl).

AMERICAN GIANTS PARK

In Chicago, many games were held at the American Giants Park (previously known as South Side Park, Schlorling's Park, and Cole's Park) at the intersection of 39th Street and Wentworth Avenue. American Giants Park had been, two decades earlier, the home of the Chicago White Sox. The White Sox took up residence at South Side Park in 1900, when they moved from St. Paul, then moved to Comiskey Park in 1910. The Negro Chicago American Giants moved into the ballpark in 1911 and remained there through 1940. Gibson first played there in 1930 when the Grays defeated the Chicago American Giants in five of six games between September 5 and September 8. While with the Crawfords, he played there in 1932 and 1934. His best effort was on June 17, 1934, when he went 3-for-4 with a pair of doubles in the second game of a doubleheader.[3]

In 1937, Gibson homered at American Giants Park. On Sunday August 29, the Grays visited the American

Giants and took both games. In the opener—won by the Grays, 4–2—Gibson homered on a 3–1 pitch in the sixth inning. The ball flew over the left field fence to give the Grays a 2–1 lead.[4]

FORBES FIELD AND YANKEE STADIUM

Gibson's professional career had begun in 1929 with the Pittsburgh Crawfords. The Crawfords would not be taken over by Gus Greenlee until 1931, and at the time Gibson played for them, they were not yet the power-house team that they would become. They played their home games at Ammon Field in Pittsburgh and went 63–11 against less-than-stellar opposition.[5] On July 25, 1930, Gibson joined the Homestead Grays, the pre-eminent Negro team, and hit nine homers with them over the balance of the season, his first coming on August 22 at Akron in a 16–5 win over the Detroit Stars.[6] (Not long after joining the Grays, tragedy stuck when Gibson's wife died while giving birth to twins on August 20.[7])

Against the Baltimore Blacksox on September 13, he homered in each game of a doubleheader at Forbes Field. He made his Yankee Stadium debut on September 21. His first Yankee Stadium homer, a blast into the left-field bleachers, came in the eighth game of the Negro League World Series on September 27. His three-run first inning homer traveled an estimated 460 feet to the bleachers in left-center field, and gave the Grays the lead as they went on to defeat the Lincoln Giants, 7–3, for their fifth win of the series.[8] Per the *Baltimore Afro-American*, "it was the longest home run that has been hit at the Yankee Stadium by any player, white or colored, all season."[9] The next day, he doubled in the second game as the Grays took that contest to win the series six games to four.[10,11]

One of his best-remembered home runs took place at Forbes Field on October 23, 1934, when the Crawfords barnstormed with the Dizzy Dean All Stars. After an interruption in the game—a bench-clearing brawl that even the fans joined in on—play resumed with Dean's team leading, 3–1, but the Crawfords came back to win, 4–3. Their game-winning, two-out, eighth-inning rally featured a double by manager Oscar Charleston, a Gibson homer, a triple by Judy Johnson, and a single by Curtis Harris.[12] Gibson's homer, one of his longest, cleared the wall in left field.

CLEVELAND STADIUM AND LEAGUE PARK

Gibson rejoined the Pittsburgh Crawfords in 1932. Crawfords' owner Gus Greenlee sent his squad barnstorming, making occasional stops at big league ballparks. At the time, there were two major league ballparks in Cleveland—League Park and Cleveland Stadium. Gibson homered at each. In a doubleheader against the Cleveland Cubs on June 19, 1932, Gibson powered a homer out of Cleveland Stadium. The next year, at League Park on July 23, 1933, the Crawfords defeated the Chicago American Giants in a double-header. In the first game, Gibson had three hits—all singles—as the Crawfords won, 8–1. Chicago's only run was a ninth-inning homer by Alex Radcliffe. The second game went to the Crawfords, 13–12, in 12 innings. Gibson tripled and homered in the game, bringing the total of big league ballparks in which he had homered to four.[13] He was far from finished with his tour.

EBBETS FIELD

Gibson's first appearances at Ebbets Field were in 1935 when the Crawfords visited the Brooklyn Eagles, owned by the husband-wife team of Abe and Effa Manley. They played on July 13–14, and a Gibson clout in the first game of a doubleheader on July 14 gave him homers in two of the three New York ball-parks. Gibson started in three of the five games played by the Crawfords at Ebbets Field in 1935. In those games, he went a combined 7-for-12.

The Eagles moved to Newark after the 1935 season and over the next several years the Negro League baseball played in Brooklyn was between out-of-town teams. Most of the games were at Dexter Park but Ebbets Field was used on occasion. On September 6, 1942, the Homestead Grays played the Newark Eagles there. The Grays won, 4–2, and Gibson stroked his second Ebbets-Field homer.[14]

ORIOLE PARK

At the end of the 1937 season, the Negro League World Series was held between the Grays and the Chicago American Giants. Ten games were played, and nine ballparks were used. On September 26, the teams split a doubleheader at Oriole Park in Baltimore. Although Baltimore was not a big league city in 1937 and would not host an American League game until 1954, Baltimore had been in the Federal League in 1914–15 and had used Oriole Park, then known as Terrapin Park, for its home games. Hence, when Gibson homered there in a 14–11 loss on September 26, he had added another big league park to his list. For those counting, the list, with the additions of American Giants Park and Oriole Park, stood at eight at the end of 1937.

GRIFFITH STADIUM

Gibson's first homer at Griffith Stadium came on June 28, 1931, in a 5–2 Grays' win over Hilldale.[15] But Griffith

Gibson began his career with the Crawfords in 1929, then rejoined them in 1932 after a stint with the Grays.

Stadium would be the proving ground that defined Gibson's greatness as a home-run hitter. Witness his performance there eight years later, on July 16, 1939. As writer Sam Lacy said, "The first contest ended 8–7 in favor of the Grays, largely because of Gibson, and the nightcap concluded with a score of 6–5 in favor of the Stars in spite of Gibson."[16] In the bottom half of the ninth inning of the opener his second homer of the game broke a 7–7 tie and gave the Grays the win over the Philadelphia Stars. In the second game his second-inning homer left the stadium completely. He also tripled during the course of the doubleheader split with the Stars.[17]

After the 1939 season, Gibson left the Negro Leagues to play ball in Mexico, not returning to the Grays full-time until 1942. But he did appear with the Grays for one doubleheader at Griffith Stadium in 1940 and, to nobody's great surprise, hit a home run. In the first game of a doubleheader on August 18, his two-run blast capped a five-run rally and the Grays went on to win, 6–4, over the Philadelphia Stars.[18] By the time he returned to the Grays in 1942, the team was using Forbes Field for Saturday home games and Griffith Stadium for Sunday home games. Gibson had his only Griffith Stadium homer of the season on May 17 in a 6–5 loss to the Baltimore Elite Giants.

What Josh Gibson did at Griffith Stadium in 1943 boggles the mind. The reality of it all dwarfs the myth!

According to myth, Gibson had more homers at Griffith Stadium in 1943 than all of the visiting American League teams had, combined, against the Washington Nationals. So, again we ask about the real story. Although he did not quite hit more homers than the visiting teams, the story of the 1943 season is compelling.

In April, 1943, not a single home run was hit at Griffith Stadium—by anyone, Black or White.

In a doubleheader against the Philadelphia Stars in May, he was prolific. In the opener, he singled and doubled in the first game win, and doubled, tripled, and homered in the second game as the Grays completed the sweep in DC. His homer was reported to have traveled 440 feet. On the day, he was 5-for-8. He scored four runs and drove in seven.[19] And, on May 31, he was just showing off. The Grays demolished the Baltimore Elite Giants, 17–0. Gibson went 5-for-6 with two homers. The first one, a solo shot in the second inning, gave his team the lead. The second homer, a grand slam, put the icing on the cake in the seventh inning.[20]

Through the end of May, Gibson thus had three homers at Griffith Stadium. The entirety of the American League, in 18 games, had two, courtesy of Charlie Keller and Bobby Doerr.

And Gibson was far from finished. On June 20 against the Kansas City Monarchs and Satchel Paige, Gibson unleashed even more fury. In the opener, he went 4-for-5 with a pair of doubles as the Grays won 10–2. They had blown Paige away with a five-run first inning. In the second game, Gibson went 2-for-4 with two more doubles as the Grays won, 7–6.[21]

The Grays first played in Homestead, Pennsylvania, in 1912 and still played many games each season in the Pittsburgh area. On June 23, 1943, at Forbes Field, Gibson hit another of his signature blasts. This one sailed an estimated 20 feet over the left field scoreboard and gave the Grays a 2–1 first inning lead against the Kansas City Monarchs. The Grays went on to win, 8–3, as Gibson hit his sixth homer in 10 games.[22]

As June ended, Gibson's count at Griffith Stadium was five, as was that of the visiting American League teams. Rudy York had hit two homers for the Tigers and Elmer Valo had hit a homer for the Athletics.

Fireworks on the Fourth of July? Of course! On July 4, the Grays hosted the Newark Eagles at Griffith Stadium and swept the doubleheader by scores of 6–2 and 6–5. Gibson went 1-for-2 in the opener and then, in the seventh inning of the second game with his team trailing, 5–4, slammed a 430-foot two-run homer with Buck Leonard aboard to give the Grays the 6–5 win. For the day, he was 3-for-4 with a triple and the homer in the second game.[23]

Over the next two days the Brooklyn Bushwicks visited the Grays at each of the Grays' home fields. On July 5, the Grays took two games at Forbes Field by scores of 5–4 and 8–5. The first game went 12 innings, and the Grays' winning run scored when pitcher Edsall Walker executed a perfect squeeze play scoring Howard Easterling.[24] Gibson extended his newest hitting streak to eight games with hits in each game. Brooklyn's first game pitcher, Bots Nekola, left the game after the tenth inning.[25] Nekola had two brief tenures in the major leagues. He was in nine game with the 1929 Yankees and two games with the 1933 Detroit Tigers. After his playing days, he scouted for the Red Sox from 1949 through 1976.

The next evening, the Bushwicks traveled with the Grays to Griffith Stadium. The Bushwicks were a top semi-pro team and their lineup featured three men who played in the major leagues. In addition to Nekola, Al Cuccinello had played 54 games with the 1935 New York Giants, and Wally Holborow, a pitcher, would pitch for the Washington Nationals, appearing in nine games at Griffith Stadium in 1945. Gibson did not let up. He tripled and homered as the Grays won, 11–3.[26]

Through July 14, Gibson had seven homers at Griffith Stadium as opposed to five for the visiting American League teams. But then the Nationals had a long homestand during which the visiting clubs had four homers. At the end of July the American League's visiting teams had two more homers than Gibson.

In August, when the Grays returned to Griffith Stadium, Gibson homered against Newark and Baltimore to bring the count in Washington to nine. But by then, the count for the visiting clubs was up to 11.

On August 21, 1943, at Forbes Field, Gibson had three hits including a triple in the first game 9–1 win over the Baltimore Elite Giants. In the second game, his two homers drove in all his team's runs in a 4–1 win.[27]

On September 2 at Griffith Stadium, Gibson was honored and presented with a trophy.

On September 12, 1943, he hit his 10th and final Griffith Stadium homer of the season. He fell four short of the number posted by the visiting American League teams. However, he did hit more than the Washington Nationals. They only had nine for the season in 76 games. Gibson's came in only 38 games in Washington. To underscore his dominance as a home-run hitter that season at Griffith Stadium, only three homers were hit by Black players not named Josh Gibson. To underscore how difficult it was to hit home runs there, compare the nine homers the Senators hit at their home ballpark with their 38 on the road.

In 1945 Gibson once again had more homers at Griffith Stadium than the Nationals. He had five and the Nationals only had one, an inside-the-park homer by Joe Kuhel.

As far as some of Gibson's homers traveled at Griffith Stadium, only the one on July 16, 1939, went beyond the rear wall.

The final home run of Gibson's career was also hit at Griffith Stadium, on September 15, 1946. It came in the first game of a doubleheader against the New York

Gibson is seen here about to cross home plate at Griffith Stadium, in a game against the Newark Eagles in 1942.

NATIONAL BASEBALL HALL OF FAME AND LIBRARY, COOPERSTOWN, NY

Cubans. It was his 27th career homer at that ballpark. It is estimated that he played in 152 games there. His production (one homer per 5.63 games) is slightly less than that of Babe Ruth, who had 34 homers in 171 games (one per 5.03 games) at that ballpark.

Of those players with at least 20 homers at Griffith Stadium, the player with the best home run frequency was Rocky Colavito. He had 24 homers in 57 games (one per 2.375 games). The second-most-frequent slugger at Griffith Stadium was Mickey Mantle. He had 29 homers in 98 games (one per 3.38 games).

Here is what other noted sluggers did at Griffith Stadium:

- **Joe DiMaggio**: 30 homers (one per 4.17 games)

- **Harmon Killebrew**: 41 homers (one per 4.80 games)

- **Roy Sievers**: 91 homers (one per 5.14 games)

- **Jimmie Foxx**: 27 homers (one per 5.78 games)

- **Ted Williams**: 23 homers (one per 6.83 games)

- **Lou Gehrig**: 22 homers (one per 7.18 games)

WRIGLEY FIELD

Gibson got to display his talents at Chicago's Wrigley Field on August 29, 1943. The Grays played the Kansas City Monarchs. In the first inning, against former teammate Satchel Paige, he hit a three-run homer to give his team the early lead. He also doubled, singled twice, and walked as the Crawfords went on to win, 10–4.[29]

POLO GROUNDS

In 1944, Gibson added New York's Polo Grounds to the list, hitting two homers in a game on July 16. The game was halted by rain in the ninth inning. The game had been tied, 6–6, after eight innings, and the Grays, with Gibson hitting a triple, had scored three runs in the ninth when the rains came. The score reverted to 6–6 and the ninth inning rally was washed away.[30]

SHIBE PARK

Two days later, Gibson hit a three-run homer that traveled 405 feet in an 11–4 win over the Baltimore Elite Giants in the first game of a doubleheader at Philadelphia's Shibe Park. His first ever Shibe Park blast came in the first inning as the Grays scored five times.[31]

COMISKEY PARK

Although Gibson's hitting performance was prodigious in several appearances, it would take Gibson a bit of time to add Chicago's Comiskey Park to his list. Negro Baseball's East-West All Star game was contested at Comiskey Park beginning in 1933, and although Gibson batted .483 (14-for-29) in 9 East-West appearances in the Windy City, he did not have a home run. In the 1935 East-West Game, Gibson had four hits in his first five at-bats and came to the plate in the 11th inning with Cool Papa Bell on second base. There were two outs at the time. The opposition wanted no part of Gibson, and he was intentionally walked, setting the stage for a game-winning homer by Mule Suttles.[32] Chicago's Negro American League team, the Chicago American Giants, played games at Comiskey Park beginning in 1941. On August 13, 1944, in the East-West Game, Gibson's long, seventh-inning double in front of 46,247 fans was not enough to offset a big five-run fifth inning by the West squad. The West won the game, 7–4. It was not until July 21, 1946, that Gibson finally connected for a homer at Comiskey. In front of an estimated 10,000 fans, he homered in the sixth inning of the second game of a doubleheader. His three-run shot highlighted a four-run inning that erased a Chicago American Giants' 3–0 lead and propelled the Homestead Grays to a 9–7 win.[33]

BRIGGS STADIUM

Gibson did not get the opportunity to play in Detroit's Briggs Stadium until 1945. Although Detroit fielded Negro League teams in the early part of Gibson's career, it was not until 1941 that the Grays played at Briggs Stadium. That season, Gibson was in Mexico. They returned to Briggs Stadium for a doubleheader in 1945. On June 3, the Grays shut out the Baltimore Elite Giants by scores of 1–0 and 5–0. Gibson's double keyed a ninth-inning rally that produced the only run in the opener. In the second game, he homered to add Briggs Stadium to his remarkable list.[34]

SPORTSMAN'S PARK

Gibson got only one opportunity to play at Sportsman's Park in St. Louis, as for most of his career, St. Louis did not have a team in the Negro Leagues. The St. Louis Stars, when they were in the Negro Leagues, did not play at Sportsman's Park. A Negro team had first appeared at Sportsman's Park after the 1921 season when a barnstorming group of St. Louis Cardinals played four games against the St. Louis Colored Giants. The first Negro League game at Sportsman's Park took place on July 4, 1941, when the Chicago American Giants played the Kansas City Monarchs.[35] Gibson finally played at the ballpark on July 9, 1946, in a doubleheader between the Homestead Grays and the Cleveland Buckeyes. The crowd of 19,774 sat through a rain delay in the third inning of the first game. At the time there was no score. But the Grays won the first game, 12–2, with Gibson going 4-for-5. The second game did not start until 11:20PM and they were only able to play two and one-half innings before the midnight curfew. The Grays scored nine runs in their two times at bat, three coming on a homer by Gibson, Although the game, not having gone five innings, was not technically official, Gibson's homer was very much real.[36]

OTHER MAJOR LEAGUE PARKS

Gibson did not play in Boston. The Massachusetts city was not in the Negro Leagues, although the Boston Royal Giants did play in the Negro minor leagues. There is no hard evidence that the Royal Giants played at Braves Field or Fenway Park. There is no record of their playing against either the Grays or Crawfords. Gibson's barnstorming travels with the Grays and Crawfords never took him beyond Hartford, Connecticut when his teams played in New England. On May 26, 1944, the Grays played at Fenway Park, defeating Fore River, 1–0. Gibson didn't play. His replacement, Robert Gaston, drove in the only run of the game with a sixth-inning single off the wall in left field.[37]

In Philadelphia, he often played at Shibe Park, but never appeared at the Baker Bowl.

CROSLEY FIELD

Only one major league park remains. Did he ever homer at Cincinnati's Crosley Field?

Gibson's first appearance in Cincinnati was on August 23, 1933, and the game with Chicago was held at Crosley Field, then known as Redland Field. He went 1-for-4 as the Crawfords lost to Chicago, 6–2, but did not homer. Following the first East-West Game at Comiskey Park in 1933, the teams traveled to Redland Field for a rematch on September 14. Unfortunately, the game was rained out. Documentation of Gibson's appearances in Cincinnati is elusive. During his time with the Crawfords, and later with the Grays, Cincinnati was not regularly represented in the Negro Leagues, and there is a significant question as to whether or not Gibson homered at Crosley Field.

There is strong anecdotal evidence that he homered there. Chester Washington of the *Pittsburgh Courier* declared in 1941 that Gibson had hit the longest home run at Cincinnati's Crosley Field.[38] Barnstorming was not as commonplace during the 1930s as it had been during the prior decade, but there were still tours that crisscrossed the country each October. In 1939, during an interview, Leo Durocher remembered an encounter at Crosley Field:

About two years ago, I played against Josh Gibson in Cincinnati and found that everything they say about him is true, and then some. In that game in Cincinnati, Josh hit one of the longest balls I've ever seen. Josh caught hold of one of Monte Weaver's fast ones, and I'll bet you it's still sailing. Boy, how he could hit that ball![39]

CONCLUSION

When Gibson added Sportsman's Park and Comiskey Park to his list in 1946, Jackie Robinson was playing for Montreal. Gibson would not live to see the first Black man play in the big leagues in the twentieth century. Gibson died on January 20, 1947. The travels of Josh Gibson forge a path of great achievement, but during his lifetime he was not as well-known as contemporary major league sluggers. At the Hall of Fame Induction ceremony in 1966, Ted Williams urged the Hall of Fame to open its doors to Negro League ballplayers. Gibson's greatness was acknowledged with his induction into the Hall of Fame in 1972. On July 6, 2000, a stamp with Gibson's image was issued by the United States Postal Service as part of its *Legends of Baseball* series. ∎

Sources

In addition to the sources shown in the notes, the author used Baseball-Reference.com, Seamheads.com, and the following:

Burick, Si. "Si-ings: Time (Magazine) Points Out," Josh Gibson of Homestead Grays as One of Greatest Sluggers of Pastime," *Dayton Daily News*, July 21, 1943:12.

Jones, Lucius Melancholy. "Sports Slants," *Atlanta Daily World*, August 16, 1942:8.

Snyder, Brad. "Black Baseball's Return Caught On," *Detroit Free Press*, March 21, 2008:4E.

Washington, Chester. "Sez Ches," *Pittsburgh Courier*, February 22, 1941:16.

Notes

1. Jimmy Powers, "The Powerhouse," *New York Daily News*, September 18, 1937, 27.
2. "Grays Jar Giants; Tie Stars, 4–4," *Philadelphia Inquirer*, July 19, 1944, 24.
3. Al Monroe, "Giants Drop Crawfords from Lead," *Chicago Defender*, June 23, 1934, 17.
4. "Giants Drop 2 to Grays: Gibson Stars," *Chicago Defender*, September 4, 1937, 19.
5. William Forsythe, Jr., "Jolly's Jottings," *Pittsburgh Courier*, August 31, 1929.
6. "Grays Defeat Stars by 16–5," *Akron Beacon Journal*, August 23, 1930, 16.
7. "Wife of Homestead Gray Catcher Dies," *Pittsburgh Courier*, August 23, 1930, 4 (second section), and "Helen Gibson," *Baltimore Afro-American*, August 30, 1930, 18.
8. W. Rollo Wilson, "Grays Win Eastern World Series," *Pittsburgh Courier*, October 4, 1930, 2–5.
9. "Giants Drop Championship," *Baltimore Afro-American*, October 4, 1930, 15.
10. "Lincolns Split; Grays Capture Colored Title," *New York Daily News*, September 29, 1930, 38.

11. Gibson also homered at Philadelphia's Bigler Field as the Grays won the fifth game, 11–3. As described in the *Philadelphia Tribune*, Gibson "clouted the longest home-run ever seen at Bigler Field, the ball clearing the leftfield fence and even the roofs across Bigler Street."; "Rivals Divide Double Bill Here; Grays Win 11–3, Lincolns on Top 6 to 4," *Philadelphia Tribune*, October 2, 1930, 10.

12. Balinger.

13. "Crawfords Trip Colored Rivals," *Cleveland Plain Dealer*, July 24, 1933,: 17.

14. William E. Clark, "Grays Clinch Pennant in Final Series with Eagles," *New York Age*, September 12, 1942, 11.

15. "Hilldale Series Thrills; Grays Set for Balto.," *Pittsburgh Courier*, July 4, 1931, A5–A6

16. San Lacy, "Josh Gibson Clouts 3 Homers as Grays Divide," *Baltimore Afro-American*, July 22, 1939, 22.

17. "Grays' Catcher Hits 3 Homers; Team Takes 2," *Washington Post*, July 17, 1939, 14.

18. "Homestead Grays Take Doubleheader," *Washington Post*, August 19, 1940, 18.

19. "Grays Defeat Stars, 9–3, 8–2," *Pittsburgh Post-Gazette*, May 24, 1943, 16, and "Homestead Grays Knock off Philadelphia Stars in Two Tilts," *New York Amsterdam News*, May 29, 1943, 15.

20. "Josh Gibson's Homers Help Grays Win," *Washington Post*, June 1, 1943, 15.

21. Harold Jackson, "Grays Take Two from Monarchs," *Baltimore Afro-American*, June 26, 1943, 23.

22. Paul Kurtz, "Gibson's Bat Spurs Grays to 8–3 Win," *Pittsburgh Press*, June 24, 1943, 24, and Al Abrams, "10,350 See Grays Defeat Monarchs in Night Game," *Pittsburgh Post-Gazette*, June 24, 1943, 15.

23. "Grays Twice Victors over Newark Nine," *Washington Post*, July 5, 1943, 11.

24. "Grays Win Twice, 5–4, 8–5," *Pittsburgh Post-Gazette*, July 6, 1943, 15.

25. "Bushwicks Set for Cubans After Road Trip," *Brooklyn Daily Eagle*, July 6, 1943, 14.

26. "Grays' Blasts Beat Bushwick Here by 11 to 3," *Washington Post*, July 7, 1943, 16.

27. "Gibson Stars as Grays Win," *Pittsburgh Sun-Telegraph*, August 22, 1943, 2–3.

28. "Grays Murder Ball to Win 5 Over Weekend: To Honor Josh Gibson, Home Run King, at Stadium," *New Journal and Guide* (Norfolk, Virginia), August 28, 1943, B19.

29. "Paige Shelled off Hill as Grays Win," *Chicago Sun*, August 30, 1943, 17.

30. "Cubans Tie Grays, 6–6," *The New York Times*, July 17, 1944, 10, and "Cubans, Grays Tie, 6–6; Rains Cancels Twin Bill," *New York Age*, July 22, 1944, 11.

31. "Grays Jar Giants; Tie Stars, 4–4," *Philadelphia Inquirer*, July 19, 1944, 24.

32. "East-West Game Draws 25,000 Fans—West Wins," *Chicago World*, August 10, 1935: 7.

33. "Homestead Nine Wins Two from Negro Giants," *Chicago Tribune*, July 22, 1946: 26.

34. "Grays Win Pair," *Pittsburgh Sun Telegraph*, June 4, 1945: 14.

35. "19,178 Fans See Negro Twin Bill," *St. Louis Globe Democrat*, July 5, 1941: 9

36. John Hagar, "Grays Pound Bracken, Beat Buckeyes, 12–2," *St. Louis Star-Times*, July 10, 1946: 21.

37. "Homestead Grays Take Fore River," *Boston Globe*, May 27, 1944: Sports-2.

38. Chester Washington, "Says Ches," *Pittsburgh Courier*, February 21, 1941: 16.

39. Wendell Smith, "Brooklyn Dodgers Admit Negro Players Rate Place in Majors," *Pittsburgh Courier*, August 5, 1939: 16

Lou Gehrig, Movie Star

Ron Backer

As the 1937 baseball season came to a close, Lou Gehrig was still at the top of his game. Lou had a .351 batting average that year, with 37 home runs and 158 RBIs. He was fourth in voting for the American League's Most Valuable Player Award, having won the title the year before. Lou made his annual appearance in the 1937 All-Star Game, hitting a home run off legendary pitcher Dizzy Dean. Lou already held the major league record for playing in the most consecutive games and his streak was approaching 2,000 games. His New York Yankees won the 1937 World Series, beating the New York Giants, four games to one.

Lou commanded a high salary for ballplayers of the day.[1] But with the aid of his business manager, Christy Walsh, Lou also looked for moneymaking opportunities outside the game. In prior years, these had included barnstorming tours and endorsements of products.[2] Now, a new idea would be implemented—a starring role in the movies.

HOLLYWOOD BECKONS

Lou first considered an appearance in a Hollywood film just after the end of the 1936 World Series.[3] Independent producer Sol Lesser, who then had the rights to the Tarzan character, was looking for a new actor to play Tarzan in an upcoming movie. In the tradition of prior Tarzans Johnny Weissmuller, Buster Crabbe, and Herman Brix, Lesser was looking for a world-class athlete to play the part. He considered Ken Carpenter, the 1936 Olympic gold medalist in the discus; Larry Kelly, a Yale football star; Max Baer and Jimmy Braddock, heavyweight-boxing champions; and Sandor Szabo and Dave Levin, professional wrestlers.[4]

When Christy Walsh suggested to Lesser that Lou Gehrig could play Tarzan, Lesser was receptive to the idea. Before making a decision, however, Lesser wanted to see more of Lou's body than is revealed in a baseball uniform.[5] Walsh then arranged for the taking of publicity photos of Lou in jungle garb, which were sent to Lesser and also circulated to the media. The photos, not unexpectedly, met with some derision.

Edgar Rice Burroughs, the author of the Tarzan stories, sent a telegram to Gehrig, which drolly read, "Having seen several pictures with you as Tarzan…I want to congratulate you on being a swell first baseman."[6] A few weeks later, after seeing the publicity photos, Lesser nixed the idea of Gehrig as Tarzan, commenting that Gehrig's legs were "a trifle too ample" for the role.[7] The part went to Glenn Morris, another Olympic champion, and the proposed film became *Tarzan's Revenge* (1938).[8]

Despite the Tarzan disappointment, Sol Lesser retained an interest in Lou as an actor and box office draw. In March 1937, Lou flew to Hollywood for a screen test for Lesser. Afterwards, the parties announced that Lou had agreed to a one-picture deal with Lesser's studio, Principal Productions. No details of the contract were disclosed. Lou was quoted at the time as saying, "I know I'm no actor, but I am going to give 'em my best."[9]

The film turned out to be a B Western titled *Rawhide*. The movie started production on January 17, 1938, primarily at the Morrison Ranch near Agoura, California, about thirty miles from Hollywood.[10] Reflecting the short shooting schedule of B movies, filming completed in early February 1938, about three weeks later.[11] Lou's wife Eleanor accompanied Lou on the trip.[12] In an interview during production, Gehrig said, "Boy, I never had so much fun in my life as I'm having on this picture. … You ought to see me in my boots and saddle and ten-gallon hat."[13] Gehrig purportedly made $2,500 per week during filming.[14]

While Lou Gehrig was the obvious draw for the making of *Rawhide*, the producers knew even though Lou was playing himself in the film, he did not have the acting skills to carry a feature-length (58 minutes) movie on his own. Other experienced performers were brought in to assist. The top-billed performer in the movie is Smith Ballew, a Texas native who entered show business in the 1920s, quickly becoming a well-known singer, leader of his own band, and a recording artist. By 1935, Ballew was a regular on the radio and in 1936, he appeared in his first feature film. When producer Sol Lesser decided to do a series of Westerns with a singing cowboy, he chose Ballew as his leading man. It turned out that there would only be five films in the series, the fourth being *Rawhide*.[15]

Evalyn Knapp, an experienced B movie actress, plays Lou Gehrig's sister, Peggy. Most of the heavies are familiar faces, such as Cy Kendall as the crooked sheriff and Dick Curtis as a henchman. The most recognizable actor in the film, though, is probably Si Jenks, who plays Pop Mason, the bewhiskered and toothless old codger who assists Lou in the movie. Jenks was a character actor who appeared in numerous films over the years, including many Westerns.

Christy Walsh received an unusual mention in the film's credits: "Lou Gehrig by Arrangement with Christy Walsh." According to *The Hollywood Reporter*, this was the first time that a manager received screen credit in a motion picture.[16]

THE FILM

Rawhide is a fairly standard B Western, in a modern setting, with Lou Gehrig and his sister Peggy buying a ranch out West near the town of Rawhide, which is tightly controlled by a criminal enterprise known as the Ranchers Protective Association. The Association, by threats and force, coerces the area's ranchers into paying high dues, buying supplies from the Association at inflated prices, and turning over a part of their profits to the combine. Local attorney Larry Kimball has been fighting the Association for some time, with little success, but with the arrival of Lou Gehrig, he now has an ally in his fight to clean up the area. After the usual fisticuffs, gunfights, and chase scenes, along with standard characters such as a crooked sheriff, thug-like henchmen, and an old-codger sidekick, Larry and Lou clean up the town, providing a happy ending for its citizens and the movie's viewers.

While *Rawhide* is routine, at best, it is the presence of Gehrig in the cast that distinguishes the film from standard B Westerns of the era. Gehrig was not simply thrown into the film for his name value and nothing else. Instead, scenes and dialogue were written especially for him, giving the movie a special flavor. For example, in a fight in a bar, Gehrig, recognizing that his pugilistic skills may not be up to Western standards, foregoes punches and instead throws pool balls at the bad guys, knocking many of them out and winning the fight. Who knew that baseball-throwing skills could be so important in the New West? Actually, Gehrig seems a little out-of-practice early in the scene, as he breaks windows and bottles in the bar, but once warmed up, he is very accurate.

A publicity still of Lou Gehrig in Tarzan garb.

Later, as Peggy Gehrig is about to sign a contract with the Protective Association on the second floor of a building, bandits on the ground floor prevent Lou from entering the building to stop her. Lou goes to the back of the building and sees some kids playing baseball. He borrows a bat, and fungoes a ball through the narrow second floor window, breaking the glass and preventing Peggy from signing. Who knew that baseball-hitting skills could be so important in the New West? Gehrig accomplishes this feat on his first try, contrasted with his throwing skills with the pool balls, suggesting that Lou may have been a better hitter than a fielder.

There is also self-deprecating humor inserted into the movie at the expense of Gehrig. Trying to mount a horse for the first time, Gehrig and his rear end quickly find the ground. All Lou can say is, "Strike One." Once Gehrig finally goes out for his first ride, he finds that bouncing on the saddle is very painful for his Eastern posterior. There is even some modern satire. Saunders, the lead villain, threatens Gehrig, saying, "You're not in New York now," to which Gehrig responds, "For a minute, I thought I was." Saunders also tells him, "You don't want to be a holdout, do you?" to which Lou replies, "Well, I've been a holdout before." The latter retort is a reference to some pre-season contract disputes that Lou had with the Yankees, including one before the 1928 baseball season.[17] Another resulted in him missing several spring training games in 1937.[18] (Lou never had a holdout during the regular season.)

As to Gehrig's performance, while he wasn't the natural in front of a camera that Babe Ruth was, Gehrig gives an acceptable performance in the film, delivering his lines with all of the sincerity he can muster. *Rawhide* was not Shakespeare in the Park and the movie did not require the greatest of performances to be effective. In fact, *Variety* gave Gehrig a good review, commenting that he "can act, and should his baseball career come to an end, he might develop into another Bill Boyd or Buck Jones type."[19] *Newsweek* wrote, "Fully dressed from sombrero to spurs, the Tarzan candidate [Gehrig] photographs well and handles an important role with assurance."[20] Unfortunately, Gehrig's hometown newspaper, *The New York Times*, was less enthusiastic, opining, "The Iron Man appears to be painfully conscious of the fact that acting is one of his lesser accomplishments."[21] Generally, however, Gehrig received good reviews for his screen performance.

It turns out that Lou Gehrig was not just a ballplayer and a cowboy star, he was also a singing cowboy. There are four songs sung in the film, with Smith Ballew carrying the heavy load on three of them.[22] Lou, while riding in a wagon, gets a chance to sing a few verses of one of the songs, "A Cowboy's Life." Those verses are specific to Lou's experiences in the West. For example, Lou warbles the following lyrics: "Oh, the city cowboy had his fun/So I took my bats/I traded them for riding boots and seven gallon hats."

Lou has a surprisingly good singing voice in the movie, but, of course, it is not really Lou singing.

Buddy Clark, a popular singer of the 1930s and '40s who sometimes dubbed other actor's voices, dubbed Lou's voice.[23] Lou's "singing" in the film continued a practice of Yankees Hall-of-Famers singing in the movies. In addition to Lou Gehrig, Joe DiMaggio sang a bit of a song in *Manhattan Merry-Go-Round* (1937) and Babe Ruth talked his way through a song in *Home Run on the Keys* (1937).

RELEASE AND PROMOTION

The premiere of *Rawhide* took place on March 23, 1938, in St. Petersburg, Florida, then the home of the New York Yankees' spring training facilities. The festivities included a parade down Central Avenue, a marching band, and fireworks. Yankees owner Colonel Ruppert, manager Joe McCarthy, Eleanor Gehrig, Christy Walsh, and players from the New York Yankees and the St. Louis Cardinals, who also trained in St. Petersburg that year, were present for the event. Al Schacht, the famous baseball clown, rode a trick bicycle. The Oklahoma Mud Cat band, composed of several St. Louis Cardinals players—including its leader, outfielder Pepper Martin—played hillbilly music for the crowd.[24] According to a newspaper report, thousands of the curious thronged the streets to get a glimpse of the celebrities of the sports world.[25]

The opening, which took place at the Capitol Theater, was advertised as "A Real Hollywood Premiere."[26] At the entrance, there was a red carpet, Klieg lights, and a microphone for anybody who had something to say.[27] Inside the theater, Lou gave a speech to the fans in attendance, saying, "People think I'm modest when I say I'm lucky. I'm not—I am lucky, and if anyone wants to argue with me about it, I'll stand and argue with him about it all day."[28] That would not be the last time in Lou Gehrig's life that he referred to himself in a speech as lucky.

Rawhide premiered in New York City at the Globe Theater in midtown Manhattan on Saturday, April 23, 1938. Although there was no Hollywood-style opening, Gehrig and his teammates made a personal appearance at the theater on the evening of Sunday, April 24, 1938, after beating the Washington Nationals earlier that day, 4–3.[29]

THE LIFE OF LOU GEHRIG

For those who are familiar with the facts of Lou Gehrig's life, there are

The three stars of Rawhide, *(L to R): Evalyn Knapp, Smith Ballew, and Lou Gehrig.*

AUTHOR'S COLLECTION

An ad for the premiere of Rawhide in St. Petersburg, Florida.

some strange moments in *Rawhide*. Lou quits baseball at the beginning of the film and returns to baseball at the end of the film, but surprisingly never mentions the New York Yankees by name. In real life, Lou never had a sister named Peggy. In fact, Lou Gehrig did not have any siblings who survived childhood.[30] Lou was married to Eleanor at the time the movie was made, but she is never mentioned in the film. In this fictionalized version of Lou's life, there is no reference to Lou being married.

Of course, the fictional character of Peggy was inserted into the film to provide Larry Kimball with a mild love interest. If Eleanor had bought the ranch with Lou in the movie, *Rawhide* would have been bereft of a romantic subplot, a B Western staple.

While not true at the time of the film's release in 1938, *Rawhide* now has a form of dramatic irony. As a result of the disease amyotrophic lateral sclerosis (ALS), Gehrig played his last regular season game of baseball in real life on April 30, 1939. Thus, Gehrig was through with baseball only about a year after the first showing of *Rawhide* in New York City. Accordingly, when Gehrig tells the reporters at the beginning of the film, "Take it or leave it. I'm through with baseball," those lines now take on added meaning. Also, because of the quick onset of ALS, some viewers may scrutinize the film to see if there are any signs of Gehrig's oncoming disease. They would conclude, as seems apparent, that Gehrig was in excellent health during the filming of the movie. In fact, he lifts a henchman over his head in the fight scene in the bar and leaps over a porch chair in the film's concluding scene.[31]

THE END OF A FILM CAREER

Rawhide contains Lou Gehrig's only role in films.[32] Although not disclosed at the time of the signing of Gehrig's contract in March of 1937, Principal Productions apparently negotiated an option for the use of Gehrig in an additional movie. The studio let that option lapse in October of 1938, with Sol Lesser announcing

that going forward, he was only interested in making kids pictures.[33] Whether another studio may have been interested in working with Lou will never be known as, by then, Lou was already showing the first signs of the disease that eventually took his life.[34] ∎

Notes

1. *The New York Times* reported that Lou's salary for 1937 was $36,000 plus a signing bonus of $750. James P. Dawson, "Two-Gun Gehrig, Movie Job Ended, Turns Thoughts to Baseball," *The New York Times*, February 3, 1938, 27. This is confirmed by "Training Camp Notes," *The Sporting News*, March 25, 1937, 8.
2. Gehrig did ads for Camel cigarettes and Aqua Velva. He was the first athlete to have his face on a Wheaties box. Louis Menand, "How Baseball Players Became Celebrities," *The New Yorker*, June 1, 2020, https://www.newyorker.com/magazine/2020/06/01/how-baseball-players-became-celebrities.
3. "Gehrig Seeks Role as Tarzan in Films," Associated Press, *The New York Times*, October 21, 1936, 40.
4. Scott Tracy Griffin, *Tarzan on Film* (London, UK: Titan Books, 2016), 58.
5. Dan Joseph, *Last Ride of the Iron Horse* (Mechanicsburg, PA: Sunbury Press, 2019), 10.
6. "Author Ridicules Gehrig as Tarzan," *Atlantic Constitution*, November 19, 1936, 12.
7. Jonathan Eig, *Luckiest Man: The Life and Death of Lou Gehrig* (New York, NY: Simon & Schuster, 2005), 220.
8. Eig, 219–20. Morris won the gold medal in the decathlon in the 1936 Olympic games in Berlin.
9. Bob Ray, "Lou Hits the Screen," *The Sporting News*, March 11, 1937, 5.
10. Joseph, 26.
11. American Film Institute Catalog of Feature Films ("AFI"), *Rawhide*, https://catalog.afi.com/Film/5451-RAWHIDE?sid=e3fb05f4-1f85-4e26-a54e-414249ec5c70&sr=0.8563489&cp=1&pos=4.
12. Bob Ray, "'Two-Gun' Lou Gehrig Stars as Rootin', Tootin', Shootin' Hero of the Wild West," *The Sporting News*, January 27, 1938, 10.
13. Ray, "'Two-Gun' Lou Gehrig."
14. Joseph, 24, 26.
15. Don Creacy, "Smith Ballew," *Classic Images*, posted June 2, 2010, http://www.classicimages.com/people/article_6a695f92-3a23-5fba-89d6-87cf2e422bf2.html
16. "Ghost Shreds Shroud," *Hollywood Reporter*, January 21, 1938, 2. Christy Walsh was never afraid to promote himself. In the 1930s, he produced several short subjects, including a five film series with Babe Ruth, with the overall title, "A Christy Walsh All America Sportreel." In *The Pride of the Yankees* (1942), he received mention in the film as follows: "Appreciation is expressed for the gracious assistance of Mrs. Lou Gehrig and for the cooperation of Mr. Ed Barrow and the New York Yankees arranged by Christy Walsh."

17. James Lincoln Ray, "Lou Gehrig," SABR Biography Project. https://sabr.org/bioproj/person/ccdffd4c.

18. Richard Hubler, *Lou Gehrig: The Iron Horse of Baseball* (Boston: Houghton Mifflin Company, 1941), 174; "Training Camp Notes," *The Sporting News*, March 25, 1937, 8.

19. *Variety*, April 6, 1938, 14. William "Bill" Boyd and Buck Jones were stars of many B movie Westerns, with Boyd playing Hopalong Cassidy in a series of films.

20. "Baseball's Iron Man Fails as Tarzan But Qualifies as Western Two-Gun Hero," *Newsweek*, April 18, 1938, 24.

21. *The New York Times*, April 25, 1938, 19.

22. Albert Von Tilzer, the man who composed "Take Me Out to the Ball Game," composed two of those songs.

23. Eig, 238.

24. Ray Robinson, *Iron Horse: Lou Gehrig In His Time* (New York: W.W. Norton & Company, Inc.: 1990) 231–32; Eig, 242; "Lou Gehrig's Film in World Premiere Here Tonight," *St. Petersburg Times*, March 23, 1938, 8.

25. Jack Thale, "Premiere Here Honors Gehrig," *St. Petersburg Times*, March 24, 1938, 6.

26. *St. Petersburg* Times, March 23, 1938, 9.

27. Gayle Talbot, "St. Louis and New York Players See Lou Gehrig's New Moving Picture," *Tampa Daily News*, March 24, 1938, 14.

28. Thale, 6.

29. Advertisement for *Rawhide*, *The New York Times*, April 23, 1938.

30. An older sister Anna died when she was just three months old. Another sister, Sophie, died when she was less than two years old and an unnamed brother died almost immediately after birth. James Lincoln Ray, "Lou Gehrig," SABR Biography Project. https://sabr.org/bioproj/person/ccdffd4c.

31. According to an article published in 2007 in *Neurology*, a scientific journal, a careful examination of *Rawhide* by medical professionals disclosed that Lou functioned normally in January 1938, when the film was shot. No evidence of hand atrophy or leg weakness appears in the movie. Melissa Lewis and Paul H. Gordon, "Lou Gehrig, *Rawhide*, and 1938," 68 *Neurology*, February 20, 2007, 615-618.

32. In *Speedy* (1928), his only other screen appearance, Lou photo bombed a scene outside Yankee Stadium with Harold Lloyd and Babe Ruth. Lou appears in the background of the scene for only a second or two. He has no dialogue.

33. "Lesser Benches Gehrig," *Variety*, October 5, 1938, 5.

34. Joseph, 137.

Spahn's Insane Stats at the Twain

Randy S. Robbins

As a young southpaw, I naturally felt an affinity for major league left-handers. Lefties, by nature, are outsiders. The consensus of sources spanning more than three decades states that only about 10 percent of the population is left-handed, making we portsiders indeed a rare breed.[1] I, personally, never experienced the forced switching of penmanship meant to "cleanse" left-handed schoolchildren of earlier generations—a barbaric act harmful to one's self-esteem, if not to the wiring of the brain itself. However, I was encouraged to slant my lined paper at a right-hander's angle. And many a classroom offered a dearth of one-piece desks built for left-handers, my left elbow hanging humiliatingly in midair while my "normal-handed" classmates wrote in fully supported olecranal luxury.

When you're left-handed, it dominates your whole being in a way that the majority of the world cannot understand simply because the world is fitted to them.

Still, even from a young age, I was told that baseball teams are forever on the lookout for left-handers who can throw with control, which made me feel special, even if my backyard catches with Dad hadn't yet graduated from tennis ball to horsehide.

Thus, it's no surprise that I felt an innate connection to southpaws who took the mound at Veterans Stadium, on television, and on my baseball cards: hometown Phillies Steve "Lefty" Carlton, Tug McGraw, Jim Kaat, and Randy Lerch (a lefty with my name!), Randy Jones (a *Cy Young–winning* lefty with my name!), Don Gullett, Mickey Lolich, Fred Norman, Paul Splittorff, Frank Tanana, Jerry Koosman. And, of course, the deity of all southpaws, Sandy Koufax, who, though just before my time, commanded the highest respect in my household because the electrifying southpaw, by virtue of his Jewish heritage, single-handedly revived my Flatbush-born father's interest in baseball after his beloved Brooklyn Dodgers broke his heart. (Sadly, that renewed vigor for the game abandoned my father once and for all upon Koufax's retirement.)

Of course, I also knew of the great lefties of old: Lefty Grove, Lefty Gomez, Eddie Plank, Carl Hubbell,

even Babe Ruth himself! But the southpaw who loomed largest, of course, was Warren Spahn. One of my baseball magazines contained his lifetime record. Thirteen 20-win seasons. *Thirteen*?! And a win total, 363, to which no other lefty stood remotely close. For me, and perhaps other young southpaws, 363 became something akin to Babe Ruth's *714* and Ty Cobb's *4191* (before many sources revised his hit total to 4189), an instantly identifiable benchmark in baseball history that spoke for itself.

Yet in examining Spahn's record more closely, one finds a statistic that should make one wonder beyond simple coincidence:

During a career in which Spahn pitched 363 victories, the multitalented hurler also recorded 363 batting hits.

When one takes into account the myriad variables that go into this curious confluence—from the fact that a starting pitcher's at-bats vary from game to game depending on how well his hurling keeps him in each contest, to the fact that Spahn relieved in 85 games, further fluctuating his at-bats—one further wonders how unusual this could be.

And then there's the additional confounding variable that Spahn appeared in 18 games as a pinch-hitter, which chance could employ to further skew two totals rather than bring them together.

Macroscopically, how could one total derived from a pool of 750 (games) end up equaling another from a pool of 1872 (at-bats)—especially considering the first is accrued at a maximum of one per game whereas the second is almost always accrued multiple times per game?

It is for strange cases such as this that I wish I were a mathematician so that I could calculate the odds of two wholly unrelated totals, incurred at vastly different per-game rates (0 to 1 for wins; 0 to infinity for hits), somehow matching up perfectly over the course of 21 seasons. Still, it doesn't leave me exactly hollow to state abstractly that the chance of both totals landing on *363* seem merely *astronomical*.

Yet, is it?

Among all pitchers with at least 100 victories, three others matched Spahn's accomplishment: Dick Ruthven (123 wins/123 hits), Dave Roberts (103/103), and Tex Carleton (100/100).

Ten other pitchers had victory and hit totals separated by exactly 1, and 57 pitchers had a difference of between 2 and 10 (including Smoky Joe Wood's tenure as a pitcher with Boston and Phil Niekro's totals as a Brave, because he never batted for another franchise). These 70 other pitchers range from some of the most talented moundsmen ever, such as Grover Cleveland Alexander and Three Finger Brown, to the mediocre likes of Don Cardwell and Chuck Stobbs.

Whether one attributes it to less formidable pitching or to pitchers, themselves, possessing better-honed batting skills in a less specialized time, this seems largely to be a phenomenon of bygone days. Only five of these 70 pitchers played most or all of their career during the designated-hitter era, and none are active (although Madison Bumgarner had a difference of just 14 at the end of the 2019 season). Warren Spahn, however, took this statistical quirk to the next level.

One of the best batsmen among pitchers, the crafty Buffalonian possessed an uncanny (though surely unrecognized) knack for knocking as many hits in a season as he tossed victories. Eleven times, Warren's win total of any given season equaled his hit total of any given season, including an incredible eight times in the *same* season. That is some serious synchronicity, if such a concept can be applied to the baseball diamond.

Yet there exists *another* layer to this algebraic madness. Spahn, who seemed as if he would continue winning forever, going 23–7 at age 42, finally was snared by Father Time in 1964. After suffering only his second losing campaign since breaking into the big leagues more than two decades earlier, he was purchased from Milwaukee by the young New York Mets just before Thanksgiving.

As the ledger closed on his Braves career, Spahn boasted 356 victories—again, the exact number of hits he notched as a Boston/Milwaukee Brave.

Struggling through 20 games with the ever-floundering Mets, Spahn staggered to a 4–12 record, his bloated 4.36 ERA hardly helping the punchless New Yorkers. Yet in those 20 games, as well as one in which he pinch-hit, Spahn collected four hits, equaling his victory total.

Going nowhere, New York released Spahn on July 17. Two days later, the San Francisco Giants, tangled in fourth place yet only 5½ games off the lead, signed Spahn, hoping to coax a last bit of magic from his left arm for the stretch drive. Perhaps revitalized by taking

Warren Spahn: true statistical anomaly?

the mound once again for a contender, Spahn pitched better, for a time. As a Giant, he cut his ERA by nearly a run and chipped in three victories, although four of his last five appearances were spent in relief, as the Giants came up two games short at the wire.

Yet with eerie consistency, Spahn once again managed to collect as many hits as victories, rapping a trio of singles to match the 3–4 record he put up with San Francisco. The Giants released Spahn after the season, ending his remarkable major league career.

Not only had Spahn managed to produce equal victory and hit totals across 21 seasons (interestingly, he stroked his first hit in 1942 yet had to wait, because of highly decorated military service in World War II, until 1946 for his initial victory) but he, improbably, registered matching numbers of hits and victories with each franchise for which he played.

Warren even remained true to his nature in the postseason, slapping four singles to complement his four World Series victories.

Spahn's peculiar proclivity was not exclusive to the major leagues. Between his pair of appearances at both the opening and closing of the 1942 season, his apprenticeship with the Hartford Bees of the Eastern League saw him register 17 hits en route to a team-leading 17 victories. And just for good measure, when Warren pitched seven innings over three games while managing the Pacific Coast League's Tulsa Oilers in 1967, he failed to get a hit in four at-bats, matching the 0–1 record of his minor league swan song.

And if all that weren't enough, the breakdown of Spahn's corresponding pitching wins and batting hits achieved as a Brave by city very nearly match as well: As a Boston Brave, Spahn won 122 games while collecting 120 hits, which, of course, leaves his totals after the Braves moved to Milwaukee at 234 pitching wins and 236 hits.

(In pale reflections of Spahn's strange achievement, Steve Carlton logged both 77 victories and hits as a St. Louis Cardinal, though his totals in Phillie pinstripes are significantly farther apart, whereas Curt Davis did the same *for* the Phillies but none of the other three teams for which he hurled. Joe McGinnity matched his league-leading 28 victories in each of his first two seasons with 28 hits during each campaign. Additionally, George Mogridge's career included 68 wins and 68 hits for the Washington Senators, and General Crowder's hit total is exactly one less than his victory total for each of the three teams for which he pitched.)

Warren Spahn's almost preternatural ability to achieve pitching victories and batting hits with the same frequency on multiple "levels" seems to represent a true statistical anomaly in baseball annals.

Perhaps southpaws should take a bit of pointless pride that this odd phenomenon appears well suited to our "eccentric" minority: Of the 71 pitchers (including Spahn) with at least 100 victories and a difference of 10 or fewer between victories and batting hits, 26 (36.6%) were lefties—an amount noticeably higher than the 28.0%–29.7% of left-handed starters populating major league rosters since 1904.[2] ■

Notes

1. "World's Biggest Study of Left-handedness." NeuroscienceNews.com, April 3, 2020. https://neurosciencenews.com/left-handedness-study-16070/.
2. Mike Petriello. "Where Have All the Top Lefty Pitchers Gone?" MLB.com, May 20, 2020. https://www.mlb.com/news/left-handed-pitchers-decreasing.

What's in a Name?

Examining Reactions to Major League Baseball's Change From the Disabled List to the Injured List via Twitter

Mary A. Hums, Evan Frederick, Ann Pegoraro, Nina Siegfried, and Eli A. Wolff

A batter takes a fastball to the ribs. An outfielder crashes into the wall trying to make a circus catch. A baserunner steps on the side of first base and sprains an ankle. All of these rather common occurrences take place on baseball diamonds on a regular basis. Sometimes the mishap results in a player being unable to play for a period of time due to the injury. In the past, a player in Major League Baseball (MLB) with this type of injury would be placed on what was known as the Disabled List or the DL. But is he injured—or disabled? And does it matter how he is labeled? Recently, MLB decided to examine its use of the term Disabled List and changed the name to the Injured List or the IL. While this seems like a rather insignificant change, baseball fans took to social media to express their opinions and perceptions of MLB's decision. The purpose of this study is to examine that reaction. We will begin with an overview of the history and usage of the terms, provide context for the analysis of effects of language on societal attitudes, and review previous work in analysis of social media with regards to societal attitudes toward sport, before we present our own analysis of reactions to MLB's announcement.

POLICY LANGUAGE USED TO DESCRIBE INJURED PLAYERS

MLB first used the term Disabled List at the end of the nineteenth century. According to Dawkins and Glass, disabled or injury lists first regularly appeared in MLB in the early 1900s.[1] The National League codified the term Disabled List in 1915 and it referred to a list of players who were removed from a roster for a 10-day period.[2] The Disabled List began to more closely resemble the current version back in 1941. Over the years, the length of time a player could be placed on the Disabled List has varied.

All of the major North American professional sports leagues have their own terms for their lists of athletes who are unable to play due to injuries. The NFL has an Injured Reserve List, Physically Unable to Perform List, a Non-Football Injury List, and a Personnel (Injury) Report Policy.[3] The NBA uses a general Inactive List for players who are not able to play for various reasons which is "the list of players, maintained by the NBA, who have signed Player Contracts with a Team and are otherwise ineligible to participate in a Regular Season game."[4] The NBA also has what is known as the Disabled Player Exception whereby a "Disabling Injury or Illness means any injury or illness that, in the opinion of the physician…., makes it substantially more likely than not that the player would be unable to play through the following June 15."[5] Lastly, the NHL uses an Injured Reserve List.[6]

Major League Baseball currently defines the Injured List as follows:

> The 10-day injured list (known as the 10-day disabled list until the end of the 2018 season) allows clubs to remove players from the 25-man active roster while keeping them on the 40-man roster. Players can be placed on the 10-day injured list for any type of injury, though players with concussion symptoms are first sent to the 7-day injured list. Players on the 10-day injured list must remain out of action for at least 10 days, though a player can also stay on the list for considerably longer than 10 days, if necessary.[7,8]

Two authors of the current study were directly involved with the nearly 15-year process advocating for the name change from the Disabled List to the Injured List. In 2003, an initial inquiry was made to the MLB Commissioner's Office suggesting the name be changed.[9] The Commissioner's Office responded with a letter acknowledging receipt of the request and indicating the matter was of interest. Over the years, the authors, along with other disability advocates, reached out again to follow up. Finally, in 2018, the authors contacted the Ruderman Family Foundation, a disability advocacy group based in Boston, about helping with getting the name changed. Link20, an initiative of the Ruderman Foundation, took up the effort and directly contacted MLB Commissioner Rob Manfred and also copied Billy Bean, MLB Vice President and Special Assistant to the Commissioner.[10] Bean is the representative in the Commissioner's Office who works with MLB's social responsibility and diversity initiatives. With Bean's assistance in the League office, the change was agreed upon. Teams were notified in a memo from Jeff Pfeifer, MLB's Senior Director of League Economics and Operations:

> In recent years, the commissioner has received several inquiries regarding the name of the 'Disabled List,'…The principal concern is that using the term 'disabled' for players who are injured supports the misconception that people with disabilities are injured and therefore are not able to participate or compete in sports. As a result, Major League Baseball has agreed to change the name 'Disabled List' to be the 'Injured List' at both the major and minor league levels. All standards and requirements for placement, reinstatement, etc., shall remain unchanged. This change, which is only a rebranding of the name itself, is effective immediately.[11]

When the renaming occurred, no changes were made to the actual policy itself.[12] The only change was replacing the word Disabled with the word Injured. (Unrelated to the name change, via the recent Collective Bargaining discussions, at the end of 2020 the shortest length of stay on the Injured List for a non-concussion injury will be changed from 10 days to 15 days.)

LITERATURE REVIEW

The Importance of Language—Disabled v. Injured

The importance of language cannot be overstated. "The words that we use shape the image of the world in which we live."[13] This holds true in the world of disability as well. Over the years, the proper terms to describe people with disabilities have evolved. "Proper" terms at various times included words such as crippled, handicapped, wheelchair-bound, lame, and impaired, language which by today's standards is clearly offensive and marginalizing.[14] Acceptable terms today use what is known as *person first language*. According to the American Psychological Association:

> For decades, persons with disabilities have been identified by their disability first, and as persons, second. Often, persons with disabilities are viewed as being afflicted with, or being victims of, a disability. In focusing on the disability, an individual's strengths, abilities, skills, and resources are often ignored.[15]

Hence, we now see the term "person with a disability" as opposed to saying "a disabled person," although there are still some groups who hold that the person first language inadequately captures the breadth of disability identity.[16] According to the United Nations:

> The term persons with disabilities is used to apply to *all* persons with disabilities *including* those who have long-term physical, mental, intellectual or sensory impairments which, in interaction with various attitudinal and environmental barriers, hinders their full and effective participation in society on an equal basis with others.

According to the Americans with Disabilities Act, a person with a disability is defined as:

> someone who has as a physical or mental impairment that substantially limits one or more major life activities, a person who has a history or record of such an impairment, or a person who is perceived by others as having such an impairment.[17]

On the other hand, the definition of *injured* is someone who is or has been "hurt or physically harmed."[18] WebMD supplies a list of sports injuries which includes ACL injuries, dislocated shoulders, muscle strains, rotator cuff tears, running injuries, turf toe, and the ulnar collateral ligament injuries that lead to Tommy John surgery, among others. The most common injuries in baseball for hitters are muscle strains, meniscus tears, hand/wrist injuries, elbow tendinitis, and rotator cuff tendinitis, and for pitchers labral tears, dead arm, ulnar collateral ligament injuries (Tommy John), and oblique strains.[19] Beyond these simple definitions, however, are the societal expectations that differ between persons who are "injured" and persons who are "disabled." Persons who are injured are typically seen as having a finite time for healing, whereas people with disabilities often live with their conditions on a long-term, and sometimes lifelong, basis depending on how/when they acquired their disability (i.e. at birth or adult onset). Beyond living with a disability and its associated physical challenges, however, there is a societal stigma placed on people who are "disabled." According to Garland-Thompson:

Because disability is defined not as a set of observable, broadly predictable traits, such as femaleness or skin color, but rather as any departure from the physical, mental, and psychological norms and expectations of a particular culture, disability highlights individual differences. In short, the concept of disability unites a heterogeneous group of people whose only commonality is being considered abnormal.[20]

People with disabilities face stigma in many forms including social avoidance, stereotyping, discrimination, condescension, blaming, internalization, hate crimes, and violence.[21] As LeClair states, "Disability is often equated with inferiority and deficiency rather than a neutral difference that may require some adaptation."[22] At times, people who are injured may become disabled as a result of their injury, but the injury itself and the disability are two different situations. The differences between the terms disabled and injured, then, are quite clear, and attitudes differ toward the people who wear those labels. In this particular study, MLB's use of the term injured is actually a more accurate term to describe baseball players who are unable to play for a designated period of time. They are injured (or ill), but not disabled.

It is important to note, however, that just because a person has a disability does not mean they are unable to participate in sport. Sport for people with disabilities has been increasing in popularity in the recent years. To put the growth into perspective, the cumulative audience watching the Paralympics has grown by 127 per cent in the last 12 years.[23] Reports on the 2020 Tokyo Summer Paralympic Games indicate ticket sales demand at an all-time record high.[24] While these numbers are encouraging, people with disabilities still face stigmatization when they seek full inclusion in society generally and specifically in the sport industry.[25] One way that inclusion can be encouraged is through the use of proper language. This includes no longer using words such as handicapped or impaired, but rather using terminology like persons with disabilities or athletes with disabilities because these terms are more accurate.[26]

According to the United Nations Department of Economic and Social Affairs, "The unique ability of sports to transcend *linguistic* [italics added for emphasis], cultural and social barriers makes it an excellent platform for strategies of inclusion and adaptation."[27] With that in mind, it becomes paramount to understand how society reflects upon and discusses these terms within a sport context. Framing is a useful theoretical framework to employ when examining the context of narratives disseminated via media platforms and whether these narratives challenge or embrace the decisions made by entities within the realm of sport.

FRAMING

The framing process refers to the selection, emphasis, and exclusion of information within media messages.[28] To frame a message is to essentially create a package of information that can thereby be interpreted by the audience.[29] Framing has traditionally been examined within the context of a top-down model, which puts the emphasis on how narratives crafted by media outlets impact public perception. A plethora of research has applied a top-down approach to the examination of framing within sport. This line of research has primarily examined coverage of the Olympic Games,[30] framing regarding social or political issues within a country,[31] and the framing of race, nationality, and the personal scandals of professional athletes.[32] The emergence of the Internet and social media platforms has provided the opportunity to examine narratives created by everyday content contributors rather than traditional media entities. This is referred to as bottom-up framing.[33] According to Meraz and Papacharissi, bottom-up framing is evident on social media, as non-elite actors can produce and reiterate certain frames via these platforms.[34]

A growing body of research has applied a bottom-up framing model to sport. Much of this sport-related research has analyzed content via Twitter and Facebook. In terms of bottom-up framing via Twitter, one study examined Twitter content pertaining to the Vancouver Riots following Vancouver's loss in the NHL's Stanley Cup Finals.[36] The authors found that many users utilized Twitter to counter negative perceptions of Canadian hockey fans, which included showing embarrassment and disassociating from those engaging in the riots. Ultimately, Twitter provided an avenue to counter traditional media coverage of the riots. Another study examined the hashtag #Sochi2014 during the Sochi Winter Olympic Games.[36] While most dialogue discussed Games-related material such as results and medal counts, dissent existed on the periphery. Much of the dissent discussed unsuitable accommodations in Sochi and Russia's political stance on the LGBTQ community. Along similar lines, Frederick, Pegoraro, and Burch performed a comparative analysis of traditional media and social media framing during the Sochi Olympic Games.[37] The analysis revealed an echo chamber from traditional media to social media in terms of political discussions. Organic content related to sub-par accommodations existed primarily on Twitter, without being amplified by traditional platforms. Additionally, Billings, et al., found a divergence between newspaper and Twitter content. Specifically, those authors examined coverage of Jason Collins coming out as gay. The analysis revealed that newspapers framed Collins' coming out as a watershed moment, while Twitter focused on ancillary items such as TV appearances.[38]

With regard to bottom-up framing via Facebook, various issues have been explored such as athlete transgressions and the framing of controversial sport leagues. In 2014, NASCAR driver Tony Stewart hit and killed Kevin Ward Jr. after Ward Jr. vacated his car on the racetrack. Following this incident, Stewart posted a message on Facebook where he expressed sadness and offered thoughts and prayers to Ward Jr.'s family and friends. Frederick, Stocz, and Pegoraro found that users responded to Stewart's message by levying judgment, displaying and debating racing knowledge with other users, and calling for a further examination of the "evidence" related to the incident.[39] With regard to controversial sport leagues, Frederick, Pegoraro, and Burch analyzed user framing of the Legends Football League (LFL) on Facebook. The LFL is a professional league where scantily-clad women play football indoors. Overall, users discussed the games, athletes, and results, thereby framing the league as a legitimate entity despite the existence of peripheral dialogue that sexualized the appearance of the athletes.[40]

Recently, sport-specific framing research has explored bottom-up framing on Facebook as it pertains to issues of racism and athlete activism. Frederick, Sanderson, and Schlereth examined user comments pertaining to protests by football players at the University of Missouri following various racially charged incidents on campus.[41] Utilizing Critical Race Theory (CRT) along with framing, the authors found that users often framed the protests as incompatible with the sporting environment and that the athletes engaging in advocacy were manufacturing racism where it did not exist. Along similar lines, Frederick, Pegoraro, and Sanderson examined responses via Facebook following LeBron James, Chris Paul, Dwayne Wade, and Carmelo Anthony's ESPYs speech during which the athletes discussed police violence against African Americans in the United States. The findings highlighted deeply ingrained racial stereotypes, as individuals debated the nature of race relations and racially charged incidents (i.e., police shootings). These debates focused on "accurate" crime rate statistics, the "facts" of recent racially-charged incidents, and the nature of racism in

the United States. A common refrain was that racism against African Americans no longer exists.[42] Finally, Schmidt, et al. examined bottom-up framing with regard to the protests by Colin Kaepernick and Megan Rapinoe during the playing of the US National Anthem. Utilizing CRT, the authors found that users framed Kaepernick's activism efforts by questioning his masculinity and expressing often misinformed and racist arguments. These racist arguments again leveraged "accurate" crime rate statistics. Users also declared that Kaepernick was anti-American and should leave the country. Similar sentiments were expressed about Rapinoe, however, there was very little discussion of race, sexual orientation, gender, etc. in her comments.[43]

Limited research has explored bottom-up framing in terms of social media reactions to policy change in sport. Cranmer and Sanderson employed bottom-up framing to examine user commentary on Twitter and online news comments pertaining to the Ivy League's decision to restrict full-contact tackling during football practices. Their thematic analysis revealed two over-arching frames including *traditionalism* and *progressivism*.[44] Comments within the *traditionalist* perspective focused on the detrimental impacts of the tackling policy and its long term consequences. Sub-themes within the *traditionalist* perspective discussed how the tackling policy would lead to an "erosion of masculinity," while also undermining American values.[45] Additionally, many advocated for preserving the norms of football, stating that the tackling policy would threaten the existence of football. Comments within the *progressivism* perspective framed this policy decision as a positive step forward. Specifically, users discussed this policy in terms of health advocacy on behalf of players, and as a significant benchmark for risk management within the Ivy League. Overall, the authors witnessed much resistance to this policy. Additionally, with regard to bottom-up framing, the authors argued, "discourse within the public sphere is much more varied than that within the media."[46]

In summary, scholars have commonly applied a bottom-up framing model to analyze sport commentary via social media platforms such as Twitter and Facebook. Bottom-up framing shifts the focus from traditional media outlets and their impact on the public to the public themselves who create their own narratives on social media. While research has explored the framing of political controversies, athlete transgressions, gender, and race, the authors could not locate research examining the framing of disability as it relates to sport. MLB changing the name of the Disabled List to the Injured List provided an intriguing opportunity to examine how individuals discussed disability within the realm of sport and beyond. The researchers were guided by the following research question:

What was social media reaction to Major League Baseball's name change from the Disabled List to the Injured List?

METHOD
Data Collection and Data Analysis

Data for this research were collected from Twitter using Twitonomy, a Twitter data collection and analysis program. The tweets were collected using the search term "injured list" for a two-day period starting from the date of the announcement on February 7, 2019, and ending on February 9, 2019. Similar abbreviated time frames have been utilized when examining the immediate impact of an announcement, event, transgression, etc. on audience perception and subsequent framing via social media (see Frederick and Pegoraro 2018; Sanderson, Frederick, and Schlereth 2017). This yielded a dataset of 5,880 tweets. The researchers then examined this tweet corpus and removed any tweets that may have contained the search term "injured list" but did not pertain to the MLB announcement of the name change, resulting in a final dataset of $N = 1,822$ tweets.

This study was rooted in discovery rather than confirmation of a previously established codebook or framework. Therefore, the researchers conducted an inductive thematic analysis with each tweet serving as the unit of analysis. In order to generate themes, two researchers independently viewed the entire dataset (1,822 tweets). The initial step in the analysis consisted of the researchers reading through the tweets and familiarizing themselves with the nuances and unique qualities of the dataset. The first round of forma coding, referred to as open coding (see Strauss, 1987) consisted of the researchers generating initial descriptors from the tweets. During this stage, categories are "built, named, and have attributes ascribed to them."[47] In order to reduce the descriptors into themes, the researchers engaged in axial coding. This process involves placing similar categories of descriptors into emergent thematic categories. Specifically, axial coding takes place when connections are made between categories, effectively bringing separate categories together under the umbrella of an "overarching theory or principle."[48]

The two researchers who conducted the coding have extensive experience and expertise in either social media use in sport or perceptions of disability as it relates to sport. Open communication took place between the researchers during the coding process if there were any misunderstandings of specific tweets. Categories were summarized and compared to ascertain similarity, and the researchers reduced the categories as much as possible while still preserving meaning. The researchers met and reviewed the themes and discussed any differences until a consensus was reached.

Results

A total of 1822 tweets were analyzed for the study. Of these, 379 were simple retweets which contained no additional content. An additional 77 contained disparate responses which did not group together to form themes. The following themes emerged from the remaining 1366 tweets:

1. Opposition (615)
2. Sarcasm (420)
3. Support (331)

Several subthemes emerged under opposition and also support.

THEME 1 – OPPOSITION

By far, the primary theme that emerged from the tweets was negative in nature. The 615 opposition tweets could be broken down further into two subthemes—(1) hostility/denial (515 tweets) and (2) deflection (100 tweets).

Subtheme 1 – Hostility/Denial. In this subtheme, tweets reflected an open hostility to the change. For example, "So today MLB renamed the DISABLED LIST to the Injured List because DISABLED LIST may be offensive to people. If you are offended by the term DISABLED LIST please unfriend me now and choke on a cupcake." "Another example of our snowflake pussy ass culture we live in. Changing the name because disabled is offensive? Disabled is a word and it describes players that can't play. Are there REALLY people that sit out there who REALLY get offended by this stuff? Fuuuuuuck" was another example of this content.

Some of the tweets decried what people saw as the onset of politically correct (PC) culture into the game. "Here we go... this is just the begging of hypersensitive babies ruining the best sport on Earth" and "Is nothing sacred from the PC police anymore?" Others saw it as a reflection of US culture becoming soft. "Because disabled offends ppl? Lol what has happened to our country. So soft" and "When the world is run by pussies, shit like this happens."

Other tweets gave a sense that people were so opposed to the change they would not even bring themselves to use the new terminology. "Always going to call it the DL. Stop trying to fuck up the sport" and "I am not calling it this" exemplify that opposition.

Subtheme 2 – Deflection. Some people indicated that MLB leaders should be spending their time on matters deemed more important to fans. "What about the advocates that are disabled from line drives and broken bats? When will you listen to us? And when are you going to address the fatal accident at Dodger Stadium?" and "MLB more offended by disabled than by Indians." Another example stated, "Let's not fix the NL's DH, tanking, shifts, blackout restrictions, sharing highlights on social media, service time manipulation, minor league wages, pitcher substitutions, slow pace. None of that. The name of the list for injured players. Unreal. Get your priorities straight @MLB."

Others just did not like the name change word choice saying, "Players go on the DL for mental issues, drug & alcohol issues, in addition to actual physical injuries" and "Calling it the Injured List creates ambiguity when a player requires time away for illness." Another tweet stated, "If you want the name changed because it is offensive, fine. But don't pretend the Injured List is more accurate or that disabled applies specifically to one group of people and it isn't just a word with multiple definitions." These statements indicate opposition but were more about the language used than the change itself.

THEME 2 – SARCASM

A large number of tweets (420) appeared to be sarcastic responses to the change. People did not make specific suggestions but just seemed to want to vent in a sarcastic manner. "MLB now channeling their inner progressiveness... Look how woke we are!", "Well, that will fix everything....", "Next for MLB they will change the name of the first baseman to avoid position privilege", "I am embarrassed for the world I live in" and "Wow—Injured List replaces Disabled List. That's a game changer. Like saying I'll rename cloudy days to overcast days" are all examples of the sarcastic commentary.

While some tweets that fell into the sarcasm category could possibly also have been classified under hostility/denial, many seemed to have a different tone. They were not attacking MLB for the change or saying they would not use the new terminology, but on some level mocked the change that was being made.

THEME 3 – SUPPORT

While two of the first three themes that emerged from the data were less than positive, numerous tweets did indicate a level of support for the change. These 331 tweets fell into two subthemes—(1) understanding (207 tweets) and (2) advocating (124 tweets).

Subtheme 1 – Understanding. Tweets in this category tended to be rather matter-of-fact and in agreement that the change made logical sense because it is more accurate. "Never thought about that but this change really shouldn't bother anyone and should be welcomed by people who did take offense to it. Good on you MLB." Other examples stated, "Well, I am not offended by the term....but to be accurate, they aren't disabled. They are injured" and "Injured List is more accurate anyway. There's no reason to be upset over changing a name that is both outdated and inaccurate anyway." These tweets, along with others, agreed that the new name brought MLB in line with industry language. "Every other sport uses Injured Reserve. I mean even taking away the offensive nature, it makes MLB more in line with what everyone else does."

Subtheme 2 – Advocating. People whose tweets fell into the advocating subtheme were supportive but went beyond and actually cheered MLB for its action. "THANK YOU BASEBALL FOR UPDATING THIS TO BE PRECISE AND ACCURATE. It's time for sports culture and media to respect what disability really means." "We never believed that a disability means you can't play the game. Props to MLB for making this important change." "MLB's Disabled List is now the Injured List. The injured might not be able to compete. The disabled still can. Community Connections applauds this change by #MLB." Others took an opportunity to display their fandom and pride with tweets such as "For my part, I am a big time fan of this move. Shout out to MLB for thinking about inclusion and the messages they send" and "Proud of the activism of Link20 a group of advocates for #disability rights and the leadership of MLB." Finally, one person simply said, "Good move—language matters." These tweets indicated there are fans who recognize the logical rationale for the change and accept or celebrate it for what it is.

DISCUSSION

In reflecting on the results section, a number of points arose which bear elaboration. These include (a) discussions of other potential MLB changes which may have influenced participants' responses, (b) reasons why baseball fans may have been resistant to the change, (c) looking at other policy changes involving disability and (d) the evolution of terms to describe traditionally under-represented groups.

First, prior to the time the name change took place, MLB had been involved in public discussions of ways to improve the game. Some of the hotly debated topics included abolishing (or expanding use of) the designated hitter, instituting a pitch clock, and requiring relief pitchers to face a minimum of three batters[49]. The name change from Disabled List to Injured List was not mentioned in these discussions. This may have influenced user framing as some saw MLB making the name change as insignificant or even diversionary compared to issues that would directly impact the pace of play.

Second, baseball fans may be an audience which does not favor change, particularly change that appears to have a political bent. Sport fans in general seem to think that politics and sport should be kept separate. A recent *Washington Post* poll revealed that 50% of respondents strongly or somewhat agreed with the statement "Sports and politics should not mix."[50] Conservatives were also more likely to oppose the mixing of sports and politics.[51] Baseball fans may be seen as unlikely to be open to change, particularly if the change involves language one could interpret as being "politically correct" in nature. This resistance to change, evident within user comments in the current study, is consistent with previous research exploring policy change in sport (see Cranmer and Sanderson, 2018). Resistance to "politically correct" language aligns well with the *traditionalist* perspective frame as discussed by Cranmer and Sanderson, as it was clear that individuals perceived the change from the DL to the IL as an affront to history and a symbolic softening of culture.

The findings of this study are also in line with the work of Kaufman, who keenly observed that athletes who engage in activism will likely receive backlash for their efforts.[52] Additionally, Cunningham and Regan have noted that athletes may be less likely to engage in activism due to public focus on athletic achievement instead of political or social advocacy within the realm of sport.[53] While the subtle advocacy of the name change was performed by a league and not an athlete, users adopted adversarial frames similar to responses following athlete activism and advocacy efforts. Specifically, the hostility theme aligns with the work of Frederick, Pegoraro, and Sanderson, who found that users attacked advocacy efforts, stating that they were misguided and misinformed.[54] The practice of trolling (leaving incendiary comments with the intention of causing offense and eliciting a response) is common in discussions of socially charged issues and further amplifies the polarity of these conversations as they unfold on social media (see Frederick, Pegoraro, and Sanderson, 2019; Smith et al., 2014). The sarcasm theme in the current study is similar to that identified by Frederick, Sanderson, and Schlereth, who noted that individuals often utilized social media to trivialize and/or downplay the significance of advocacy efforts with sarcastic overtones or ill-fated attempts at humor.[55] Overall, the most prominent themes in this study highlight a general resistance to change. The resistance to MLB's change was further illustrated by a number of blogs and websites which spoke out against or disparaged the change in language.[56] As MLB Executive Billy Bean observed in a podcast on this topic:

> I think it's more about people being afraid of where we're going to take the sport, if we start changing things that they're just accustomed to, and not the actual understanding that we were underserving a segment of our community and our population, and it was time to change and stop doing that.[57]

Third, it is useful to examine how another policy change in the representation of disability was received. A non-sport example of a policy which changed a long-standing depiction of disability occurred when the state of New York passed legislation to alter "existing law to require the removal of the word handicapped from new or replaced state signage, as well as update and destigmatize the accessibility logo."[58] The state adopted the use of the new Accessible Icon on any signs dealing with accessibility. A few years later, the state of Connecticut followed as well, changing to the use of the newer Accessible Icon and changing the wording on signs on parking spaces from "handicapped" to "reserved." According to Gazda:

> "It's 45 years old," said Connecticut Governor Daniel Malloy about the outgoing symbol. "It was developed at a different time, when our own ideas of a culture and a society were much more about concentrating on that which held people back, as opposed to that which moves people forward and so it was time."[59]

Can MLB say the same for its language change? While MLB may view the change as a progressive and obvious move forward, it was clear from user framing via Twitter that the notion of changing Disabled List to Injured List was viewed as neither evident nor necessary.

Finally, language changes over time and words related to under-represented groups have evolved. For example, gendered terms such as chairman or policeman have now become chair and police officer to avoid sex bias. Regarding race, the terms Negro or Colored used to be in common usage but were replaced by Black or African-American, and Oriental has been replaced by Asian. It is important to note that the advocacy efforts examined in the present study aimed to remove the word disability because it was not an accurate description within the particular context of injured players. While many advocacy initiatives center around inserting disability into the language and diversity dialogue, this MLB initiative perhaps created some confusion and misunderstanding for the layperson who may have believed that now the disability community does not agree with the term "disability." In fact, the use of the word disability is strongly encouraged when needed and necessary, but in the context of describing injury it is not an accurate term. It is possible that the extraction of the term disability may have increased opposition by the everyday fan who lacked an understanding of the nuances of the situation, possibly contributing to the overall negative responses via Twitter.

LIMITATIONS AND DELIMITATIONS

One delimitation to this study was that the data were collected only from Twitter, which has been a common approach in sport communication research (see Blaszka et al., 2016; Burch et al., 2015). Other social media platforms such as Instagram or Facebook were not used for data collection. Another delimitation was the time frame involved in data collection. The time frame took place between the time ESPN reported the change would occur and lasted for 48 hours in order to capture the initial responses. A limitation in the study was an unrelated occurrence that coincided with when the name change story went public. On that same day, Hall of Fame outfielder Frank Robinson passed away. Because he was a prominent MLB player and manager, this may have deflected some commentators who were more interested in the story of Robinson's death than the change in the name of the Disabled List to the Injured List.

FUTURE RESEARCH

As a follow up to this study, more work is needed in examining disability in a sport industry context. Much work has focused on participation in sport for people with disabilities, but the work being suggested here should focus on disability from a management perspective. For example, while researchers have extensively examined the sport consumption behavior patterns of women and racial ethnic minorities, this has not been done for people with disabilities. In addition, while work exists on the numbers of women and racial ethnic minorities working in sport management (see Lapchick, 2020), this work has not been replicated for sport managers with disabilities. Representation is important and having sport managers with disabilities who are visible to fans, sponsors, media, athletes, and coaches will create a more welcoming environment for all. Finally, assessing sport organizations on how disability is present in various aspects of the organization needs to be undertaken. A tool such as the Criteria for Inclusion put forth by Hums, et al. in 2019 could be used to assess how well people with disabilities are represented in sports organizations in terms of funding/sponsorship, media/information distribution, awards/recognitions, philosophy, awareness/education, policy environment, and attitudinal environment.[60] Finally, research should continue to monitor how disability is discussed and how information related to disability is disseminated via social media in order to determine how perceptions and reactions change with time.

IMPLICATIONS FOR PRACTITIONERS

In general, organizations should work to promote diversity for two primary reasons: (a) it is the right thing to do, and (b) it makes business sense.[61] This includes using inclusive language since it has a positive effect in business environments. According to Pecoraro, "Valuing diversity should be part of the communications brand you build for your business, if you want to reflect the customers you're serving."[62] Approximately 35% of households in the United States have a member with a disability and these households are more loyal to brands than other households.[63] People with disabilities living in the US combine for nearly $175 billion in annual discretionary spending.[64] Clearly, this is a market with great potential. People with disabilities also are quite interested in sport and attending sporting events despite the fact they often encounter barriers when wanting to do so. Some teams have made an effort to make their games more inviting to people with disabilities. MLB's Arizona Diamondbacks host Autism Awareness Day at their ballpark, and the New York Yankees celebrated a Disability Awareness Night, while minor league baseball's Lake Elsinore Storm and Lancaster Barnstormers have done the same. MLB teams have successfully promoted events such as Ladies Days, Pride Nights, and Hispanic-themed celebrations to appeal to fans from specific demographics. Sending out the message that people with disabilities are welcome, as MLB has done with the change in the Injured List language, can go a long way in newly cultivating a potentially very loyal fan base.

CONCLUSION

The importance of language cannot be overstated. "Language powerfully reflects and influences attitudes, behaviour and perceptions,"[65] but language is never static. Changes in everyday language occur all the time. According to the Linguistic Society of America, "Language is always changing, evolving, and adapting to the needs of its users."[66] This study examined how social media users reacted to a change in language related to people with disabilities in the context of a name change to a sport organization's policy. It illustrated that however simple and straightforward changing one word may appear, that change can still elicit strong emotions from people who are fans of a particular sport. Language can be used to include or exclude. MLB made the decision to change language to be more inclusive of people with disabilities. Social media users reacted both positively and negatively. It was a sure sign that language related to disability in sport needs further research and there is much for sport managers to learn about how to implement changes such as these. ■

References

Allentuck, Danielle. (2019, June 29). "Paralympians See a Big Welcome in Small Title Change." *The New York Times*, June 29, 2019, https://www.nytimes.com/2019/06/29/sports/olympics/usoc-paralympians-.html.

American Psychological Association. "Guidelines for Nonhandicapping Language in APA Journals." 2019. https://apastyle.apa.org/manual/related/nonhandicapping-language.

Angelini, James, MacArthur, Paul, and Billings, Andrew. "Spiraling Into or Out of Stereotypes? NBC's Primetime Coverage of Male Figure Skaters at the 2010 Olympic Games." *Journal of Language and Social Psychology* 33, no. 2, (2014). 26–35.

Associated Press. "MLB is Focused on Pace of Play Game Changes for 2019." *The New York Times*. February 8, 2019. https://www.nytimes.com/2019/02/08/sports/baseball/rob-manfred-rule-changes.html.

Atcheson, Sheree. "Embracing Diversity and Fostering Inclusion is Good for Your Business." *Forbes*. September 9, 2018. https://www.forbes.com/sites/shereeatcheson/2018/09/25/embracing-diversity-and-fostering-inclusion-is-good-for-your-business/#7d9f3c6472b1.

Baseball Reference. "Disabled List." No date. https://www.baseball-reference.com/bullpen/Disabled_list.

Bell, Stephania. "Injury Primer: A Guide to Common Baseball Injuries." ESPN. March 30, 2009. https://www.espn.com/fantasy/baseball/flb/story?page=mlbdk2k9_injuryprimer.

Billings, Andrew, Moscowitz, Leigh, Rae, Coral, and Brown-Devlin, Natalie. "The Art of Coming Out: Traditional and Social Media Frames Surrounding the NBA's Jason Collins." *Journalism and Mass Communication Quarterly* 92, no. 1, (2015). 142–60.

Bishop, Ronald. "The Wayward Child: An Ideological Analysis of Sports Contract Holdout Coverage." *Journalism Studies* 6, no. 4, (2005): 445–59.

Blaszka, Matthew, Frederick, Evan, Newman, Tim., and Pegoraro, Ann. "Was Dissent Being Displayed During the Sochi Olympics? Examining the #Sochi2014 Hashtag for Dissent." *Global Sport Business Association Journal* 4, no. 1, (2016). 1–13.

Blum, Ronald. "31 MLB Players and 7 Staff Test Positive for COVID-19 — A Rate of 1.2%." *Chicago Tribune*. July 4, 2020. https://www.chicagotribune.com/sports/breaking/ct-mlb-covid-19-test-results-20200704-46mgzdfv2bepzcyvugc6op56tu-story.html.

Bogage, Jacob. (2019, February 9). "'Baseball Got It': Disability Rights Advocates Hail MLB's Decision to Shelve the Disabled List." *Washington Post*, February 9, 2019. https://www.washingtonpost.com/sports/2019/02/08/baseball-got-it-disability-rights-advocates-hail-mlbs-decision-shelve-disabled-list/?noredirect=on&utm_term=.29f9a4b9f56d.

Bowman, Karlyn. "Polls on Political Correctness." *Forbes*. June 5, 2017. https://www.forbes.com/sites/bowmanmarsico/2017/06/05/polls-on-political-correctness/#5c3e81af6093.

Burch, Lawrence, Frederick, Evan, and Pegoraro, Ann. "Kissing in the Carnage: An Examination of Framing on Twitter During the Vancouver Riots." *Journal of Broadcasting & Electronic Media* 59 no. 3, (2015). 399–415.

Cambridge University Press. "Definition of Injured." Cambridge University Press. 2019. https://dictionary.cambridge.org/us/dictionary/english/injured.

Cranmer, Gregory and Sanderson, Jimmie. "'Rough Week for Testosterone'": Public Commentary Around the Ivy League's Decisions to Restrict Tackle Football in Practice." *Western Journal of Communication* 82, no. 5, (2018). 631–47.

Cunningham, George. B., and Regan, Jr., Michael. "Political Activism, Racial Identity, and the Commercial Endorsement of Athletes." *International Review for the Sociology of Sport* 47, (2012), 657–69.

Dawkins, Corey, and Glass, Rebecca. "Collateral Damage: The Disabled List—A History." Baseball Prospectus. February 3, 2012. https://www.baseball-prospectus.com/news/article/15967/collateral-damage-the-disabled-list-a-history.

Eagleman, Andrea. (2011). Stereotypes of race and nationality: A qualitative analysis of sport magazine coverage of MLB players. *Journal of Sport Management*, 25, 156–68.

Eagleman, Andrea, Rodenberg, Ryan, and Lee, Soonhwan. "From 'Hollow-eyed Pixies' to 'Team of Adults': Media Portrayals of Women's Gymnastics Before and After an Increased Minimum Age Policy. *Qualitative Research in Sport, Exercise & Health* 6, no. 3, (2014), 401–21.

Entman, Robert. "Framing: Toward Clarification of a Fractured Paradigm." *Journal of Communication* 43, no. 4, (1993), 51–58.

European Parliament. "Gender Neutral Language in the European Parliament." 2018. http://www.europarl.europa.eu/cmsdata/151780/GNL_Guidelines_EN.pdf.

Ferrigon, Phillip. (2019). "Person-first Language vs. Identity First Language: An Examination of the Gains and Drawbacks of Disability Language in Society." *Journal of Teaching Disability Studies*. (2019). https://jtds.commons.gc.cuny.edu/person-first-language-vs-identity-first-language-an-examination-of-the-gains-and-drawbacks-of-disability-language-in-society.

Fisher, Marc. (2015, April 5). "Baseball is Struggling to Hook Kids—and Risks Losing Fans to Other Sports." *Washington Post*. April 5, 2015. https://www.washingtonpost.com/sports/nationals/baseballs-trouble-with-the-youth-curve--and-what-that-means-for-the-game/2015/04/05/2da36dca-d7e8-11e4-8103fa84725dbf9d_story.html?utm_term=.2d552bd5d64a.

Frederick, Evan and Pegoraro, Ann. "Scandal in College Basketball: A Case Study of Image Repair via Facebook." *International Journal of Sport Communication* 11, no. 3, (2018) 414–29.

Frederick, Evan, Pegoraro, Ann, and Burch, Lawrence. "Legends Worthy of Lament: An Analysis of Self-presentation and User Framing on the Legends Football League's Facebook Page." *Journal of Sports Media* 12, no. 1, (2017) 169–90.

Frederick, Evan, Pegoraro, Ann, and Burch, Lawrence, "Echo or Organic: Framing the 2014 Sochi Games." *Online Information Review* 40, (2016) 1–19.

Frederick, Evan, Pegoraro, Ann, and Sanderson, Jimmie. "Divided and United: Perceptions of Athlete Activism at the ESPYS." *Sport in Society* 12, (2019), 1919–36.

Frederick, Evan, Sanderson, Jimmie, and Schlereth, Nicholas. "Kick These Kids Off the Team and Take Away Their Scholarships: Facebook and Perceptions of Athlete Activism at the University of Missouri." *Journal of Issues in Intercollegiate Athletics* 10, (2017), 17–34.

Frederick, Evan, Stocz, Michael, and Pegoraro, Ann. "Prayers, Punishment,and Perception: An Analysis of the Response to the Tony Stewart—Kevin Ward Jr. Incident on Facebook." *Sport in Society* 19, (no. 10), (2016), 1460–77.

Gamson, William and Modigliani, Andre. "The Changing Culture of Affirmative Action." *Research in Political Sociology* 3, (1987), 137–77.

Garland-Thomson, Rosemarie. "Reshaping, Rethinking, Redefining: Feminist Disability Studies." Women Enabled. 2001 https://www.womenenabled.org/pdfs/Garland-Thomson,Rosemarie,RedefiningFeministDisabilities StudiesCWPR2001.pdf.

Gazda, Maureen. (2017, January 13). "Connecticut Assesses Law Updating Access Symbol." *New Mobility*. January 13, 2017. http://www.newmobility.com/2017/01/connecticut-updates-access-symbol.

Howe, David. "From Inside the Newsroom: Paralympic Media and the 'Production' of Elite Disability." *International Review for the Sociology of Sport* 43, no. 2, (2008), 135–50.

Huang, Ying and Fahmy, Shahira. "Picturing a Journey of Protest or a Journey of Harmony? Comparing the Visual Framing of the 2008 Olympic Torch Relay in the US Versus Chinese Press." *Media, War & Conflict* 6, no. 3, (2013), 191–206.

Hums, Mary, Wolff, Eli, and Legg, David. "Leadership in Disability Sport." In *Sport leadership in the 21st century*. Edited by Laura Burton, G. Kane, and John Borland, 283–300. Sudbury, MA: Jones & Bartlett. 2019.

International Paralympic Committee. "Rio 2016 Paralympics Smash All TV Viewing Records." 2017 https://www.paralympic.org/news/rio-2016-paralympics-smash-all-tv-viewing-records.

Jimenez, Abdel. "The Spending Power of Americans with Disabilities." *Business Journalism*. 2018. https://businessjournalism.org/2018/09/the-spending-power-of-americans-with-disabilities.

Kastel, Matthew. "Our National Pastime Collides with Political Correctness." Newsmax. April 10, 2019. https://www.newsmax.com/matthewkastel/baseball-political-correctness-sports/2019/04/10/id/911083.

Kaufman, Peter. "Boos, Bans, and Other Backlash: The Consequences of Being an Activist Athlete." *Humanity & Society* 32, (2008), 215–37.

Lapchick, Richard. "Racial and Gender Report Card." TIDE Sport. 2020. https://www.tidesport.org/racial-gender-report-card.

Laucella, Pamela. "Arthur Ashe, Privacy, and Media: An Analysis of Newspaper Journalists' Coverage of Ashe's AIDS Announcement." *International Journal of Sport Communication* 2, no. 1, (2009), 56–80.

Laucella, Pamela. "Michael Vick: An Analysis of Press Coverage on Federal Dogfighting Charges." *Journal of Sports Media,* 5, no. 2, (2010), 35–76.

Le Clair, Jill. "Global Organizational Change in Sport and the Shifting Meaning of Disability." *Sport in Society*, 14, no. 9, (2011), 1072–93.

Liang, Limin. "Framing China and the World Through the Olympic Opening Ceremonies, 1984—2008." *Sport in Society* 13, no. 5), (2010), 819–32.

Lindlof, Thomas and Taylor, Bryon. *Qualitative Communication Research Methods* (3rd ed.). Thousand Oak, CA: Sage Publications. 2011.

Linguistic Society of America. "Is English Changing?" 2019. https://www.linguisticsociety.org/content/english-changing.

Major League Baseball. "10 Day Injured List." 2019. http://m.mlb.com/glossary/injuries/10-day-injured-list.

Mataxas, Panagiotis., and Twitter Trails Research Team. "Retweets Indicate Agreement, Endorsement, Trust: A Meta-analysis of Published Twitter Research." Wellesley. 2017.http://cs.wellesley.edu/~pmetaxas/WorkingPapers/Retweet-meaning.pdf.

Mather, Victor. "The 'Disabled List' in Baseball Gets Deactivated." *The New York Times*. February 8, 2019. https://www.nytimes.com/2019/02/08/sports/disabled-list-baseball.html.

Meraz, Sharon and Papacharissi, Zizi. "Networked Gatekeeping and Networked Framing on #Egypt." *The International Journal of Press/Politics* 18, (2013), 138–66.

NBA. "Collective Bargaining Agreement." 2017. https://cosmic-s3.imgix.net/3c7a0a50-8e11-11e9-875d-3d44e94ae33f-2017-NBA-NBPA-Collective-Bargaining-Agreement.pdf.

NBA Media Ventures. "Inactive v. Active List Rules." 2018. https://www.nba.com/news/inactive_rules_0506.html.

Neff, Jack. "Nielsen's First Dive into Households with Disabilities Finds Poorer but Loyal Customers." *Ad Age*. October 26, 2016. https://adage.com/article/cmo-strategy/nielsen-households-disabilitles-skew-poorer-loyal/306474.

New York State. "Governor Cuomo Signs Legislation Updating New York's Accessibility Signage and Logos." *Governor of New York*. July 25, 2014. https://www.governor.ny.gov/news/governor-cuomo-signs-legislation-updating-new-yorks-accessibility-signage-and-logos.

NFL. (2017). "Personnel (Injury) Report Policy." 2017. https://operations.nfl.com/media/2683/2017-nfl-injury-report-policy.pdf.

NHL. "Hockey Operations Guidelines." http://www.nhl.com/ice/page.htm?id=26377.

Nightingale, Bob. "MLB to Implement New Rule Changes That Will Shake Up Look of Sport." *USA Today*. March 14, 2019. https://www.usatoday.com/story/sports/mlb/2019/03/14/mlb-new-rule-changes-roster-3-batter-minimum/3157226002.

Nisbet, Matthew. "Knowledge Into Action: Framing the Debates Over Climate Change and Poverty." In *Doing Frame Analysis: Empirical and Theoretical Perspectives*, edited by Paul D'Angelo and Jim Kuypers, 43-83. London: Routledge, 2010.

Passan, Jeff. "Major League Baseball to Rename Disabled List to Injured List." ESPN. February 7, 2019. https://www.espn.com/mlb/story/_/id/25947020/major-league-baseball-rename-disabled-list-injured-list.

Pecararo, Grazia. "The Business Impacts of Inclusive Language." *Employment Law Matters*. August 27, 2018. https://employmentlawmatters.com/health-wellbeing-eeo/the-business-impacts-of-inclusive-language/#.XUChpZNKi4s.

Portnoy, Howard. "The Latest Victim of Political Correctness: The Disabled List in Baseball." *Liberty Unyielding*. February 28, 2019. https://libertyunyielding.com/2019/02/08/the-latest-victim-of-political-correctness-the-disabled-list-in-baseball.

Rehabilitation Research and Training Center. "Disability Stigma and Your Patients." No date. http://agerrtc.washington.edu/info/factsheets/stigma.

Ruderman Foundation. "Episode 13: Diversity and Inclusion in Major League Baseball." April 15, 2019.https://rudermanfoundation.org/podcast/episode-13-diversity-and-inclusion-in-major-league-baseball.

Reuters. "Tokyo Receives Unprecedented Demand for Paralympic Tickets." *The Guardian*. December 10, 2019. https://www.theguardian.com/sport/2019/dec/10/tokyo- receive-unprecedented-demand-2020-paralympics-tickets-athletics.

Schmidt, Samuel, Frederick, Evan, Pegoraro, Ann, and Spencer, Tyler. "An Analysis of Colin Kaepernick, Megan Rapinoe, and the National Anthem Protests." *Communication & Sport* 7, (no. 5), (2019). 653–77.

Serazio, Michael and Thorson, Emily. "Sports Fans Were Already Politicized. And Sports Culture is Deeply Conservative." October 2, 2017. *Washington Post*. https://www.washingtonpost.com/news/posteverything/wp/2017/10/02/sports-were-already-politicized-and-sports-culture-is-deeply-conservative/?utm_term=.25671c966c26.

Silva, Carol and Howe, David. "The (In)validity of Supercrip Representation of Paralympic Athletes." *Journal of Sport and Social Issues* 36, no.2), (2014), 174–94.

Smith, Marc, A., Rainie, Lee, Shneiderman, Ben., and Himelboim, Itai. "Mapping Twitter Topic Networks: From Polarized Crowds to Community Clusters." Pew Research Internet Project. 2014, http://www.pewinternet.org/2014/02/20/mapping-twitter-topic-networks-from-polarized-crowds-to-community-clusters.

Strauss, Anselm. *Qualitative Analysis for Social Scientists.* London: Cambridge University Press. 1987.

Tewksbury, David and Scheufele, Dietram. "News Framing Theory and Research." In *Media Effects: Advances in Theory and Research.* Edited by J. Bryant and M. B. Oliver. 17–33. New York: Taylor & Francis. 2009.

Thorson, Emily., and Serazio, Michael. "Sports Fandom and Political Attitudes." *Public Opinion Quarterly*, 82 no. 2, (2018). 391–403. https://doi-org. echo.louisville.edu/10.1093/poq/nfy018.

Toback, Rebecca. "Explaining PUP, NFI, IR, and Other NFL Roster Designations." Cincy Jungle. September 2, 2018. https://www.cincyjungle.com/2018/8/31/17797904/explaining-pup-nfi-ir-other-injury-nfl-roster-designations-cuts-53-man-roster.

United Nations. "FAQs." 2007. https://www.un.org/esa/socdev/enable/faqs.htm.

United Nations Office of Economic and Social Affairs. "Disability and Sport." 2011. https://www.un.org/development/desa/disabilities/issues/disability-and-sports.html.

USDOJ. "Introduction to the ADA." No date. https://www.ada.gov/ada_intro.htm.

van Luijk, Nicollen and Frisby, Wendy. "(Re)Framing of Protest at the 2010 Winter Olympic Games." *International Journal of Sport Policy* 4, no. 2, (2012). 343–59.

WebMD. "Sports Injuries A-Z." 2019. https://www.webmd.com/fitness-exercise/sports-injuries-a-to-z.

Notes

1. Dawkins and Glass, 2012.
2. Baseball-Reference.com
3. NFL, 2017; Toback, 2018.
4. NBA 2017, Article 1, 5; NBA Media Ventures, 2018.
5. NBA, 2017, 200.
6. NHL.
7. Major League Baseball, Official Rules, 2019.
8. Of note is the fact that due to the COVID-19 pandemic, MLB also created a COVID-19 related injured list, which specified no minimum stay. Any of three conditions could place a player on this list:"a positive test, exposure to coronavirus or symptoms that require isolation or additional assessment," as quoted by Blum, 2020.
9. Author, personal communication, September 3, 2003.
10. Link20, personal communication, November 27, 2018.
11. Passan, 2019.
12. Bogage, 2019; Mather, 2019.
13. Mary Hums, as quoted in Allentuck 2019, 1.
14. Ferrigon, 2019.
15. APA, 2019.
16. Ferrigon, 2019.
17. USDOJ.
18. Cambridge University Press, 2019.
19. Bell, 2009.
20. Garland-Thomson, 2001, 2.
21. Rehabilitation Research and Training Center, n.d.
22. LeClair, 2011, 1078.
23. International Paralympic Committee, 2017.
24. Reuters, 2019.
25. Howe, 2008; Silva and Howe, 2012.
26. American Psychological Association, 2019.
27. United Nations Department of Economic and Social Affairs, 2011.
28. Entman, 1993.
29. Gamson and Modligliani, 1987; Tewksbury and Scheufele, 2009.
30. Angelini, et al. 2014; Billings, et al. 2014; Eagleman, et al. 2014.
31. Huang and Fahmy, 2013; Liang, 2010; van Luijk and Frisby, 2012.
32. Bishop, 2005; Eagleman, 2011; Laucella, 2009, 2010.
33. Nisbet, 2010.
34. Meraz and Papacharissi, 2013.
35. Burch, et al., 2015.
36. Blaszka, et al., 2016.
37. Frederick, Pegoraro, and Burch, 2016.
38. Billings, et al., 2015.
39. Frederick, Stocz, and Pegoraro, 2016.
40. Frederick, Pegoraro, and Burch, 2017.
41. Frederick, Sanderson, and Schlereth, 2017.
42. Frederick, Pegoraro, and Sanderson, 2019.
43. Schmidt, et al., 2019.
44. Cranmer and Sanderson, 2018.
45. Cranmer and Sanderson, 638.
46. Cranmer and Sanderson, 642.
47. Lindlof and Taylor 2011, 251.
48. Lindlof and Taylor 2011, 252.
49. Associated Press, 2019; Nightingale, 2019.
50. Serazio and Thorson, 2017.
51. Thorson and Serazio, 2018.
52. Kaufman, 2008.
53. Cunnigham and Regan, 2012.
54. Frederick, Pegoraro, and Sanderson, 2019.
55. Frederick, Sanderson, and Schlereth, 2017.
56. Kastel, 2019; Portnoy, 2019.
57. Rudeman Foundation, 2019.
58. New York State, 2014.
59. Gazda, 2017.
60. Hums, et al, 2019.
61. Atcheson, 2018.
62. Pecoraro, 2018.
63. Neff, 2016.
64. Jimenez, 2018.
65. European Parliament, 2018.
66. Linguistic Society of America, 2019.

The Houston Asterisks

Analyzing the Effects of Sign-Stealing on the Astros' World Series Season

Will Melville and Brinley Zabriskie

In November 2019, *The Athletic* published an article that credibly accused the Houston Astros of electronically stealing catcher signs in 2017.[1] Stealing catcher signs can potentially provide an advantage to batters since they know in advance the type of pitch the pitcher will throw. Late in the 2017 season, Major League Baseball (MLB) forbade the use of electronics to steal catcher signs and relay those signs to hitters, with Commissioner Rob Manfred issuing a memo to that effect in September 2017.[2] *The Athletic* article sparked outrage in the baseball world, with many fans demanding the Astros be stripped of their 2017 World Series title.

As a result of the article and ensuing outrage, MLB began investigating the Houston Astros. The results of that investigation were published in January 2020, and it was determined that the Astros did break the rules by electronically stealing signs.[3] Reportedly, the Astros had two distinct methods of sign-stealing.

For the first method, Astros employees in the video replay review room used the live game feed from the center-field camera to attempt to decode the opposing catcher's signs using a program called "Codebreaker."[4] If the employees were able to decode the sign sequence, they would relay that information to the players. Then, if an Astros player reached second base, the player could decode the catcher's signs and signal the next pitch to the current batter, thereby giving their team an advantage against the opposing team's pitcher. It is believed that the Astros used this method to steal signs throughout the 2017 season and partway into the 2018 season during both their home and away games.

The Astros began a second method of sign-stealing apparently on May 28, roughly two months into the 2017 season.[5] A group of players, as well as bench coach Alex Cora, set up a monitor outside the team's dugout that displayed the center-field camera feed. They then used that feed to steal the opposing catcher's signs and signal the next pitch to the batter by banging on a trash can. One or two bangs typically corresponded to off-speed or breaking pitches, whereas no bangs corresponded to a fastball. The Astros used this method to steal signs throughout the 2017 season (after May 28) during their home games.

In his official report on the Astros investigation, Rob Manfred stated that he was unable to determine if the sign-stealing actually helped the Astros win games. Many Astros players stated that they felt the banging was more distracting than helpful. Not only that, but many baseball fans, as well as high-ranking baseball officials, believe that the sign-stealing issue is widespread and not confined to the Astros alone. Thus, it is possible that the Astros' sign-stealing, while illegal, did not actually provide them a significant advantage during the 2017 season. However, it is also possible that their sign-stealing did provide an unethical advantage.

The aim of this article is to identify and describe evidence that cheating by electronic sign-stealing provided or did not provide the Astros with an advantage over the other MLB teams. To that end, we analyze a variety of offensive statistics to determine if the Astros appear to have had a significant advantage offensively compared to other MLB teams. Specifically, we analyze swing rates, walk and strikeout rates, overall hitting as measured by weighted runs created plus (wRC+), rare run-scoring events, and comeback rates. We compare the Astros' performance during their home games (where trash-can-banging and "Codebreaker" were used) versus their away games (where only "Codebreaker" was used) to determine if the trash-can-banging scheme significantly aided the Astros. (The home-field advantage effect is not substantial in baseball.[6]) Additionally, we compare the Astros' home games before and after May 28, since that is when they started using the trash-can-banging scheme. We did not include the three "home" games that the Astros played in Tampa Bay as a result of Hurricane Harvey. As a baseline for comparison, we also look at the rest of the league's performance.

We present the swing rates, walk and strikeout rates, overall hitting, rare scoring events, and comeback rates data analyses in Section 1. In Section 2, we summarize our findings in terms of the evidence that sign-stealing provided or did not provide the Astros a significant advantage during the 2017 season. Finally, we end with our conclusions. Overall, we do not believe the evidence we present offers definitive proof that the Astros significantly benefitted, or did not benefit, from their cheating during the 2017 season.

SECTION 1.
Data Analysis

In this section, we analyze several metrics to try to measure if the Astros' sign-stealing provided them an unfair advantage during the 2017 season. We analyze metrics that would likely have been directly impacted by sign-stealing, like swing rates, walk rates, and strikeout rates. We also look at metrics that may have been indirectly affected by sign-stealing, like wRC+, rare run-scoring events, and comebacks. Swing rate data were obtained from Baseball Savant's Statcast.[7] The walk rates, strikeout rates, and wRC+ data were taken from FanGraphs.[8] Finally, Retrosheet provides the data used in the rare run-scoring event and comeback analyses through their game logs and play-by-play files.[9] We compare the Astros' performance during their home games (where they supposedly used trash-can-banging and "Codebreaker") against their away games (where they just used "Codebreaker") in an attempt to quantify the effects of their sign-stealing schemes. We also compare the Astros' home games before May 28 (29 games) and after May 28 (49 games) to determine if the trash-can-banging scheme alone helped the Astros. Additionally, we compare the Astros' performance with the rest of the league's performance to see if they had a significant advantage over other MLB teams.

Throughout these analyses, we will often report *p*-values. A *p*-value is the probability, under a certain statistical model, that a summary of the data (e.g., the average difference between two groups) would be equal to or more extreme than its observed value.[10] For the swing rate analyses, a *p*-value would represent the probability of seeing the given difference, or larger difference, in home and away swing rates if we assume that the true swing rates are equal. A small *p*-value indicates statistical incompatibility of the observed data with what we assumed to be true, which, for the swing rate analysis would indicate evidence of a significant difference in the home and away swing rates. It should be noted that we do not support using arbitrary cut-offs to determine if a *p*-value is significant. For more information about *p*-values and their correct interpretations, see reference 9.

Swing Rate Comparisons

One potential advantage of sign-stealing is foreknowledge of a pitch, which could affect a hitter's choice to swing, which would affect their overall swing rate. When comparing the Astros' swing rates, we consider three different pitch types: fastballs, breaking balls, and off-speed pitches. We also consider pitches outside the strike zone. We compare the Astros' home swing rates with their away swing rates, and we compare their home swing rates before May 28 against their home swing rates after May 28. To make these comparisons, we apply a two-sample t-test, a basic statistical hypothesis test to compare the swing rate of one set of games to the swing rate of another set of games, to each type of pitch. We use a two-sided test to determine if there is a significant difference in swing rates at home versus away, as well as at home before and after May 28. A significant difference in swing rates in any of these tests would provide evidence that the trash-can-banging scheme had an effect on swing rates, and, consequently, an effect on the game.

Note that "Codebreaker" may also have had a small effect on swing rates. However, stealing signs via "Codebreaker" required having a runner on second base, which is relatively uncommon, so most pitches and swings would have occurred with no runner on second. Additionally, the Astros used "Codebreaker" at home and on the road, so by comparing home and away swing rates, we are essentially treating "Codebreaker" as a baseline for assessing the effectiveness of the trash-can-banging scheme.

In addition to testing for a difference in swing rates between home and away games, we also test for a difference in swing rates for the rest of the league's home and away games. This will act as a baseline for comparison for the Astros' swing rates. For instance, if the rest of the league and the Astros have similar differences in their home and away swing rates, then this would suggest the sign-stealing did not significantly aid the Astros.

Figure 1 (next page) shows the 2017 home and away swing rates for the Astros and the rest of the league. There is weak evidence that the Astros were more likely to swing at fastballs at home than they were on the road (*p*-value of 0.04). Conversely, there is weak evidence that the rest of the league was less likely to swing at fastballs at home (*p*-value of 0.05). Since the Astros were more likely to swing at fastballs at home, but the rest of the league was less likely to, this could indicate that sign-stealing influenced the Astros' fastball swing rates.

For breaking balls, there is weak evidence that the Astros were less likely to swing at these pitches at

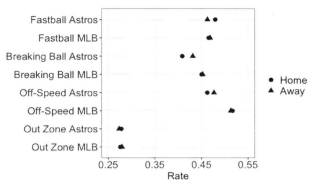

Figure 1. 2017 home and away game swing rates for the Astros and the rest of the MLB teams

home than they were on the road (*p*-value of 0.05). On the other hand, there is no significant difference in the rest of the league's swing rates at breaking balls at home or away (*p*-value of 0.37). These results suggest that the trash-can-banging may have helped the Astros avoid swinging at breaking balls during their home games.

Neither the Astros nor the rest of the league saw significant differences in their home and away swing rates at off-speed pitches (*p*-values of 0.43 and 0.32, respectively). Likewise, the Astros saw no significant difference in their swing rates at pitches outside the strike zone during their home or away games (*p*-value of 0.55). However, there is evidence that the rest of the league was more likely to swing at pitches outside the strike zone on the road than they were at home (*p*-value of 0.02). These results suggest that trash-can-banging had no effect on the Astros' swing rates at off-speed pitches or pitches outside the strike zone.

Figure 2 shows the Astros' home swing rates before and after May 28, the day they started trash-can-banging to steal signs. There are no significant differences in the Astros' swing rates at fastballs (*p*-value of 0.28)

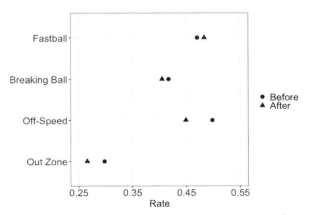

Figure 2. 2017 home game swing rates for the Astros before and after May 28

or at breaking balls (*p*-value of 0.51) before and after May 28. There is weak evidence (*p*-value of 0.06) that the Astros were less likely to swing at off-speed pitches after May 28. There is fairly strong evidence (*p*-value of 0.01) that the Astros were less likely to swing at pitches outside the strike zone after May 28. Overall, the results in Figure 2 suggest that sign-stealing may have affected the Astros' swing rates at off-speed pitches and pitches outside the strike zone, but it did not seem to affect their swing rates at fastballs or breaking balls.

Walk Rates, Strikeout Rates, and wRC+

Next, we consider walk rates, strikeout rates, and wRC+. A team's walk rate is the total number of times they walked divided by their total number of plate appearances. Similarly, their strikeout rate is the total number of strikeouts divided by plate appearances. Weighted runs created (wRC) quantifies a player's offense in terms of runs, and wRC+ simply compares a player's wRC to the league average wRC after adjusting for ballpark effects.[11] Swing rates naturally have an effect on strikeout and walk rates, and walk rates and strikeout rates have an effect on overall offense, which can be measured with wRC+. To determine if the sign-stealing schemes had a significant effect on the Astros' walk rates, strikeout rates, and wRC+, we employ t-tests, as outlined earlier.

We start by comparing walk and strikeout rates for the Astros' home and away games. The Astros had no significant difference in walk rates at home (rate of 0.078) versus away (rate of 0.085) (*p*-value of 0.33). Similarly, their strikeout rates were not significantly different at home (rate of 0.167) than they were on the road (rate of 0.179) (*p*-value of 0.21). The Astros wRC+ was the same value, 121, at home and away. It appears that sign-stealing via trash-can-banging did not significantly impact the Astros' walk rates, strikeout rates, or wRC+ when comparing their home and away games.

Next, we compare walk and strikeout rates from the Astros' home games before and after May 28. There was no significant difference in the Astros' walk rates before May 28 (rate of 0.077) and after May 28 (rate of 0.079) (*p*-value of 0.89). Strikeout rates were also not significantly different for the Astros' home games before May 28 (rate of 0.178) and after May 28 (rate of 0.160) (*p*-value of 0.21). Sign-stealing via trash-can-banging appears not to have helped the Astros' walk more or strike out less when comparing their home games before and after May 28.

The change in the Astros wRC+, on the other hand, is rather interesting when comparing this value before and after May 28. The Astros wRC+ at home before May 28 was 112, and their wRC+ at home after May 28 jumped up to 126. To determine how common it is to see an increase as large as the Astros', we compare every MLB team's 2017 home wRC+ before May 28 and after May 28.

Figure 3 shows a scatterplot with the home wRC+ values before and after May 28 for every MLB team in 2017. The plot shows that it was not uncommon to see an increase in wRC+ of fourteen. In fact, the Giants (SFG), Padres (SDP), Royals (KCR), Rockies (COL), Orioles (BAL), Rangers (TEX), Marlins (MIA), and Twins (MIN) all saw similar, or even larger, increases (marked on the plot). However, these teams all started out with a below average wRC+ before May 28, whereas the Astros (HOU) started out with an above average wRC+ before May 28 (note that 100 is considered average for wRC+). It could be argued that the increase in wRC+ for the other teams is expected due to a regression-to-the-mean effect. However, that same argument cannot be made for the Astros since their wRC+ before May 28 was already above average. One could perhaps argue that the Astros wRC+ increased after May 28 because they were stealing signs with the trash-can-banging scheme, but then we would also expect their home wRC+ (121) to be larger than their away wRC+ (121), which is not the case. These inconsistencies make it difficult to say with confidence that the Astros' sign-stealing led to their increase in wRC+ after May 28.

The dashed diagonal line in Figure 3 marks the points where teams would have the same wRC+ before and after May 28. Teams above the dashed line improved their wRC+ after May 28, while teams below the dashed line saw a decrease in their wRC+ after May 28. Teams with an increase in wRC+ of

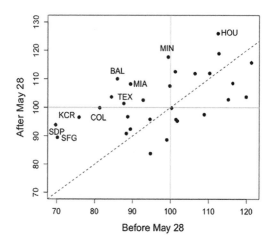

Figure 3. 2017 MLB teams' home wRC+ scores.

more than 14 are labelled. The grey horizontal and vertical lines mark the average, as defined, for wRC+.

Rare Run Scoring Events

We now consider two rare offensive events: big run innings and big run games. Though the sign-stealing would not have had a direct impact on rare offensive events, it is possible that consistent sign-stealing would have helped the Astros have significantly more big run events than their opponents. We define big run innings as an inning where a team scores four or more runs, and we define big run games as a game where a team scores eleven or more runs. Innings of four or more runs occurred 2.7% of the time in 2017, and games with eleven or more runs occurred about 5.6% of the time in 2017. We compare the Astros' home and away games to see if they were more likely to have these rare offensive events at home (where they were stealing signs with the trash can method and "Codebreaker") than on the road (where they were just using "Codebreaker") compared to the likelihood of the rest of the league.

Traditional statistical methods are insufficient to analyze rare event data such as these. Accordingly, we employ the methods of Zabriskie and Fisher's exact test, which are designed to handle rare events. We use the method of Zabriskie for the big run innings analyses.[12] This method was designed originally for rare event meta-analyses and is a way to pool information from multiple sources to produce one overall conclusion. This method will pool the evidence across the Astros' 81 away games and 78 home games during the 2017 season, while accounting for the natural clustering of each game. We apply Fisher's exact test to the big run games analyses to determine if the Astros were more likely to have more big run games than their opponents.[13]

For both rare events, we perform two separate analyses: one for the Astros' home games, the other for the Astros' away games. For the Astros' i^{th} home game ($i = 1,2,...,78$), we compare the Astros' (the home team) performance with their competitor's (the away team) performance. We do the same for the Astros' i^{th} away game ($i = 1,2,...,81$), where we compare the Astros' (the away team) performance with their competitor's (the home team) performance. For big run innings, we count the number of times four or more runs were scored during the n_i innings in the ith game (n_i ranged from 8 to 13 in the Astros' 2017 season). For big run games, we count the number of games with eleven or more runs ($n_i = n = 1$ for all games).

In summary, for the Astros' home and away game comparisons, we perform four statistical tests, one for each combination of rare events (big run innings and big run games) and game location (home and away). Additionally, we conduct similar tests to compare the Astros' home games before and after May 28, when the trash-can-banging scheme began.

Table 1 shows the results of the rare big run innings tests on the Astros' home and away games. There is no significant difference in big run innings between the Astros and their competitors. This suggests that sign-stealing at home did not aid the Astros in having more big run innings than their opponents, nor did "Code-breaker" help the Astros have more big run innings on the road than their competitors.

Table 1. Average big run innings percentages for the Astros' home and away games in 2017 for the Astros and their competitors. Also reported are the one-sided *p*-values for testing if the Astros had significantly more big run innings than their competitors.

	Big Run Innings for the Astros' Home Games	Big Run Innings for the Astros' Away Games
Astros' Average Event Rate	3.92%	4.63%
Competitors' Average Event Rate	2.14%	3.50%
p-value	0.92	0.91

Table 2 displays the results of the rare big run games tests on the Astros' home and away games. For the home games, there is no evidence to suggest that sign-stealing at home helped the Astros have big games more frequently. For the away games, there is some evidence that the Astros had significantly more big run games than their opponents. Perhaps "Code-breaker" aided the Astros offensively by helping them achieve big run games more often on the road.

Table 2. Average big run games percentages for the Astros' home and away games in 2017 for the Astros and their competitors. Also reported are the one-sided *p*-values for testing if the Astros had significantly more big run games than their competitors.

	Big Run Games for the Astros' Home Games	Big Run Games for the Astros' Away Games
Astros' Average Event Rate	6.41%	14.81%
Competitors' Average Event Rate	2.56%	6.17%
p-value	0.22	0.06

We also compare the Astros' and their competitors' performance during the Astros' home games before and after May 28. The results for big run innings and big run games are identical to what was found for all of the Astros' home games because all big run innings and big run games occurred after May 28. Namely, there is no evidence that sign-stealing aided the Astros' in achieving more big run innings or big run games than their competitors when comparing the Astros' home games before and after May 28 (*p*-values greater than 0.21).

Comebacks

Finally, we consider comebacks. Stealing signs could potentially help a team stay competitive in games that they are expected to lose. For example, knowing the opposing team's signs might help a batter hit a home run or an extra-base hit late in a one-run game. Additionally, the Astros would have been more motivated to steal signs in games where they needed to make a comeback than in games where they already had a lead. We are interested in determining if the Astros had an unusually good ability to come back in games where they were down, so we analyze their comeback rates by inning. We define comeback rate by inning as the total number of times a team won a game when they were down in the given inning divided by the total number of times they were down in that inning. We compare the Astros' comeback rates to the rest of the league's comeback rates to see if they came back more frequently than expected. We compare home and away comeback rates separately since the cheating tactics were different at home than they were on the road. We also compare the home comeback rates before and after May 28.

Figure 4 (next page) shows the Astros' home comeback rates and the rest of the league's home comeback rates. The vertical lines represent 95% confidence intervals for the true comeback rate. These confidence intervals represent a range of values that we can say with a high level of confidence include the true comeback rate. If the Astros' vertical lines overlap MLB's vertical lines at an inning, then we conclude that there is no significant difference in home comeback rates between the Astros and MLB teams. From Figure 4, we see that the confidence intervals for the Astros and the rest of the league overlap in each inning. Thus, there is no evidence to suggest that banging on trash cans or "Codebreaker" helped the Astros come back when they were down in their home games.

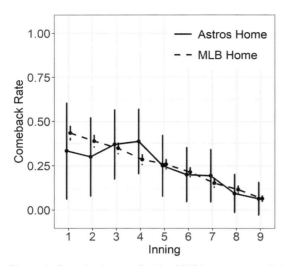

Figure 4. Comeback rates for the 2017 home games. Data are split for the Astros and the rest of the MLB teams with 95% confidence intervals plotted for each inning.

Figure 5 displays the Astros' away game comeback rates and the rest of the league's away game comeback rates. The confidence intervals for the Astros and the other MLB teams overlap in the fifth, sixth, eighth, and ninth innings, but they do not overlap in the second, third, fourth, or seventh innings. This suggests that the Astros were significantly more likely to come back when they were losing on the road in those innings (second, third, fourth, and seventh) than the rest of the league. This provides evidence that "Codebreaker" may have helped the Astros come back on the road. However, the Astros used "Codebreaker" at home, along with the trash-can-banging scheme, but they were not significantly more likely to come back at

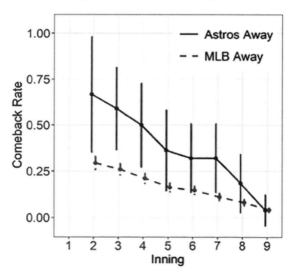

Figure 5. Comeback rates for the 2017 away games. Data are split for the Astros and the rest of the MLB teams with 95% confidence intervals plotted for each inning.

home than the rest of the league for any inning. This inconsistency makes it hard to attribute the Astros' unusual ability to come back on the road in some innings to sign-stealing.

We also compared comeback rates for the Astros and the rest of the league before and after May 28 and found no significant differences in comeback rates for any inning. This is to be expected due to the small sample size for the Astros' games. The Astros were not down at home in any inning more than twelve times before May 28.

SECTION 2. SUMMARY OF THE EVIDENCE

We will now summarize our findings in terms of which results provide evidence that (i) the Astros' performance was improved by sign-stealing and (ii) sign-stealing did not have a significant effect on the Astros' performance.

Evidence Sign-Stealing Provided a Significant Advantage

In this section we list the evidence we found that indicates the Astros' sign-stealing schemes aided their offense. We consider the possible effects of "Codebreaker" (used during both home and away games) and trash-can-banging (used only at home games).

- There is weak evidence that the trash-can-banging scheme helped the Astros swing at fastballs more frequently during their home games and at breaking balls less frequently during their home games.

- There is some evidence that the trash-can-banging scheme aided the Astros in swinging less often at off-speed pitches and pitches outside the strike zone during the Astros' home games after May 28.

- The trash-can-banging scheme may have contributed to a large increase in the Astros' home wRC+ after May 28. Although it was not uncommon for a team's home wRC+ to increase by as much as the Astros' after May 28, the Astros were the only team whose wRC+ increased by that much and who also had an above average wRC+ before May 28.

- The Astros had significantly more big run games than their opponents during the Astros' away games. This suggests that "Codebreaker" may have helped the Astros have more big run games on the road. However, the Astros did not have significantly more big games at home, so it is difficult to conclude if this result is because of "Codebreaker" (which was used both at home and away).

- The Astros were significantly more likely than an average MLB team to come back in away games in the second, third, fourth, and seventh innings, which suggests that "Codebreaker" may have helped them come back more than expected. But, since "Codebreaker" was also used during home games, and this trend was not apparent for home games, we cannot be certain that the Astros' comebacks in away games are due to "Codebreaker."

Evidence Sign-Stealing Did Not Provide a Significant Advantage
In this section we summarize the evidence we found that the Astros' sign-stealing schemes did not affect their offense. We consider the possible effects of "Codebreaker" (used during both home and away games) and trash-can-banging (used only at home games).

- There were no significant differences in the Astros' home and away swing rates at off-speed pitches and pitches outside of the zone, which suggests that trash-can-banging did not have an effect on those swing rates.

- Trash-can-banging may not have had an effect on fastball and breaking ball swing rates, as there were no significant differences in the Astros' home swing rates at fastballs or breaking balls before and after May 28.

- There were no significant differences in the Astros' home and away walk and strikeout rates, and there were no significant differences in the Astros' home walk rates and strikeout rates before and after May 28. Together, these results suggest that trash-can-banging did not affect walks and strikeouts.

- The Astros' year-long wRC+ was identical at home and on the road, which is unusual because most teams have a higher wRC+ at home than they do on the road. Overall, this suggests that trash-can-banging did not improve the Astros' overall offense.

- The Astros did not have significantly more home or away big run innings than their opponents. This suggests that neither the trash-can-banging scheme nor "Codebreaker" helped the Astros increase their big run innings.

- The Astros did not have significantly more home big run games, which suggests that neither "Codebreaker" nor the trash-can-banging helped the Astros increase their home big run game rate.

- The Astros were not more likely than an average MLB team to come back at home in any inning, so trash-can-banging did not seem to help them come back. Likewise, they were not more likely to come back on the road in the fifth, sixth, eighth, or ninth innings, which suggests that "Codebreaker" may not have helped them come back, either.

CONCLUSION
The goal of this article was to compile and present evidence that the Astros' sign-stealing tactics did or did not give them an unfair advantage on offense in 2017. We considered metrics that would have been directly affected by sign-stealing, like swing rates, and metrics that would have been indirectly affected by sign stealing, like comeback rates. As we have shown, there is compelling evidence in both directions, and we leave it to the readers to draw their own conclusions about the effects of the Astros' sign-stealing schemes. When readers think critically of the evidence presented, they will realize there are likely other factors involved that we did not consider and that are not related to cheating. For example, we found that the Astros were more likely to come back during certain innings of away games than the rest of the league. This could be because of "Codebreaker," but it is also possible that the Astros were just really good at hitting. Likewise, we found that the Astros were more likely to swing at fastballs at home than they were on the road. This could be because of sign-stealing, but maybe there's something about the batter's eye in the Astros' home stadium that helps hitters see fastballs better. Additionally, some of the metrics we used to measure the effects of cheating provided contradictory evidence, like wRC+, which was the same for the Astros at home and on the road, but it also increased dramatically after May 28. Overall, the evidence we present does not offer definitive proof and should not be interpreted as such. There are potentially other explanations for the phenomena we discovered, and cheating just happens to be one of them.

Despite the evidence shown in both directions, one thing is crystal clear: the Astros' sign-stealing scandal has shaken the baseball world and tainted the integrity of America's pastime. Whether sign-stealing unethically aided them or not, their actions are inexcusable, and their 2017 World Series title will always be associated with an asterisk of illegitimacy. ■

Notes

1. Ken Rosenthal and Evan Drellich, "The Astros stole signs electronically in 2017—part of a much broader issue for Major League Baseball," *The Athletic*, accessed March 30, 2020, https://theathletic.com/1363451/2019/11/12/the-astros-stole-signs-electronicallyin-2017-part-of-a-muchbroader-issue-for-major-league-baseball.
2. Billy Witz, "Red Sox Are Fined Over Theft Of Signals," *The New York Times*, September 16, 2017, Sec D, 1. Accessed October 27, 2020, https://www.nytimes.com/2017/09/15/sports/baseball/red-sox-fined-stealing-signs-yankees.html.
3. Robert D. Manfred, Jr., Commissioner of Baseball, "Statement of the Commissioner," accessed March 30, 2020, https://img.mlbstatic.com/mlb-images/image/upload/mlb/cglrhmlrwwbkacty27l7.pdf.
4. Jared Diamond, "'Dark Arts' and 'Codebreaker': The Origins of the Houston Astros Cheating Scheme," *Wall Street Journal*, accessed March 30, 2020, https://www.wsj.com/articles/houston-astros-cheating-scheme-dark-arts-codebreaker-11581112994.
5. Tony Adams, "Sign Stealing Scandal," accessed March 30, 2020, http://signstealingscandal.com.
6. Michael J. Lopez, Gregory J. Matthews, and Benjamin S. Baumer, "How often does the best team win? A unified approach to understanding randomness in North American sport," *The Annals of Applied Statistics* 12, no. 4 (2018): 2483–2516, https://projecteuclid.org/euclid.aoas/1542078053.
7. Bill Petti, "Data Aquisition Functions," accessed March 30, 2020, http://billpetti.github.io/baseballr/data-acquisition-functions.
8. "Splits Leaderboards," FanGraphs, accessed March 30, 2020, https://www.fangraphs.com/leaders/splits-leaderboards?splitArr=.
9. Retrosheet, accessed March 30, 2020, https://www.retrosheet.org.
10. Ronald L. Wasserstein and Nicole A. Lazar, "The ASA's statement on p-values: context, process, and purpose," *The American Statistician* 70, no. 2 (2016): 129–133, http://dx.doi.org/10.1080/00031305.2016.1154108.
11. Steve Slowinski, "wRC and wRC+," Fangraphs, accessed March 19, 2020, https://library.fangraphs.com/offense/wrc.
12. Brinley Zabriskie, "Methods for Meta-Analyses of Rare Events, Sparse Data, and Heterogeneity" (PhD diss., Utah State University, 2019), 18–75.
13. Ronald A. Fisher, *Statistical Methods for Research Workers* (Edinburgh: Oliver & Boyd, 5th Edition, 1934).

The Art of the Brushback

Theo Tobel

"Pitching is the art of instilling fear."[1]
—Sandy Koufax

In Major League Baseball, the difference between a winning team and a losing one can be mental preparation and psychological advantage. It is a game of streaks, slumps, and momentum. A team that can get inside its opponent's head will find it much easier to win games. There are many ways that mental strategy has been used in the game. After a questionable call, managers may purposely get ejected to fuel their team. Hitters may use certain routines to get into the pitcher's head, such as the well-known "Soto Shuffle."[2] And for pitchers, the brushback pitch is a tool that is commonly used to intimidate batters or to move them off the plate. Even though a brushback pitch may lead to dangerous outcomes such as hit-by-pitches, when executed correctly, it is believed to negatively affect the hitter's performance.[3]

A "brushback pitch" is defined as a pitch that, when it crosses home plate from the catcher's perspective, falls within the batter's specified box, but does not hit the batter. In this paper, I analyze the use of the brushback pitch by count and pitch type to determine which one has the greatest effect on hits (by use of the chi-square test) and walks.

DATA COLLECTION

The width of the plate is almost 17 inches, the width from the edge of the plate to each of the batter's boxes is 6 inches, and the width of each batter's box is 4 feet (or 48 inches).

In order to determine which pitches qualify as brushbacks, I used 2018 regular season data from Daren Willman's Baseballsavant.com.[4] As defined by Baseball Savant's documentation glossary, "plate_x" is the horizontal position of the ball when it crosses home plate from the catcher's perspective.[5] Also, on Baseball Savant, the strike zone spans from -0.8 to 0.8 "plate_x" units.[6]

To convert "plate_x" to inches, I used the plate dimensions to make a ratio. By setting 1.6 "plate_x" units (absolute value of -0.8 – 0.8) to 17 inches, I found that 1 "plate_x" unit equals 10.625 inches, or 1 inch equals $1 \div 10.625$, or about 0.09 units.

Next, "Flag 1" was classified as the right-handed batter's box, and "Flag 2" was designated as the left-handed batter's box. Since the distance from the edge of the plate to each batter's box is 6 inches, I used the conversion calculated above to find that 6 inches equals $6 \div 10.625$, or about 0.56 units. Since the width of the batter's box is 48 inches, I also used the conversion to find that 48 inches equals $48 \div 10.625$, or about 4.52 units. Therefore, Flag 1 ranges from (-0.8 – 0.6) to (-0.8 – (0.6 + 4.5)) "plate_x" units, or about -1.4 to -5.9 units (0.6 is an estimate of 0.56 and 4.5 is an estimate of 4.52). On the other side of the plate, Flag 2 ranges from (0.8 + 0.6) to (0.8 + (0.6 + 4.5)) "plate_x" units, or about 1.4 to 5.9 units. This makes sense, because the middle of home plate has a "plate_x" value of 0, so the values of the batter's boxes are absolutes of each other, as the plate and boxes are symmetric across the "plate_x" = 0.

Three columns were added to the CSV file from Baseball Savant, "Result" (Column A), "Flag 1" (Column B), and "Flag 2" (Column C). The "Result" column states whether a pitch is a brushback. The code below states that any pitch in the "plate_x" range -1.4 to -5.9 units returns a 1 in the "Flag 1" column. Similarly, any pitch in the "plate_x" range 1.4 to 5.9 units returns a 1 in the "Flag 2" column. If a pitch isn't in the specified ranges, a 0 is returned. Basically, any pitch that falls within a batter's box is labeled a 1, and otherwise a 0. To determine whether a pitch was a brushback from the data, if the equation of "Flag 1" + "Flag 2" resulted in a 1, the "Result" was "YES." A pitch can't be in both batters' boxes, so if either of the Flags equaled 1, it appeared as a brushback pitch since $0 + 1$ or $1 + 0 = 1$.

The Excel code is shown below:

In "Flag 1":

```
=(K2="R")*(N2<=-1.36470588235)*
(N2>=-5.88235294118)*(I2<>"hit_by_pitch")
```

In "Flag 2":

```
=(K2="L")*(N2>=1.36470588235)*
(N2<=5.88235294118)*(I2<>"hit_by_pitch")
```

In "Result":
=IF((B2+C2)=1,"YES","NO")
where Column K is "stand" = Side of the plate batter is standing,
where Column I is "description" = Description of the resulting pitch,
and
where Column N is "plate_x,"
and "R" is right and "L" is left.

After brushbacks were classified in the "Result" column as a "YES," I wrote a code that looked through the data and classified pitches in a brushback at-bat. I added a fourth column, "Is BBAB?" to classify brushback at-bats. Pitches in brushback at-bats were classified with a "Y."

The code is shown below:
=IF((SUMPRODUCT(($A$2:$A$35000="YES")*($O$2:$O$35000=O2)
*($E$2:$E$35000=E2)*($G$2:$G$35000=G2),$E$2:$E$35000))>0,
"Y",""))
where Column A is "Result" (see above),
where Column O is "at_bat_number" = Plate appearance number of the game,
where Column E is "game_date" = Date of the Game, and
where Column G is "batter" = MLB Player ID tied to the play event.

The code marks a "Y" in Column D ("Is BBAB?")on every pitch with the same at-bat number, game date, and batter if there is a brushback pitch. (See Figure 1)

Now that the data are processed and sorted, statistical significance must be determined to see if there is a correlation between batting statistics and brushback pitch usage. In order for the results to be significant following a chi-square test for independence, the p-value must be less than the significance level, 0.05

or 5 percent. Also, three conditions must be met: a random sample, ideal values more than 5, and a sample size of less than 10% of the population.

THE EFFECT OF THE BRUSHBACK PITCH ON BATTING AVERAGE

For this test of statistical significance, I am going to use the chi-square test for independence because it is appropriate for the data being analyzed. The chi-square test will give two tables, one real and one ideal, and will also give a p-value. My null hypothesis (H0) is that a brushback pitch does not affect batting average, while my alternative hypothesis (Ha) states that brushback pitches affect batting average.

First, events with null, other out, pickoff 1b, pickoff 2b, pickoff 3b, pickoff caught stealing 2b, pickoff caught stealing 3b, pickoff caught stealing home, caught stealing 2b, caught stealing 3b, caught stealing home, walk, field error, sac bunt, sac fly, sac bunt double play, sac fly double play, catcher interf, and hit by pitch were removed from the data because each of these outcomes is not counted as an at-bat, so they do not affect batting average.

Second, I randomly picked 15,000 at-bats as a sample size since there were around 165,000 at-bats in the 2018 regular season.[7] The amount 15,000 is less than 10% of 165,000, but not so small that the results would be skewed. This group of 15,000 at-bats was labeled "Sample 1."

I filtered the data by classifying at-bats as brushback or no-brushback at-bats, and then as a hit or no hit. Any event with "single," "double," "triple," or "home_run" was classified as a hit. These values were placed in the real table. Then, an ideal table was used to find the difference between the real and ideal values. If there was statistical significance, the difference was deemed note-

Figure 1. An example of Athletics 2018 data

Result	Is BBAB?	game date	player name	batter	pitcher	events	description	stand	balls	strikes	plate x	at bat number	pitch name
NO		9/30/18	Beau Taylor	607333	605301	strikeout	swinging strike	L	1	2	-0.5263	50	4-Seam Fastball
NO		9/30/18	Beau Taylor	607333	605301	null	ball	L	0	2	-2.6236	50	Slider
NO		9/30/18	Beau Taylor	607333	605301	null	foul	L	0	2	-0.2095	50	4-Seam Fastball
NO		9/30/18	Beau Taylor	607333	605301	null	swinging strike	L	0	1	-0.1199	50	4-Seam Fastball
NO		9/30/18	Beau Taylor	607333	605301	null	foul	L	0	0	1.1525	50	4-Seam Fastball
NO		9/30/18	Beau Taylor	607333	628333	double	hit into play no out	L	1	1	0.1909	34	Changeup
NO		9/30/18	Beau Taylor	607333	628333	null	ball	L	0	1	0.144	34	Changeup
NO		9/30/18	Beau Taylor	607333	628333	null	called strike	L	0	0	-0.2904	34	Cutter
NO		9/20/18	Beau Taylor	607333	516472	field out	hit into play	L	1	1	-0.2479	80	Curveball
NO		9/20/18	Beau Taylor	607333	516472	null	foul	L	1	0	-0.1559	80	Curveball
NO		9/20/18	Beau Taylor	607333	516472	null	ball	L	0	0	0.7359	80	Curveball
NO		9/20/18	Beau Taylor	607333	592547	walk	ball	L	3	1	-1.7692	64	4-Seam Fastball
NO		9/20/18	Beau Taylor	607333	592547	null	ball	L	2	1	-1.1357	64	4-Seam Fastball
NO		9/20/18	Beau Taylor	607333	592547	null	ball	L	1	1	-1.7516	64	Changeup
NO		9/20/18	Beau Taylor	607333	592547	null	blocked ball	L	0	1	0.1541	64	Curveball
NO		9/20/18	Beau Taylor	607333	592547	null	foul	L	0	0	0.079	64	4-Seam Fastball
NO	Y	9/19/18	Beau Taylor	607333	628333	field out	hit into play	L	1	2	-0.3508	60	Slider
YES	Y	9/19/18	Beau Taylor	607333	628333	null	ball	L	0	2	1.4497	60	4-Seam Fastball
NO	Y	9/19/18	Beau Taylor	607333	628333	null	foul	L	0	2	0.6704	60	4-Seam Fastball
NO	Y	9/19/18	Beau Taylor	607333	628333	null	foul	L	0	1	-0.6031	60	Changeup
NO	Y	9/19/18	Beau Taylor	607333	628333	null	called strike	L	0	0	-0.2142	60	Cutter

worthy, and if the values were alike then I determined there was little to no statistical significance.

Real

	Hit	No Hit	Totals
Brushback	x	y	$x + y$
No Brushback	a	b	$a + b$
Totals	$x + a$	$y + b$	$N = x + y + a + b$

Ideal (expected data assuming no association):

	Hit	No Hit
Brushback	$\dfrac{(a + x)(x + y)}{N}$	$\dfrac{(b + y)(x + y)}{N}$
No Brushback	$\dfrac{(a + b)(x + a)}{N}$	$\dfrac{(b + y)(a + b)}{N}$

Sample 1: Real

	Hit	No Hit	Totals
Brushback	317	1098	1415
No Brushback	3348	10237	13585
Totals	3665	11335	15000

Sample 1: Ideal

	Hit	No Hit
Brushback	≈ 345.7	≈ 1069.3
No Brushback	≈ 3319.3	≈ 10265.7

Since all of the values in the ideal table are above 5, the third condition of statistical significance for a chi-square test for independence is met.

Degrees of Freedom (DF) = (r-1)(c-1), where r is the number of rows and c is the number of columns
Degrees of Freedom (DF) = (2-1)(2-1) = 1
Chi-Squared = Σ (R - I) ^ 2 / I, where R is the real value for a given data cell and I is the ideal for that cell.
Chi-Squared ≈ 3.49

Using an online calculator,[8]
P-value ≈ 0.062, and $0.062 > 0.05$, so the result is *not significant and fails to reject null hypothesis*.

Based on the Sample 1 test results, ***brushback pitches do not significantly affect batting average*** and are thus not a good strategy for pitchers if their goal is to reduce batting average. However, this sample could be an outlier, so a chi-square test for Sample 2, chosen the same way as Sample 1 with replacement from previous samples, as shown:

Sample 2: Real

	Hit	No Hit	Totals
Brushback	331	1115	1446
No Brushback	3423	10131	13554
Totals	3754	11246	15000

Sample 2: Ideal

	Hit	No Hit
Brushback	≈ 361.9	≈ 1084.1
No Brushback	≈ 3392.1	≈ 10161.9

Chi-Squared ≈ 3.89.
P-value ≈ 0.049, and $0.049 < 0.05$, which is slightly ***significant and rejects null hypothesis***.

Since Sample 1 was slightly insignificant and Sample 2 was slightly significant, a third test was run, called Sample 3.

Sample 3: Real

	Hit	No Hit	Totals
Brushback	383	1087	1470
No Brushback	3429	10101	13530
Totals	3812	11188	15000

Sample 3: Ideal

	Hit	No Hit
Brushback	≈ 373.6	≈ 1096.4
No Brushback	≈ 3438.4	≈ 10091.67

Degrees of Freedom = 1.
Chi-squared ≈ 0.353365.
P-value ≈ 0.55, and $0.55 > 0.05$, which is ***not significant and fails to reject null hypothesis***.

The results of these three samples suggest that there is little to no significance between brushback pitches and batting average. The first sample shows significance at the 0.10 level but not at 0.05; the p-values vary greatly and thus the null hypothesis cannot be entirely rejected.

All in all, this shows that brushback pitches do not have a significant effect on batting average, and so the common misconception that hitters are "intimidated" after a brushback pitch cannot be proven by the data.

THE EFFECT OF THE BRUSHBACK PITCH ON WALK PERCENTAGE

Brushback pitches do not affect batting average, so they do not significantly help a pitcher reduce the "hit" portion of Walks and Hits per Innings Pitched, or WHIP. The other factor of WHIP is walks, or base on balls. Since brushbacks are not strikes (they are in the batter's boxes far away from the plate), my null hypothesis (H0) is that brushback pitches do not affect walk percentage (BB%), while my alternative hypothesis (Ha) states that brushback pitches have an effect on walk percentage.

Two samples, labeled Sample 4 and 5 are shown below. Like Sample 1, 2 and 3, these are randomly chosen and are less than 10% of the data. The only difference is that walks are included in the "events" column and all other at-bat outcomes, including hits, are under no walk.

Sample 4: Real

	Walk	No Walk	Totals
Brushback	327	1372	1699
No Brushback	925	12376	13301
Totals	1252	13748	15000

Sample 4: Ideal

	Walk	No Walk
Brushback	≈ 141.8	≈ 1557.2
No Brushback	≈ 1110.2	≈ 12190.8

Degrees of Freedom = 1.
Chi-squared ≈ 297.6.
P-value < 0.00001 and < 0.05, *which is significant and rejects null hypothesis*.

This shows that there is a strong significance between walk percentage and brushback pitches. However, this sample may be an outlier (even though that would be very unlikely because of Sample 4's remarkably low p-value), so Sample 5 is shown below chosen the same way.

Sample 5: Real

	Walk	No Walk	Totals
Brushback	301	1328	1629
No Brushback	863	12508	13371
Totals	1164	13836	15000

Sample 5: Ideal

	Walk	No Walk
Brushback	≈ 126.4	≈ 1502.6
No Brushback	≈ 1037.6	≈ 12333.4

Degrees of Freedom = 1.
Chi-squared ≈ 293.3.
P-value < 0.00001 and < 0.05, which is *significant and rejects null hypothesis*.

Based on these two very low p-values, the relationship between walk percentage and brushback pitches is significant.

ANALYZING THE EFFECT OF THE BRUSHBACK PITCH ON WALK PERCENTAGE

Since brushback pitches affect walk probability, the only question is whether brushbacks raise or lower the BB% (walk percentage). The alternative hypothesis (brushback pitches affect walk percentage) is supported because brushbacks add 1 additional ball to a walk (4 balls).

For Sample 4:
- BB% of at-bats with brushbacks: 19.25%
- BB% of at-bats without brushbacks: 6.95%

For Sample 5:
- BB% of at-bats with brushbacks: 18.48%
- BB% of at-bats without brushbacks: 6.45%

As shown, BB% is nearly three-fold in at-bats with brushbacks. In conclusion, brushback pitches do not affect batting average but they *increase* the likelihood of a walk, which is not beneficial for pitchers.

BRUSHBACK USAGE BY PITCH TYPE

A common use of brushbacks is as an intimidation tool, as pitchers can use extremely fast pitches to scare batters and keep them off the plate. Some believe that brushbacks are thrown "accidentally" by a pitcher—that they are pitches where the ball slipped, and were not intended to scare the batter. The data in Figure 2 prove this belief wrong.

In the 2018 MLB season, 80.2% of pitchers were right-handed, and 65.2% of batters were right-handed.[9] The majority of brushbacks were thrown to right-handed batters by right-handed pitchers. The three pitches that are most commonly thrown inside to a right-handed batter by a right-handed pitcher are the 2-seam fastball, the changeup, and the sinker. The 4-seam fastball could be used as an intimidation pitch, but since it is the natural tendency of this pitch to tail *away* from the right-handed batter, the effectiveness and usage of the pitch as a brushback is diminished, as reflected in the data. The graph shows that on non-brushback pitches, the 2-seam fastball and changeup are thrown at the same rate while the sinker is thrown slightly less often. However, on brushback pitches, both the 2-seam fastball and the sinker are thrown significantly *more often* than the changeup. The fact that the more intimidating "fastball" pitches (2-seam and sinker) are thrown as brushbacks significantly more often than the non-intimidating "off-speed" pitch (changeup) demonstrates intent by the pitchers to throw hard inside. If brushbacks were thrown accidentally, the incidence of brushbacks would be consistent across all three pitch types.

BRUSHBACK USAGE BY PITCH COUNT

The count when a brushback is thrown can also suggest intent and determine effectiveness. Pitchers tend to throw brushbacks once they have thrown a strike. The highest percentage of brushbacks thrown is on 0–1 (4.15%), 0–2 (3.85%), and 1–2 (4.01%) counts. A possible reason for this is that pitchers feel more comfortable "messing" with batters once they are ahead

in the count, in order to intimidate them and more firmly establish control of the strike zone.

The lowest percentage of brushbacks thrown is on 3-ball counts: 1.64% of the time on 3–0 counts, 1.86% on 3–1 counts, and 2.23% on 3–2 counts. On 3–0 counts, the pitcher is so behind that they have no benefit of throwing at a batter, especially considering that a brushback is a ball the majority of the time. On 3–1 and 3–2, a pitcher's priority is to prevent a walk, so a brushback pitch wouldn't be useful.

Figure 3 shows brushbacks thrown by count divided by total pitches thrown by count. It shows that a pitcher is most likely to throw a brushback on an 0--1 count.

Figure 2. Dark (Brushback Pitches) vs. Light (Non-Brushback Pitches)

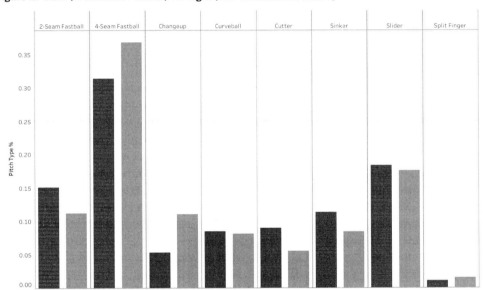

Figure 3. Count vs. Brushback Pitch Percentage, 2018 MLB

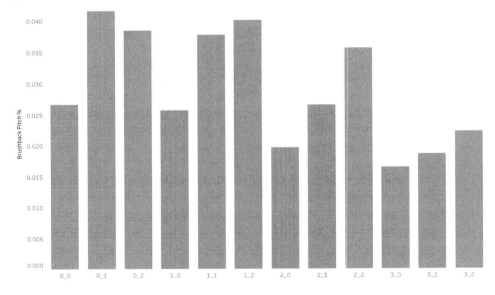

CONCLUSION

In conclusion, the brushback pitch has no significance in regard to batting average, but it increases walk percentage by a substantial amount. The 2-seam fastball and sinker are the inside fastball pitches most commonly used to throw the brushback, which suggests intent to intimidate (as opposed to being thrown accidentally). Brushbacks are also thrown most often in pitcher-friendly counts, furthering the evidence of strategic intent.

There are many additional studies that can be performed with these data. For example, do brushback pitches affect other hitting statistics, such as strikeout or slugging percentage? The door is open to further data-driven exploration of this under-studied aspect of baseball performance and psychology. ■

Notes

1. Robert E. Hood, *The Gashouse Gang* (New York: Morrow, 1976).
2. Alden Gonzalez, "'It's a Fight, Just the Pitcher and Me': What's behind the Juan Soto Shuffle." ESPN. ESPN Internet Ventures, October 21, 2019. Accessed May 8, 2020. https://www.espn.com/mlb/story/_/id/27868944/fight-just-pitcher-the-juan-soto-shuffle.
3. "Brushback Pitch." Baseball-Reference.com Bullpen. Accessed May 8, 2020. https://www.baseball-reference.com/bullpen/Brushback_pitch.
4. "Baseball Savant: Trending MLB Players, Statcast and Visualizations." baseballsavant.com. Accessed May 8, 2020. https://baseballsavant.mlb.com.
5. Daren Willman, "Statcast Search CSV Documentation." baseballsavant.com. Accessed May 8, 2020. https://baseballsavant.mlb.com/csv-docs.
6. "Statcast Search." baseballsavant.com. Accessed May 8, 2020. https://baseballsavant.mlb.com/statcast_search.
7. "2018 Major League Baseball Season Summary." Baseball-Reference.com. Accessed May 8, 2020. https://www.baseball-reference.com/leagues/MLB/2018.shtml.
8. "Chi-Square Calculator." Chi Square Calculator 2x2 (includes Yates correction). Accessed April 10, 2020. https://www.socscistatistics.com/tests/chisquare/default2.aspx.
9. "Handedness Report." Baseball-Reference.com. Accessed September 21, 2020. https://www.baseball-reference.com/friv/handedness.cgi.

"This compilation, a distillation of all that is important to the society's members . . . showcases the SABRite at his or her baseball-loving, stat-obsessed best."
—Paul Dickson, *Wall Street Journal*

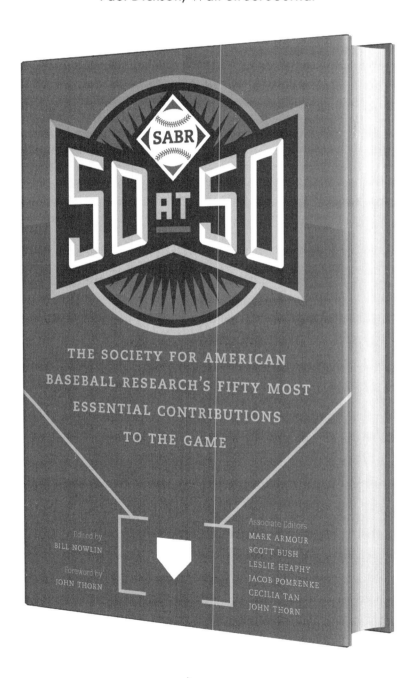

nebraskapress.unl.edu

Competitive Balance in the Free Agent Era

The Dog that Didn't Bark

David J. Gordon, MD, PhD

This paper examines competitive balance in the free agent era by comparing the old reserve clause system versus the modern collectively bargained system.

Baseball's reserve system began modestly on September 29, 1879, when the National League owners introduced a new rule that would eventually be incorporated into every player contract and would allow each franchise to retain the services of five designated players for the following season.[1] Their explicit intent was to hold down labor costs and thereby insure franchise stability: "The financial results of the past season prove that salaries must come down. We believe that players in insisting on exorbitant prices are injuring their own interests by forcing out of existence clubs which cannot be run and pay large salaries except at a large personal loss."[2] Indeed, the movement of players from team to team, even in midseason, had helped sink the old National Association (1871–75) four years earlier, as weaker teams were often unable to complete their schedules, generating a revolving door of failed and replacement franchises. However, having gained a foothold, the NL pushed the "reserve clause" concept forward aggressively, gradually increasing the number of reserved players and instituting a rigid salary structure in 1889. This set off a mass rebellion, led by John Montgomery Ward and his Brotherhood organization, which formed a rival league in 1890.[3] Indeed, the 1890 Players League was but one of five new leagues that challenged the NL's dominance in the first 35 years of the reserve rule—along with the American Association (1882–91), Union Association (1884), American League (1901–present), and Federal League (1914–15).

The competition from each new league provided a temporary boost in player salaries, but in time each new league either joined the NL in adopting the reserve rule or went out of business.[4] In 1922, the US Supreme Court in effect gave its imprimatur to the reserve rule by holding MLB exempt from the Sherman Anti-Trust Act of 1890.[5] Subsequently, the reserve rule's encroachment on player freedom grew ever more onerous and monopolistic and eventually encompassed all players who signed contracts in professional baseball, even those on minor league rosters, binding each player in perpetuity to the team that held his contract. MLB's anti-trust exemption was upheld as recently as 1972, when the US Supreme Court ruled against Curt Flood, 5–3.[6] However, the courts also ruled that MLB was subject to regulation by the National Labor Relations Board and in 1975 upheld arbitrator Peter Seitz's decision to grant free agency to two players, Dave McNally and Andy Messersmith, who had played without contracts that season, thereby ending the reserve system as it had been constituted and forcing the owners to create the system of arbitration, seniority, and free agency in place today.[7]

During those 96 years, the rationale for the reserve rule shifted subtly.[8] In 1956, economist Simon Rottenberg wrote, "The defense most commonly heard is that the reserve clause is necessary to assure an equal distribution of playing talent among opposing teams; that a more or less equal distribution of talent is necessary if there is to be uncertainty of outcome, and that uncertainty of outcome is necessary if the consumer is to be willing to pay admission to the game. This defense is founded on the premise that there are rich baseball clubs and poor ones and that, if the players' market was free, the rich clubs would outbid the poor for talent, taking all the competent players for themselves and leaving only the incompetent for other teams."[9] Never mind that the reserve rule system did not prevent the 1956 New York Yankees from winning their 22nd AL pennant and 17th World Series in 36 years! Rottenberg argued that competitive balance would be preserved in a free market, because rich teams would be constrained by diminishing returns from hoarding excessive talent and because each team's success ultimately depends on a competitive environment. Even under the reserve rule, he argued, rich teams have a competitive advantage in acquiring and retaining talent via amateur signings and trades. "It seems, indeed, to be true," he concluded, "that a market in which freedom is limited by a reserve rule such as that which now governs the baseball labor market distributes players among teams about as a free market would."[10] Now, 45 years after the replacement of the old reserve system with the modern collectively bargained system, in which player movement and compensation is less constrained, we have the opportunity to assess the impact of this change on competitive balance.

METHODS

This article will address two important aspects of competitive balance:

1. **Static Parity**: Are the pennant races in each league closely contested each year?

2. **Dynamic Parity**: How much upward and downward mobility exists from year to year? Are there perennial "haves" and "have-nots" or is there genuine hope for the teams at the bottom?

Lack of static parity is no fun for the fans of losing teams, but as Cubs and Astros fans can attest, dynamic parity is what keeps fan interest alive through the lean years.

STATIC PARITY

I have used two methods to evaluate static parity:

- The simplest metric is to count the number of outstanding, good, average, poor, and terrible teams in each season. In periods of relative balance, the percentage of teams in or near the middle rises and the percentage of outstanding and terrible teams falls. In periods of relative imbalance, the percentage of teams at either extreme grows, and the middle of the distribution shrinks. I have used a ≥ 0.600 winning average (98–64 in a 162-game season or 93–61 in a 154-game season) as the lower threshold for "outstanding," a ≥ 0.550 winning average (90–72 in a 162-game season or 85–69 in a 154-game season) as the lower threshold for "good," a ≤ 0.450 winning average 72–90 in a 162-game season or 69–85 in a 154-game season) as the upper threshold for "bad," and a ≤ 0.400 winning average (64–98 in a 162-game season or 61–93 in a 154-game season) as the upper threshold for "terrible." Teams with a winning average below 0.550 but above 0.450 are considered "average."

- The Noll-Scully ratio (NS) provides a more sophisticated and comprehensive way to quantify competitive balance. This metric is the ratio of the observed standard deviation of winning percentage in a league to the "theoretical ideal" standard deviation of a league in which all the teams have equally talented rosters.[11] In the "perfect parity" scenario, it is as if each game were decided by a coin flip. The standard deviation of winning average in such a league is the mean winning average divided by the square root of the average number of games played per team (not counting ties). This comes out to 0.0393 when the mean winning average is 0.500 and each team plays 162 games but was higher in strike-shortened seasons and before expansion, when the schedule was shorter. A league that was so balanced that the outcome of every game was random would not generate much interest. Obviously, a sport generally thrives best in a competitive environment in which there are clear favorites and underdogs but where the underdogs stand a fighting chance.[12] Historically, NS ratios in MLB have ranged from 1.25 to 3.3 but have remained mostly between 1.5 and 2.5 since 1960. I have combined both major leagues in my analyses to smooth out yearly fluctuations and to guarantee a mean winning average of 0.500 even after the introduction of interleague play. Since the NS ratio measures the top-to-bottom spread of all MLB teams, not just the parity of teams at the top, a low NS ratio does not guarantee close pennant races, nor does a high NS ratio preclude this possibility (especially with divisional play and wildcard teams).

DYNAMIC PARITY

I have used three methods to evaluate the even more important issue of dynamic parity:

- I have compared Pearson correlation coefficients of winning percentages in seasons separated by one to five years during different historic periods. The greater the dynamic parity, the faster the correlations decline toward zero.

- I have compiled a simple descriptive tabulation of the longest streaks of winning and losing seasons by individual teams at different points in MLB history.

- I used a standard life table method, introduced by Kaplan and Meier to analyze survival curves in clinical trials using a non-parametric long-rank (chi-squared) statistic to assess statistical significance, to compare the "longevity" of streaks of winning and losing seasons in different eras.[13,14] As applied to baseball winning (or losing) streaks, one calculates the cumulative probability that a streak survives for a given number of consecutive seasons and compares streaks that begin in different historic eras.

I have confined my analysis to post-1900 since MLB franchises and leagues were not stable before then. All the team records are taken from Baseball-Reference.com.[15] I have used the Student t-test to assess statistical significance of differences between means in NS ratio and inter-season correlation coefficients in different historic periods. Microsoft Excel built-in functions STDEV.P, CORREL, and T.TEST were used to calculate all standard deviations, correlation coefficients, and t-tests, respectively.

RESULTS

Static Parity
In Table 1, I have divided MLB history into three periods: the pre-expansion era (1901–60), a transition period (1961–75), in which MLB underwent rapid growth with the old reserve rule still intact, and the modern free agency era (1976–2020).

Table 1. Distribution of Winning Averages in Three Historic Periods

Period	Winning Average (%)					Total
	≥ .600	.550–.599	.451–.549	.401–.450	≤ .400	
1901–60	16.0	17.5	34.9	14.8	16.8	100
1961–75	8.9	15.0	51.2	13.8	11.0	100
1976–2020	6.8	19.1	49.7	16.8	7.7	100

"Extreme" teams (with winning average exceeding .600 or below .400) were more than twice as frequent before the 1961 expansion as after the 1975 downfall of the reserve rule. About half of all post-1975 teams resided in the middle part of the distribution, compared with 35% of all pre-1961 teams. Thus, competitive balance clearly did not suffer from the introduction of voluntary free agency. However, competitive balance during the 1961–75 transitional period more closely resembled the post-1975 than the pre-1961 period. It therefore seems that the post-1960 increase in competitive balance anteced the modification of the reserve rule and was not caused by it.

The more sophisticated Noll-Scully (NS) ratio analysis confirms this general picture (Figure 1).

The drop in NS ratio seems to have taken hold sometime between 1958 and 1966, with the exact timing muddled by expansion-related spikes in 1961–62 and 1969. The average NS ratio was 2.36 in 1901–60 versus 1.75 in 1976–2020; the difference was strongly statistically significant (P < 0.0001). The high NS ratio during the pre-expansion era pre-dated the Yankees dynasty of 1921–64 and did not differ systematically between the two major leagues.[16] Indeed, NS ratio often exceeded 3.0 in the Deadball era, reaching an all-time high of 3.29 in 1909, when five out of 16 teams, led by the 110–42 Pirates, won > 60% of their games, and four teams, "led" by the 42–110 Senators, won < 40% of their games. Despite the introduction of eight expansion teams in 1961–75, the average NS ratio during this period was 1.90, significantly less than in 1901–60 (P < 0.0001), and not statistically different from the 1976–2020 average.

My analysis also confirms that the small uptick in NS ratio in the first decade of the twenty-first century, attributed by Baumer and Zimbalist to an increasing competitive advantage enjoyed by the large market teams, has continued in 2011–17 The NS ratio for both leagues combined increased from 1.64 in 1980–99 to 1.82 in 2000–20. The difference in means was statistically significant (P = 0.02), although the test for a linear trend was not (P = 0.30). There was a recent surge in NS ratio in the AL to 2.77 in 2018 and 2.89 in 2019, thanks to three 100-win and three 100-loss teams in each season; the NS ratio remained below 2.0 in the NL, which had only one 100-win team (the Dodgers) and one 100-loss team (the Marlins) in 2019 and none of either in 2018. The NS ratio for both leagues combined reached 2.45 in 2019, its highest level since 1954, but fell back to 1.47 in the pandemic-shortened 2020 season.

Dynamic Parity. There is more to competitive balance than a series of static snapshots of the distribution of winning averages in a succession of seasons. Any meaningful analysis of competitive balance must bring dynamic parity into the mix. While greater static parity implies that bad teams don't have to climb as far to

Figure 1. Competitive Balance in MLB

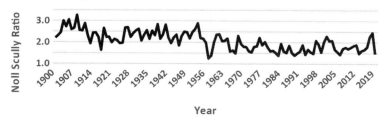

become contenders (and that good teams don't have to fall as far to slip from contention), one must also have a high enough season-to-season turnover rate to give realistic hope to the fans of have-not teams. Most fans will tolerate a terrible team for a few years if those lean years are followed by a similar period of excellence.

A useful way of approaching dynamic parity is to analyze how closely team winning averages are correlated from one season to another and how quickly this correlation dissipates over time. In Figure 2, I have plotted the mean correlation of team winning averages in seasons separated by one to five years during the three eras defined above—the pre-expansion era (1901–1960), the transitional period between the first expansion and the overthrow of the old reserve system (1961–75), and the modern free agency era (1976–2020). Since each correlation coefficient includes two seasons, only teams that were in existence during both seasons were included in each calculation. Because most new expansion teams have little upward mobility in their early years, the correlation coefficients for 1961–75 was calculated both including (solid line) and excluding (dashed line) the first five seasons of the eight expansion teams debuting in that period. Omitting the first five seasons of the six post-1975 expansion teams made no difference.

As would be expected, within each era the correlations of winning averages in two seasons grow weaker as the seasons are further separated in time, reflecting the arrival, emergence, decline, and departure of key personnel. However, the correlations were consistently far stronger in 1901–60 than in 1976–2020 (P < 0.0001). Indeed, in the pre-expansion era, the winning average was correlated by 30% (on the average) with its winning average as long as five years later. By contrast, in the modern free agency era, the winning average of a given team was essentially uncorrelated (on the average) with its winning average five years later. The correlation coefficients from the transitional period (1961–75) are intermediate between those of the pre-expansion and free agency eras. Because this relatively short 15-year period included the introduction of eight expansion teams, the correlation coefficients are strongly influenced by whether one includes or excludes the first five seasons—mostly dismal—of these teams. With expansion teams included, the correlation coefficients do not differ significantly from those of 1901–60 and differ significantly (P = 0.001 to 0.014) from those of 1976–2020. However, the situation is reversed when those new expansion teams are excluded; the correlation coefficients do not differ significantly from those after 1976 and differ significantly (P = 0.007 to 0.04) from those before 1960. Note that correlation coefficients during the current era (1976–2020) are unaffected by whether the first seasons of the 1977, 1993, and 1998 expansion teams are included. This reflects both the relatively small number of such teams (six in 44 years) and the rapid success of the Diamondbacks (1998) and Marlins (1993), who won the World Series in their fourth and fifth seasons, respectively.

Because of the simultaneous improvements in both static and dynamic parity, we now see far fewer long streaks of winning and losing seasons than we did before 1960. Table 2 (page 52) lists the 20 teams in modern MLB history that have maintained a 0.550-plus winning average for six or more consecutive seasons.

All but five of these long winning streaks (and 10 of the top 11) were compiled before 1960. The longest post-1960 winning streak, 10 seasons, was by the 1991–2000 Atlanta Braves, who won five NL pennants and one World Series during that decade-long streak. However, five pre-expansion teams compiled even longer winning streaks, led by the 1926–43 Yankees, who won 11 AL pennants and nine World Series in 18 years, and the 1946–58 Yankees, who won 10 AL pennants and eight World Series in 13 years. But it wasn't just the Yankees. In the NL, the 1901–12 Pirates, the 1903–13 Cubs, and the 1916–25 Giants, each compiled double-digit winning streaks, in which they won a combined 13 pennants and six World Series. The longest consecutive streak of 0.600-plus seasons since 1961 is five, by the 1972-76 Big Red Machine. No other post-expansion team had more than three consecutive 0.600-plus seasons. By contrast, four pre-expansion teams—the 1947–57 Yankees, the 1904–10 Cubs, the 1941–46 Cardinals, and the 1928–32 Athletics—each had streaks of five or more consecutive 0.600-plus seasons. Although static parity was slightly worse in 2000–19 than in 1980–99, dynamic parity has been better than

Figure 2. Winning Average Correlations

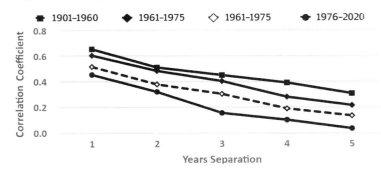

*Excluding first 5 seasons for expansion teams.

Table 2. Teams Maintaining Winning Average > 0.550 for at Least Six Consecutive Seasons

Winning Streak	Team	League	Start	End	W–L	Best Record Avg	Best Record Year	Pennants	WS Wins
18	New York Yankees	AL	1926	1943	110–44	0.714	1927	11	9
13	New York Yankees	AL	1946	1958	103–51	0.669	1954	10	8
12	Pittsburgh Pirates	NL	1901	1912	103–36	0.741	1909	4	1
11	Chicago Cubs	NL	1903	1913	116–36	0.763	1906	4	2
10	New York Giants	NL	1916	1925	98–56	0.636	1917	5	3
10	Atlanta Braves	NL	1991	2000	106–56	0.654	1998	5	1
9	St. Louis Cardinals	NL	1941	1949	106–48	0.688	1942	4	3
9	Cleveland Indians	AL	1948	1956	111–43	0.721	1954	2	1
8	Philadelphia Athletics	AL	1925	1932	107–45	0.704	1931	3	2
8	Brooklyn Dodgers	NL	1949	1956	105–49	0.682	1953	5	1
8	Milwaukee Braves	NL	1953	1960	95–59	0.617	1957	2	1
8	Los Angeles Dodgers	NL	2013	2020	43–17	0.717	2020	2*	0*
7	Chicago Cubs	NL	1932	1938	100–54	0.649	1935	3	0
7	Baltimore Orioles	AL	1977	1983	102–57	0.642	1979	2	1
7	New York Yankees	AL	2001	2007	103–58	0.640	2002	2	0
6	New York Giants	NL	1908	1913	103–48	0.682	1912	3	0
6	Philadelphia Athletics	AL	1909	1914	102–48	0.680	1910	4	3
6	New York Yankees	AL	1919	1924	98–54	0.645	1923	3	1
6	New York Giants	NL	1933	1938	95–57	0.625	1937	3	1
6	New York Yankees	AL	1976	1981	103–59	0.636	1980	4	2

* The 2020 pennant and World Series winners are unknown as this is written.

ever. All 30 MLB teams have reached the postseason at least once since 2000, with 20 different teams reaching the World Series and 14 different teams winning it. Only three teams—the 2000-01 Yankees, the 2008-09 Phillies, and the 2010–11 Rangers—won consecutive pennants during this period, and no team since the 1998–2000 Yankees has won consecutive World Series.

On the other side of the coin, 26 teams have endured losing streaks of six or more consecutive seasons with a winning average < 0.450 (Table 3).

Five of these streaks belonged to new expansion teams, topped by the 1998–2007 Devil Rays. Seventeen others, including nine of the top ten, took place before the 1961 expansion. Established teams endured only four post-1960 losing streaks of six or more seasons— the 2004–11 Pirates, the 1977–83 Mets, the 1985–90 Braves, and the 2006–11 Orioles. All four teams made the postseason within five years after their losing streaks ended; the 1986 Mets and 1995 Braves won the World Series. Fans of the inept 2019 Tigers, Orioles, Marlins, and Royals teams should consider themselves lucky when they compare their situation to that of the long-suffering fans of the hapless 1918–48 Philadelphia Phillies, who won more games than they lost only once (78–76 in 1932) in a span of 31 years. Fans of the 1937–67 Athletics, 1930–59 Browns/Orioles, 1947–66 Cubs, 1917–45 Braves, 1919–36 Red Sox, and 1947–61

Nationals/Senators/Twins didn't fare much better. Since 1960, only the 1969–74 Padres, the 1961–64 Senators, and the 1962–65 Mets—all new expansion teams—have suffered through more than three consecutive sub-0.400 seasons.

Figure 3 shows Kaplan-Meier plots of the longevity of streaks of winning and losing seasons during these three periods of baseball history. In Figure 3A, winning seasons are defined as those in which a team's winning average > 0.550; in Figure 3B, losing seasons are defined as seasons in which a team's winning average 0.450. Streaks that overlap two historic periods are considered to belong to the period in which they began. Streaks that were ongoing at the end of the 2019 season are treated as "censored" observations. Losing streaks by first-year expansion teams are not included in Figure 3B. Thus, the 1998–2007 Devil Rays, the 1962–68 Astros, 1969–75 Padres, 1961–66 Senators, the 1962–67 Mets, the 1977–81 Blue Jays, 1977–81 Mariners, the 1969–72 Pilots/Brewers, the 1969–70 Royals, the 1993–94 Rockies, the 1961 Angels, the 1969 Expos, 1993 Rockies, and 1998 Diamondbacks all got a mulligan.

It is clear once again that teams were able to sustain longer winning streaks (and forced to endure longer losing streaks) in 1901–60 than in 1976–2019. The differences between these two periods are statistically

Table 3: Teams Enduring Winning Average < 0.450 for at Least Six Consecutive Seasons

Losing Streak	Team	League	Start	End	Worst Record W–L	Pct.	Year
16	Philadelphia Phillies	NL	1933	1948	42–109	0.278	1942
12	Boston Red Sox	AL	1922	1933	43–111	0.279	1932
11	Philadelphia Phillies	NL	1918	1928	43–109	0.283	1928
11	St. Louis Browns	AL	1930	1940	43–111	0.279	1939
11	St. Louis Browns/Baltimore Orioles	AL	1946	1956	52–102	0.338	1951
10	Washington Senators/Nationals	AL	1902	1911	38–113	0.252	1904
10	Boston Beaneaters/Doves/Rustlers/Braves	NL	1903	1912	44–107	0.291	1911
10	Brooklyn Superbas/Dodgers	NL	1904	1913	48–104	0.316	1905
10	Tampa Bay Devil Rays*	AL	1998	2007	55–106	0.342	2001
9	Philadelphia Athletics	AL	1935	1943	49–105	0.318	1943
8	Philadelphia Athletics	AL	1915	1922	36–117	0.235	1916
8	Pittsburgh Pirates	NL	1950	1957	42–112	0.273	1952
8	Pittsburgh Pirates	NL	2004	2011	57–105	0.352	2010
7	Cincinnati Reds	NL	1929	1935	52–99	0.344	1933
7	Boston Bees/Braves	NL	1939	1945	59–89	0.399	1942
7	Houston Colt 45s/Astros*	NL	1962	1968	64–96	0.400	1962
7	San Diego Padres*	NL	1969	1975	52–110	0.321	1969
7	New York Mets	NL	1977	1983	63–99	0.389	1979
6	St. Louis Cardinals	NL	1905	1910	49–105	0.318	1908
6	Chicago White Sox	AL	1929	1934	49–102	0.325	1932
6	Cincinnati Reds	NL	1948	1953	62–92	0.403	1949
6	Washington Nationals/Senators	AL	1954	1959	53–101	0.344	1955
6	Washington Senators*	AL	1961	1966	56–106	0.346	1963
6	New York Mets*	NL	1962	1967	40–120	0.250	1962
6	Atlanta Braves	NL	1985	1990	54–106	0.338	1988
6	Baltimore Orioles	AL	2006	2011	64–98	0.395	2009

*New expansion teams.

Figure 3A. Streaks with >0.550 Winning Average

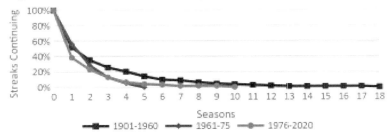

Figure 3B. Streaks with >0.450 Winning Average (excluding new expansion teams)

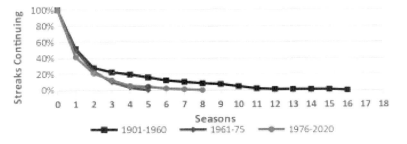

significant both for winning streaks (Chi-squared = 5.37 (1 df), $P < 0.025$) and losing streaks Chi-squared = 4.48 (1 df), $P < 0.05$). The 1961–75 transitional period between the first expansion and the end of the reserve clause again resembled the post-1975 period more than the pre-1961 period, although the sample size was too small to reach statistical significance. Thus, the observed change in dynamic parity, like the observed change in static parity, appears to have antedated the modification of the reserve rule. A similar analysis of streaks of seasons with winning averages above 0.600 or below 0.400 gave qualitatively similar results, but the sample sizes were smaller, and the differences between time periods were not statistically significant.

DISCUSSION

Competitive balance in MLB has clearly not collapsed in the 45 years since Peter Seitz handed down his historic decision; in fact, competition is significantly more balanced than it was under the old reserve system. The Yankees no longer dominate the AL, and more teams than ever before reach the World Series. Both static and dynamic parity have improved markedly, accompanied by the near disappearance of extended dynasties and perennial losers. The overwhelming dominance of the Yankees in 1921–64 undoubtedly contributed to the competitive imbalance in those seasons, but competitive imbalance was as evident in the NL (where no single team dominated) as in the AL, and was even more extreme in 1901–20, before the Yankees won their first pennant. Furthermore, the introduction of divisional play in 1969 and the addition of wild card teams in 1995 and 2012 has expanded the postseason from 12.5% (2/16) of all teams before 1960 to 33.3% (10/30) after 2012 and has enabled more teams to reach the postseason, over and above any improvements in the underlying parity of competition. Thus, many lesser teams, including four with a sub-0.540 winning average—the 1973 Mets (0.509), the 2006 Cardinals (0.516), the 1987 Twins (0.525), and the 1997 Indians (0.534)—have reached the World Series since the start of divisional play, and two (the 2006 Cardinals and 1987 Twins) have won the World Series.

So, what happened circa 1960 that might account for the observed improvement in competitive balance? I believe that the game-changer was greater parity in financial resources, due primarily to two interrelated factors:

1. **Migration/Expansion.** Starting in 1953, the second MLB teams in crowded two-team cities like Boston, St. Louis, and Philadelphia began to leave for greener pastures, thereby tapping into new markets and allowing the teams that stayed behind to thrive. This trend accelerated in 1958 when the Dodgers and Giants left New York for California, thereby opening up rich new markets and giving MLB a coast-to-coast scope for the first time. Then in 1961–77 MLB expanded into the south (Atlanta, Houston, and Dallas), west (Anaheim, San Diego, Oakland, and Seattle), and Canada (Montreal and Toronto), as well as adding Minneapolis and replacing departed teams in New York, Kansas City, and Milwaukee. This geographical expansion gave every team an ample uncontested territory from which to draw fans and created a national audience for the product.

2. **Television.**[18,19] Baseball games were first televised commercially in the 1950s, mainly locally in the larger markets, and took a distant back seat to ticket purchases as a source of revenue. There was a national TV game of the week on Saturday afternoons as early as 1953, but telecasts were blacked out within 50 miles of any major league stadium and not every team signed on. As late as 1962, TV revenue totaled $16.8M, only $4M of which was generated by national telecasts and benefited mainly the richer teams. However, this all changed in the 1960s and 1970s. Local TV revenues increased to $22.5M in 1971 and $39M in 1980. Even more importantly, national TV revenues, which were shared among all teams, grew to $18M in 1971 and $41M in 1980. By 1983, MLB's combined $153.7M in local and national TV revenue accounted for more than 30% of MLB's $500M total annual revenue. Revenue from television and other media has continued to grow since then.

By 1980, each team had not only a viable local market, but a guaranteed share of an ever-growing revenue stream with which to compete for talent. While small-market teams like the Reds, Royals, and Brewers were still not on an equal footing with behemoths like the Yankees and Dodgers, they could compete as never before for top talent.

The creation of new revenue streams was accompanied by new streams of African American and international talent. Although Jackie Robinson broke the "color barrier" in 1947, integration was slow to take hold. Only 12 African American players reached the major leagues by 1950—eight of them with the Dodgers and Indians, who (not coincidentally) rose from futility to become two of the most successful teams of the late 1940s and 1950s; the Red Sox did not integrate until 1959.[20] Even in 1957, 10 years after Jackie Robinson, baseball still had only 6.7% African Americans and 5.2% Latinos; by 1980, these percentages had climbed to 18% and 10%, respectively.[21] While these new sources of talent were offset in part by the need to staff a 50% increase in the number of teams (from 16 to 24), the influx of minority players was disproportionately rich in exceptional talent, as measured by the number of Hall of Famers and by metrics like JAWS.[22]

A third contributing factor to the increase in competitive balance was the implementation of the annual amateur draft in 1965, which gave small-market teams access to top amateur talent without having to match the large-market teams dollar for dollar.[23] Since it takes time for amateur talent to reach the major leagues, the arrival of the amateur draft in 1965 cannot explain the drop in NS ratio, which was already evident by the mid-1960s. But it did not take long for the draft's positive impact on the upward mobility of losing teams to be felt. Charles Finley's 1971–75 Oakland A's were the prototype of a longtime (1937–67) losing team using the new amateur draft to build a winner. Reggie Jackson (second overall pick in 1966), Vida Blue (second round pick in 1967), Sal Bando (sixth round pick in 1965), Gene Tenace (20th round pick in 1965), and Ken Holtzman (acquired in a 1971 trade for Rick Monday, the first overall pick in 1965) were core players on this three-time World Series champion.

So what was the impact of free agency on competitive balance? While the observed improvement in competitive balance began with the reserve clause still in place, the specter of the calamitous destruction of competitive balance and the consequent failure of small-market teams, frequently raised to justify the reserve clause, utterly failed to materialize when the reserve system was overturned in 1975. As Sir Arthur Conan Doyle might have put it, free agency was "the dog that didn't bark."[24] Indeed, exactly as Rottenberg had predicted in 1956, the replacement of MLB's reserve system by a relatively free market changed only the distribution of money between players and owners, not the distribution of talent among teams.[25] Starting in 1974, when Catfish Hunter was declared a free agent on a technicality, the Yankees used the new free agent system to acquire the services of Hunter, Reggie Jackson, and Rich Gossage, who joined a strong core of Thurman Munson, Graig Nettles, Willie Randolph,

Ron Guidry, Sparky Lyle, Mickey Rivers, and Chris Chambliss to run off four pennants and two World Series championships in 1976–81. But is this really so different from the Yankees' purchase of Babe Ruth's contract from Harry Frazee, the financially distressed owner of the Red Sox for $100,000 in 1919, or their acquisition of Joe DiMaggio's contract from the San Francisco Seals (PCL) for cash and four obscure players in 1934, or the acquisition of Roger Maris from the Kansas City Athletics (their go-to patsies in the 1950s) in 1959 in a lopsided trade? The main difference is that Hunter, Jackson, and Gossage—not the owners of their teams—got paid.

Recent articles by Edwards and Calandra have raised concern about the adverse impact of "tanking" on competitive balance during the past decade.[26,27] First, let us clarify what we mean by the term "tanking." I would use that term to describe the systematic dismantling of a competitive team by financially motivated personnel moves that relegate that team to winning fewer than 40% of its games in the near future. Connie Mack, who dismantled championship teams in 1915 and again in 1932–35, was the prototypical tanker, and (without the benefit of an amateur draft) the rebuilds took 14 and 30+ years, respectively. Within living memory, Wayne Huizenga's dismantling of the Marlins after their 1998 World Series Championship is a more successful example of tanking; they won another World Series in 2003. Note it is not tanking when a bad team trades veterans for prospects. That is merely what smart GMs have been doing since 1900, when the last-place New Your Giants traded fading Hall of Famer Amos Rusie for unproven 20 year-old Christie Mathewson, who helped pitch them to five NL pennants and three second-place finishes in 1904–13.[28]

Among the five teams that lost 100+ games in 2018 and/or 2019, only the Marlins and White Sox fit the definition of tankers. After assuming ownership of the Marlins, Derek Jeter dismantled a team that was coming off two disappointing 79- and 77-win seasons in 2016–17, trading its core of young stars (Stanton, Ozuna, Yelich, and Realmuto) to pare payroll and secure last-place finishes and attendant high draft picks in 2018–19. Rick Hahn similarly dismantled a 78-win 2016 White Sox team by trading three of their best players (Sale, Eaton, and Quintana), but these trades were motivated more by the prize prospects they received in return (Moncada, Kopech, Giolito, Dunning, Jimenez, Cease) than by financial considerations. The Orioles were already terrible (28–69, 0.289) when they kicked off their rebuild by trading Manny Machado on July 18, 2018, and actually improved slightly (to 54–108, 0.333) in 2019. Other than trading Verlander for prospects on August 31, 2017, the Tigers' fall to 100+ losses in 2019 was due more to the aging and decline of its core stars (especially Miguel Cabrera) than to salary-dumping trades. The Royals' fall to 100+ losses in 2018–19 was entirely due to the decline and departure of the core stars from its 2015 championship team, not tanking. Thus, it is incorrect to hold tanking responsible for the confluence of four 100-loss teams in 2019, which brought the NS ratio to its highest level since 1954. It is also premature at best to deem a two-year spike in NS ratio that was confined to the AL (2.77 in 2018 and 2.89 in 2019) a harbinger of a long-term trend. The AL NS ratio exceeded 2.0 only one other time since 2004 in the AL (2.08 in 2013) and not at all in the NL (where the highest NS ratio since 2004 was 1.99 in 2015). Linear regression analysis shows no statistical evidence of a significant positive trend in NS ratio since 2000 in either league or in both leagues combined. Thus, the recent spike in the AL's NS ratio is consistent with the large normal year-to-year fluctuations throughout MLB history (Figure 1). And as stated earlier, dynamic parity has never been better. Ask any Cubs or Astros fan if spending three years in the tank was worth it.

While a significant and sustained rise in NS ratio to pre-expansion levels would be undesirable, I am optimistic that this will not happen, because of limitations in the efficacy of the tanking strategy. Most teams are already growing increasingly reluctant to trade top prospects, even for established stars. Furthermore, teams like the Rays and A's have modeled creative ways to compete on a limited budget without tanking. Also, it is not clear that tanking can work for multiple teams simultaneously since there are only so many high draft picks to go around and some don't pan out. To paraphrase Yogi Berra, nobody will go there anymore if it gets too crowded.[29] MLB can always institute an NBA-style draft lottery to discourage tanking, but I doubt that this will be necessary.

CONCLUSION

Baseball's competitive balance, which left much to be desired in 1901–60, improved markedly by the mid-1960s. This improvement was manifest both in the decreased frequency of teams at either extreme of the spectrum of winning percentage each season and in greater dynamic turnover of winning and losing teams from season to season. These favorable changes in competitive balance are probably attributable mainly to MLB's expansion to new markets and the explosion of television revenues in the 1960s and 1970s. The influx of new talent streams of African American and Latino players and the implementation of the amateur draft in 1965 also contributed to this improvement.

We cannot know the impact of a true unrestricted free market on competitive balance, since baseball replaced the reserve system, not with a free market, but with negotiated Collective Bargaining Agreements (CBA) that still allow teams to control players until they accrue six years of major league service and to trade non-vested players without their consent. The current CBA also includes salary arbitration, a luxury tax on "excessive" team payrolls, compensatory draft picks, and an amateur player draft with closely regulated bonuses. However, contrary to the gloomy and self-serving predictions of the reserve rule's apologists, competitive balance in MLB has not only survived but thrived without that system's onerous constraints on player movement and compensation. The reserve rule's overthrow in 1975 did nothing to impede MLB's newfound competitive balance, which has continued to the present day. ∎

Notes

1. Edmund P Edmonds, "Arthur Soden's Legacy: The Origins and Early History of Baseball's Reserve System," *Albany Government Law Review*, 38 (2012). http://scholarship.law.nd.edu/law_faculty_scholarship/390.
2. David J Berri, Martin B Schmidt, Stacy L Brook, "Baseball's Competitive Balance Problem," *The Wages Of Wins: Taking Measure of the Many Myths In Modern Sport*, (Stanford, CA: Stanford Business Books, 2007), 46–68.
3. John Montgomery Ward (1887), "Is the Base Ball Player a Chattel?" *Lippincott's Magazine*, V40: 310–19.
4. James Quirk, Rodney D, *Fort, Pay Dirt: The Business of Professional Team Sports*, (Princeton, NJ: Princeton University Press, 1992) 180–83.
5. Wikipedia, Federal Baseball Club v. National League, https://en.wikipedia.org/wiki/Federal_Baseball_Club_v._National_League.
6. Wikipedia, Flood v. Kuhn, https://en.wikipedia.org/wiki/Flood_v._Kuhn.
7. Roger I. Abrams, "Arbitrator Seitz Sets the Players Free," *The Baseball Research Journal*, SABR, Volume 38 (1992), Number 2: 79–85.
8. Sky Andrechek, The Case for the Reserve Clause, *Sports Illustrated*, January 14, 2010, https://www.si.com/more-sports/2010/01/14/andrecheck-freeagency.
9. Simon Rottenberg, "The Baseball Players' Labor Market," *Journal of Political Economy*, Vol. 64, No. 3 (1956): 242–58.
10. Rottenberg.
11. Quirk and Fort, 245–48.
12. Quirk and Fort, Chapter 4.
13. EL Kaplan, P Meier, "Nonparametric estimation from incomplete observations." *Journal of the American Statistical Association.* 53 (282) (1958): 457–481. doi:10.2307/2281868. JSTOR 2281868.
14. Wayne W LaMorte, "Comparing Survival Curves," Survival Analysis (Boston University School of Public Health, 2016) http://sphweb.bumc.bu.edu/otlt/MPH-Modules/BS/BS704_Survival/BS704_Survival5.html.
15. Baseball-Reference.com, https://www.baseball-reference.com/teams.
16. Berti, Schmidt, and Brook, Tables 4.1–2, 51–52.
17. Benjamin Baumer, Andrew Zimbalist, "Chapter 6," *The Sabermetric Revolution*, (Philadelphia: University of Pennsylvania Press, 2014).

18. Wikipedia, Major League Baseball on Television, https://en.wikipedia.org/wiki/Major_League_Baseball_on_television.

19. Quirk and Fort (1992), 505.

20. Wikipedia. List of first black Major League Baseball players, https://en.wikipedia.org/wiki/List_of_first_black_Major_League_Baseball_players.

21. Mark Armour, Daniel R. Levitt, "Baseball Demographics 1947–2016," SABR Biography Project, http://sabr.org/bioproj/topic/baseball-demographics-1947-2012.

22. David J Gordon, "Racial Parity in the Hall of Fame," *Baseball Research Journal*, 47 (2018): 49–57.

23. Wikipedia, Major League Baseball Draft. https://en.wikipedia.org/wiki/Major_League_Baseball_draft.

24. Mike Shotnicki, "The Dog that Didn't Bark: What We Can Learn from Sir Arthur Conan Doyle About Using the Absence of Expected Facts," BrieflyWriting.com, July 25, 2012, https://brieflywriting.com/2012/07/25/the-dog-that-didnt-bark-what-we-can-learn-from-sir-arthur-conan-doyle-about-using-the-absence-of-expected-facts.

25. Rottenberg.

26. Craig Edwards, "Baseball's Competitive Balance Problem," Fangraphs, November 18, 2019. https://blogs.fangraphs.com/baseballs-competitive-balance-problem.

27. Will Calandra, "The MLB Has a Competitive Balance Issue, and It's Related to Money and Payroll Inequalities," *The Georgetown Voice*, February 18, 2020. https://georgetownvoice.com/2020/02/18/the-mlb-has-a-competitive-balance-issue-and-its-related-to-money-and-payroll-inequalities.

28. Baseball-Reference. Christy Mathewson page. Transactions. https://www.baseball-reference.com/players/m/mathech01.shtml.

29. Houston Mitchell., "Yogi Berra Dies at 90: Here Are Some of His Greatest Quotes," *Los Angeles Times*, May 12, 2015. https://www.latimes.com/sports/sportsnow/la-sp-sn-yogi-berra-turns-90-quotes-20150512-story.html.

Luck, Skill, and Head-to-Head Competition in Major League Baseball

Irwin Nahinsky

In this article I deal with two issues: the relationship between luck and skill in Major League Baseball and the role of matchups between teams in season competition. The former issue is dealt with to assess the significance of the latter.

It is generally felt that both skill and luck are factors in determining success or failure. Being in the right place at the right time is considered a matter of luck. Preparation and ability are acknowledged to be skill factors. What constitutes skill and what constitutes luck in baseball? How do we assess the relative contribution of luck or skill in determining game outcome? The spectacular catch by Willie Mays in game one of the 1954 World Series is a prime example of superb skillful performance. The bad hop over Fred Lindstrom's head in the 1924 World Series is a clear example of extremely bad luck. On the other hand, how do we evaluate the ground ball off Billy Loes's leg in the 1952 World Series that he said was lost in the sun? All of these illustrate key events in determining game outcomes. The problem to be addressed is finding out the relative contribution of luck or skill to victory or defeat.

In order to solve the problem, we must consider identifying the variables that are related to game outcome. Insofar as we can identify performance measures that relate to team outcome, we have potential indicators of skill. After such measures are applied to predict outcomes, we can observe how much variability in outcomes remains. Such variability may result from in part luck and in part skill. Here is where it is important to be able to assess how much variability in performance would occur if only randomness or "chance" (which we call luck) determines the outcome. My approach includes such an assessment, as we will see.

There is a long history of trying to find the factors that account for team success, to specify how they work, and separate them from luck. Perhaps the most notable is Bill James's Pythagorean expectation, named for its resemblance to the well known Pythagorean Theorem.[1] His basic formula is $\frac{rs^2}{\left(rs^2 + ra^2\right)}$,

where rs is runs scored and ra is runs allowed. Runs scored and runs allowed are two very direct measures of team effectiveness that are combined in the formula for predicting team success. The formula is used to estimate how many games a team "should" have won, with any difference between actual and estimated values attributed to luck. The rationale for the exponent 2 is based upon the use of the ratio rs/ra as a measure of "team quality," with reciprocal of the ratio used as the measure for a generalized opponent. However, searches were made to find an exponent that better predicted winning percentage (for example, the work of Clay Davenport and Keith Woolner,[2] and David Smith[3]). Insofar as values are based on empirical fits, they do not represent a theoretical basis for explaining the process.

Since systematic differences between actual and expected winning percentages using the formula occur (e.g., big winners "should" have won less, and big losers "should" have won more), other measures that could relate to team performance have been introduced into the formula. After all, runs may be scored as a result of luck as well as skill. Variables such as on base percentage and earned run average may help get around the luck factor. Having a measure of the possible effect of a luck factor may help us.

Using a different approach, Pete Palmer examined the variability between teams in win records over many seasons and compared it with what would be expected if teams were all equal in skill, and all variability between teams was a matter of luck.[4] Palmer concluded that since 1971 the contributions of luck and skill have become nearly equal. The apparent decreasing relative contribution of skill may reflect a trend toward parity. Luck would then play an increasing role in determining outcomes. I deal with this a little later and consider changes in the game other than increased parity.

THE HEAD-TO-HEAD PERFORMANCE VARIABLE

I have looked at the possibility that another factor related to skill contributes to differences between teams in outcomes: head-to-head competition. John Richards has developed an approach that predicts head-to-head outcome probabilities using relative overall season success of the two competing teams.[5] However, I show that a team may produce significantly more or fewer wins against a given team than would be expected by its overall season performance. Such a result may well be attributable to unique differences between teams in terms of relative strengths and weaknesses. I test the hypothesis that head-to-head performance variation may be something more than chance variation over a season.

A season for a given team may be considered as a set of "mini seasons" consisting of the season's series for two teams in contention for the pennant. In this light we may look at a team's win record as the sum total of average total season performance and performance over and above (or below) its average total season performance against certain teams. If the hypothesized impact of specific factors related to particular team matchups is found, another variable may be added to total season performance. Insofar as this factor is identified, the contribution of the skill factor is increased, and the relative contribution of luck is thereby decreased. Here is where the assessment of the skill-luck relationship becomes tricky. Although, as we will see, we may be able to calculate the variation that would exist if only pure luck determines outcomes, we can always potentially find different performance variables associated with skill that increase the contribution of the skill factor. Hence, the contribution may always increase relative to luck.

To illustrate how assessment of the head-to-head factors would work, Figure 1 shows the season win record of the Chicago White Sox against each of its seven opponents in the 1954 season. The 1954 White Sox present a clear example of overall superior performance save for unusual difficulty in beating the Yankees. Their general pattern of victories against other opponents suggests some head-to-head effects. The seven opponents are denoted in the chart in positions corresponding to the number of White Sox victories against them in their season series. The White Sox won 94 games for an average of 13.43 wins per opponent.

We would expect the average victories per opponent to converge to that value over many repetitions of the 1954 season, assuming the White Sox performance was independent of opponent played, and luck was the only factor causing variation from that average. It is, of course, assumed the White Sox remain a .610 team over all replications. The solid horizontal line from the vertical axis reflects the chance baseline value of 13.43 games. The distances from this line may represent variation attributable to either luck, skill, or some combination of the two.

To make the appropriate assessment, we need a measure of how much variation— such as shown in Figure 1—is attributable to pure random variation or luck. We also need a comparable measure of actual variation. Using Figure 1 as an example, we can find the average of the squared differences between number of White Sox victories against each of the seven teams and the mean of 13.43. The resulting value is 11.39. To generalize, we can find a measure of variability between teams for a season by subtracting mean number of victories for all teams from the number of victories for each team, and averaging the resulting squared differences for all teams. The resulting value is called the variance, which we will see has important properties.

A measure of the variability expected if only luck determines outcomes can be computed using the binomial distribution. The binomial distribution is produced by the sum of a number of independent observations on a variable that assumes two possible values: zero or one. In our example, one stands for victory and zero for defeat. For a large number of such observations, the binomial distribution approximates the normal bell-shaped distribution. Suppose $\mathbf{p}$ is the probability of victory for a team, and hence $(1 - \mathbf{p})$ the defeat probability. The expected number of victories for a team in a season is then *number of games* $\times \mathbf{p}$.

In the White Sox example, the best estimate of the value is $154 \times .610$ victories for their season total. If luck dominates, $\mathbf{p} = .50$. In a 162-game season, the expected number of wins for all teams is then $162 \times 50 = 81$. The variance for a binomial distribution is *number of observations* $\times \mathbf{p} \times (1 - \mathbf{p})$. In our White Sox

Figure 1. 1954 White Sox Wins Against

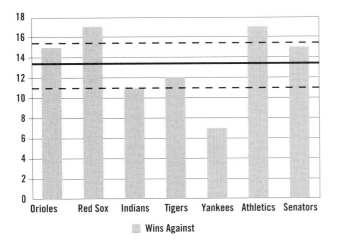

Wins Against

example, the expected variance of White Sox victories in 22 games against a given opponent if only chance variation from their usual level determines outcome is $22 \times .61 \times .39$ which equals 5.23.

Although the variance has analytic advantages, the square root of the variance, the standard deviation, produces a value in terms of games, which allows for comparisons of interest. The standard deviation in our example is 2.29. The dashed lines above and below the horizontal line in Figure 1 define a band between + and − one standard deviation from the 13.43 mean. In the bell-shaped normal distribution it is expected that values would occur about 68% of the time in this band. In this case, with Cleveland just outside the band, only three of seven teams show results that fell within the range expected by luck alone, which suggests something more than luck might be at work.

So far we have some measure of the independent effect of the head-to-head variable, insofar as variation from the average performance of a given team is measured independently of variation between teams. However, we have neglected to account for the impact of the difference between two teams in overall season performance upon the relative success in matchups between those two teams. Returning to the 1954 White Sox example, the White Sox won 17 of their 22 games against the Red Sox, 3.57 more games above the season average number of wins per opponent. However, the White Sox won 13 more games than did the Red Sox against the other six teams in the league. Dividing by six shows that on average the White Sox beat each of the other six teams in the league 2.17 times more often than did the Red Sox. Thus, 2.17 of the White Sox victories over the Red Sox could be attributed to overall superiority, and the remainder to unique factors related to the head-to-head matchup. The 3.57 games above the per-team average is reduced accordingly to produce a measure of the head-to-head factor for the two teams.

As another example, consider the season series between the Yankees and the White Sox. The White Sox record against the six American League teams other than the Yankees was 87 victories and 45 losses, while the Yankees were 88 and 44 against the same six teams. Thus, the White Sox won one fewer game than did the Yankees against the rest of the league. This means that they averaged .17 fewer victories against each of the other teams than did the Yankees. This difference is a measure of general superiority of the Yankees over the White Sox, and the White Sox would be expected to lose on average .17 more games than the Yankees against common opponents on the basis of

overall team strength. The necessary adjustment would be to add .17 to the White Sox victory total of seven for their season series to reflect a compensating head-to-head factor. We note that making adjustments to victory totals is equivalent to making adjustments to deviations from the per-opponent average in terms of calculating a variance attributable to the head-to-head factor. Table 1 shows the White Sox victories against the seven other teams together with victory values corrected as above. Standard deviations of corrected and uncorrected values are shown for comparison.

Table 1. Victories by 1954 White Sox Against League Opponents Compared with Victories Adjusted for Relative Performance by White Sox and Each Opponent Against Rest of League

Opponent	Victories	Adjusted Victories
Baltimore	15	9.67
Boston	17	14.83
Cleveland	11	13.83
Detroit	12	8.00
New York	7	7.17
Philadelphia	17	11.83
Washington	15	11.67
Standard deviation	3.64	2.87

LUCK, SKILL, AND HEAD-TO-HEAD PERFORMANCE PRIOR TO 1969

I performed an analysis to assess the relative contribution of overall team performance, head-to-head competition, and the luck factor to variability in team performance. Table 2 shows average standard deviations by decades for total season team performance for each league from 1900 to 1968, the last year before divisional play was introduced. Standard deviations for head-to-head contributions are based on the adjustments for two competing teams' differences in victories against the league. I examine the reasons for considering seasons after that separately later.

A measure that takes advantage of the additive nature of variances and sums of squared differences was used to calculate the variability attributable to head-to-head matchups. In general, the variance of a sum of independent variables is equal to the sum of their variances. The same cannot be said of standard deviations. It is possible to total the sum of squared differences, such as found in the White Sox example, over all teams in a league for a season. If we use an appropriate denominator for the sum, we get an unbiased estimate of a variance for the league season. The additive nature of variances makes it possible to estimate the relative contribution of head-to-head matchups in a way not possible for standard deviations.

The measure corrects for overall team victories for each team, and hence is independent of the variance of overall team victories. It will later be used in a technique called the analysis of variance when other comparisons are made. Table 2 shows the average square roots of the values for each decade. These function as the mean standard deviations for head-to-head contributions. Standard deviations expected for pure luck are also shown for both the total season and head-to-head factors. Results showed a tendency for contribution of total season performance to be much greater than that of head-to-head matchups. I return to these results after considering the data for the era of divisional play.

Table 2. Standard Deviations for Team Performance and for Chance Variation (1900–68)

Decade	League Seasons	Total season Performance	Chance	Head-to-head Performance	Chance
1900–09	19	16.93	6.03	2.58	2.30
1910–19	20	15.25	6.08	2.70	2.22
1920–29	20	14.55	6.17	2.92	2.35
1930–39	20	15.99	6.16	2.64	2.35
1940–49	20	14.97	6.18	2.79	2.35
1950–59	20	14.25	6.19	2.83	2.35
1960–68	18	13.11	6.06	2.43	2.15

Palmer noted a tendency for the relative contribution of the skill factor to decline after 1970. This coincided with the introduction of the divisional structure in each league. In the post-1968 era, each team within a division plays every other team in its division an equal number of times. Each team in one division plays each team in the other division an equal number of times, although usually less often than teams in its own division. The intra-divisional setup imposes the same constraints upon the schedule as was true in the pre-divisional era, where total victories must equal total defeats. This constraint does not exist in extra-divisional play. As an extreme example, all teams in one division might win all their games with all teams in the other division.

Table 3. Standard Deviations for Team Performance for Intra- and for Extra- Division Play (1969–2019)

Decade	Intra-League Division Seasons	Performance	Extra-League Division Seasons	Performance
1969–79	44	7.68	22	5.69
1980–89	40	6.64	20	5.21
1990–99	46	5.45	38	4.54
2000–09	60	6.64	60	3.28
2010–	54	6.91	54	3.15

The comparison between intra- and extra-divisional play reflects an important property of variances relevant to assessing performance factors in this situation.[6] Table 3 demonstrates the clear difference between intra- and extra-divisional play in variability of team records with intra-divisional standard deviations averaging about 1.5 times greater than extra-divisional values. Variances related to each other as those in this case can always be expected to show the relationships found. Each extra-division standard deviation was based on a season's competition between two divisions. The 1994 season was not included in the analysis, because the abbreviated season resulted in very large variations in number of games in head-to-head series that made meaningful analysis not feasible.

Most seasons featuring divisional play have schedules in which more games are played within a division than are played between two divisions. Hence, it is possible that intra-division overall variances for teams are merely larger because of this difference. I found that for the 93 cases in the two-division period in which more intra-division than extra-division games were played, the intra-division and extra-division variances were 59.44 and 32.93 respectively; for the 51 cases in which there were more extra-division games, the intra-division and extra division variances were 45.89 and 32.16 respectively. Thus, number of games within a division could not account for the observed differences in variances. The dynamic of an intra-division balanced schedule seems the most comparable to that for the pre-1969 season schedule. Since both intra- and extra-divisional records figure into the overall performance variance, the variance of overall team victories after 1968 would tend to give a lower estimate of the performance factor relative to that of pre-1969. Thus, intra-division performance should provide the most appropriate measure in making comparisons to pre-1969 performance.

A problem with using intra-divisional results stems from the fact that the smaller intra-division schedule relative to that for the full earlier seasons results in an intrinsically lower performance variance because of a smaller range of possible values. This problem can be dealt with by correcting the intra-division victories data with a constant that equalizes the range of values for all seasons. I used the 162-game season for all seasons from 1900. Using each victory record for all full seasons from 1900 to 1968, and the same data for intra-division play from 1969 on, I multiplied each victory record by 162/number of games played in a season or in a division. For example, for a 154-game season the correction factor is $162/154 = 1.052$. This transformation preserves the pattern of team values for each season and produces a common scale of values for all seasons. The change in values produces variances equal to the correction squared times the original variances. A corresponding correction was made using 18 games as a reference number for head-to-head season series.

Since variances of independent variables are additive, the total variance of season victories minus the variance for pure luck for a 162-game season equals the variance attributable to skill. The square root then equals the standard deviation, an approximate average measure in games of variation attributable to skill. An analogous measure for head-to-head series is possible. Table 4 shows these skill measures by decade for total season victory record and for head-to-head series victory record, with corrected intra-division records used after 1968.

If the head-to-head factor plays no role in determining a team's season record against each of the other teams, then we should expect that deviations of season records against specific teams from overall performance of a team should be a matter of chance. That is, when corrected for overall performance, teams would be expected to do equally well against each other on the average. Returning to the 1954 White Sox example, the number of victories corrected to reflect the head-to-head factor for each White Sox opponent produced an average of 11 games. The result reflects no advantage or disadvantage for one team against another on the average. It is possible to demonstrate that in general the expected value of number of season's victories for one team against another is one half the

games they play against each other.[7] For example, in a 162-game season two teams within a division generally play 18 games against each other with each team expected to win 9 games if no head-to-head factor is involved and there is no overall difference between the two teams. Thus, it is appropriate to use $p = 50$ to calculate variance attributable to luck in testing for significance of the head-to-head factor.

We can see that the skill standard deviation for total season wins per decades ranged from 11.01 for the 1980s to 17.55 for 1900–09. The corresponding ratio of skill to luck ranged from 1.73 to 2.76. Although there may have been a small drop-off in amount of performance attributable to skill post-1968, the skill factor still dominates, with a large part of perceived drop attributable to introduction of the divisional structure. The skill factor for head-to-head performance averaged 1.46 over decades. The values for the divisional decades may over correct for season length, and skill standard deviations without the correction are shown in parentheses. These values are somewhat lower than the corrected values. The analysis suggests that for a given team the unique matchup factor may account for between 1 and 1.5 games on the average in a given season's series. This may prove significant when considering a team's matchups against all the other teams. However, it is necessary to consider the net effect over a season. For example, the White Sox in 1954 fared poorly against the Yankees, winning only seven games, but they compensated by beating the Red Sox 17 times. Overall season records conceal much of the dynamics of a season. A team's season win record gives a smoothed-over description of a season's performance. It is true that the net sum of variations in head-to-head victories from a team's average is zero. However, the comparison of a team's head-to-head profile to the performance of its opponents against each other presents a complex picture of a season. Unlike total season record, the head-to-head factor is only a little less than half of the luck factor of 2.12 standard deviations.

Measures of the effects of performance factors become meaningful only if they are reliably greater than would be expected by luck or random variation. Pearson's Chi Square distribution provides a test of significance that allows us to determine the probability that the head-to-head factor is nothing more than the product of luck or random variation. A conservative statistical test was derived to determine this probability.[8] Results for the head-to-head factor are shown in Table 5. All the results are significant at the .01 level. This means that it is very unlikely that the head-to-head

Table 4. Standard Deviations Attributable to Skill Normed to a 162 Game Season (1900–2019).

Decade	Skill for total season[A]	Skill for head-to-head[B]
1900–09	17.55	0.65
1910–19	15.30	0.93
1920–29	14.06	1.16
1930–39	15.99	0.54
1940–49	14.46	0.89
1950–59	13.47	0.96
1960–68	11.55	1.08
1969–79	12.44	1.95 (1.83)
1980–89	11.01	2.19 (1.53)
1990–99	13.91	2.95 (1.55)
2000–09	13.49	2.22 (2.15)
2010–19	13.57	2.03 (2.20)

A – Chance standard deviation = 6.36
B – Chance standard deviation = 2.12

factor reflects nothing more than luck. It is apparent that the head-to-head factor contributes a significant amount to performance differences. Corresponding chi square tests were done to test whether total season differences between teams are a matter of chance. For the total seasons' records all results for decades through the 1970s were significant at the .01 level, the 1990s and 2010s were significant at the .05 level, and the 1980s and 2000s were nonsignificant.

Table 5. Pearson's Chi Square Values for Testing Significance of the Head-to-Head Factor.

Decade	Chi square	Degrees of freedom
1900–09	585.11	456
1910–19	623.43	480
1920–29	762.62	480
1930–39	624.18	480
1940–49	690.82	480
1950–59	707.50	480
1960–69	873.70	719
1970–79	998.14	513
1980–89	970.76	591
1990–99	854.10	453
2000–09	842.44	459
2010–19	816.12	408

Note. All chi squares are significant at the .01 level.

Next, I examined the relationship between overall season performance for teams and head-to-head performance. The analysis of variance enables us to see if the variance of season victory totals is significantly greater than that for head-to-head performance. This appears obvious, and the analysis of variance confirms it. The 387 analyses of variance found that variance for total season victories was significantly higher than that for head-to-head variance at at least the .05 level in 217 of the cases. Random differences between the two factors would predict significance for between 19 and 20 of such cases.

PREDICTING HEAD-TO-HEAD PERFORMANCE

What is the importance of the small variation in performance attributable to the head-to-head factor? Each game is, after all, a head-to-head contest and the outcome should at least in part depend upon the specific pattern of relative strengths and weaknesses of the two teams, in addition to the overall abilities of the teams in competition with all other teams in the league. I return to the 1954 White Sox example and their record against each of the seven other teams in the league. The White Sox only won seven of their 22 games against the Yankees. The deficit, corrected for overall

difference between teams of 6.26 games, may have something to do with the unique matchup between the teams in addition to the difference between the teams in overall ability. Except for their head-to-head performance, the teams were nearly equal. Of course, both finished behind the Cleveland Indians, who won 111 games (and proceeded to be swept by the Giants in the World Series, perhaps more evidence for a specific head-to-head factor?).

The problem of explaining the 6.26 game corrected deficit on the White Sox part may be of interest to those who wish to predict how teams will fare against each other apart from their overall competitive records. A natural way to approach the problem is to examine how differences between the teams in important performance variables predict differences between the teams in the unique head-to-head performance factor. An extensive exploration is beyond the scope of this article, but I made an initial try using four seasons that indicated a strong effect of the head-to-head factor with two prime performance measures which seemed to be good candidates: AERA, park adjusted earned run average, and AOPS, a park adjusted measure of on base average and slugging. These statistics I used were from the 2005 *Baseball Encyclopedia*.[9] Pete Palmer did extensive work demonstrating the effectiveness of OPS as a predictor of wins and why it works.[10] ERA would seem to be an appropriate complement to that. In our White Sox example, the difference between the White Sox and Yankees in these two measures would be used to predict the White Sox disadvantage against the Yankees, 6.26 games. The difference in 1954 between the two teams in AERA was 122–105 = 17 favoring the White Sox; however the difference in AOPS favored the Yankees, 103–118 = –15. The Yankees that year were first in AOPS, a power-laden team that out-homered the White Sox 133 to 94. The White Sox defense, on the other hand, had an advantage. In this matchup the offensive factor seemed to outweigh the defense. It is necessary to see how these variables relate to each other and to the head-to-head factor.

I used season data for the 1905, 1909, and 1962 National League seasons and the 1954 American League season to test the predictive value of the two above performance measures for the head-to-head factor. The selected seasons seemed promising because the contribution of the head-to-head factor was strong for these seasons. Of course, further research would be necessary if results generalize. Stanley Rothman used runs scored minus runs allowed as a predictor in a linear regression analysis predicting overall winning percentage.[11] His analysis was able to account for nearly

95% of variation in winning percentage. However, the predictor variable includes chance variation as well as variation attributable to skilled performance such as AOPS and AERA.

Multiple regression was used to generate a prediction equation of the form

$$a + b \cdot (AOPS_{White Sox} - AOPS_{Yankees}) + c \cdot (AERA_{White Sox} - AERA_{Yankees})$$

using our White Sox-Yankees example for predicting the head-to-head effect in this case. Value predicted would be compared to the observed value of -6.26 in this case. The equation for a season would be arrived at by determining the values of the weights in the equation that best fit the set of head-to-head performance values for all pairs of competing teams. There were 28 pairs of teams in 1905, 1909, and 1954; and 45 such pairs in 1962. The prediction equations for each season contain weights that produced the highest multiple correlation between those equations and the head-to-head performance measures.

Table 6. Multiple Regression for Predicting Head-to-Head Effects from AOPS and AERA Differences Between Teams

| League seasons | Multiple R^2 | Regression Weights | | r(AOPS, AERA) |
		AERA[A]	AOPS[A]	
1905 NL	.412**	.595	.140	.232
1909 NL	.486**	.454	.380	.395
1954 AL	.265*	.462	.068	.748
1962 NL	.403**	.346	.502	.091

A – Standardized weights
* – Significant at the .02 level
** – Significant at the .01 level

Table 6 shows the multiple correlation squared, weights for the two predictors, and correlation between the two predictors for each of the four seasons. Multiple R^2 was used, because it measures the proportion of total variance attributable to the two predictors. The correlations between the two predictors, r(AOPS, AERA), are shown, but the predictive weights indicate the contribution of each predictor apart from that of the other predictor. Although the number of team pairs in a season was not large, the multiple correlations between prediction equations and head-to-head measures were highly significant for all of the four seasons. Multiple correlations range from .515 to .697, where 1.000 is the maximum possible value. Standardized weights are shown, which makes the values comparable in terms of units of the variable measured. It is noteworthy that the AERA variable outweighed the AOPS variable in three of the four cases which highlights the importance of pitching in head-to-head matchups.

In exploring the variables that may correlate with the head-to-head factor, it is well to be aware that the pattern of measures of this factor for teams at the top or bottom range of the standings differ, from the pattern for teams near the middle. Teams near the top have a smaller chance of showing a positive head-to-head value over a given team than do teams lower in the standings. By the same token, losing teams have a better chance of showing a head-to-head advantage than do teams above them. The ceiling or floor in season performance makes this intuitive.

To illustrate for a winning team, consider the 1954 White Sox example again. The White Sox were 15 and 7 against the Orioles, demonstrating dominance. However, their score of 9.67 victories adjusted for relative performance of the two teams against the rest of the league placed them 1.33 games below the expected 11-game average against the league given no head-to-head effect. This, of course, results from the fact that the overall performance of the White Sox against teams in the rest of the league was on the average 5.33 games better than that of the Orioles. Thus, it appears that the White Sox underperformed against the Orioles.

As a counter example substitute a middle of the pack team with a 77 and 77 record for the White Sox which produces an average of 11 victories against each team in the rest of the league. This hypothetical team would have won half a game more on average against each of the other teams than did the Senators. If the hypothetical team beats the Senators 15 times, it has a four game advantage over its average. Subtracting the half game from this value produces a healthy 3.5 game head-to-head effect. Analogous comparisons to those above for losing teams would tend to result in apparent over performance. The above comparisons should be considered in evaluating head-to-head competition.

The results give support to the idea that unique factors associated with competition between certain teams can be assessed in understanding the dynamics of a season. Certainly, if measures associated specifically with head-to-head competition reflect only random variation, we could not expect any variables to provide significant predictive ability. Having an edge over another team in performance variables in five-team divisions assumes great importance. ∎

Acknowledgment

I would like to acknowledge Rodger Payne for his helpful comments as I prepared this article.

Notes

1. Pythagorean expectation, https://"Pythagorean theorem of baseball", https://baseball-reference.com/bullpen/pythagorean.
2. "Revisiting the Pythagorean Theorem," Baseball Prospectus, http://www.baseballprospectus.com/article.php?articleid=342.
3. "W% Estimators," http://gosu02.tripod.com/id69.html.
4. Pete Palmer, "Calculating skill and luck in Major League Baseball," *Baseball Research Journal* 46, no.1 (2017): 56–60.
5. John A. Richards, "Probabilities of victory in head-to-head team matchups," *Baseball Research Journal* 43, no.2 (2014): 107–17.
6. In general, twice the variance is equivalent to the average of all the squared differences between each of the possible paired observations in the distribution of values. If the correlation between pairs of observations is negative, it can be shown that the variance is greater than would be the case if observations were independent. In the period before 1969 and in intra-divisional play each team plays every other team an equal number of times, and the total number of victories within a division is fixed. The expected correlation between pairs of teams is then negative. Thus, the variance of team victories can be expected to be greater for intra-divisional play than for extra-divisional play, where observations are independent of each other.
7. Consider corrected head-to-head values for a given team against another team in the same league or division, e.g., the White Sox against the Senators. Let x_i be total victories for team i, and let y_j be total victories for team j. Let $x_{i,j}$ be the number of victories for team i against team j, and let $y_{i,j}$ be the number of victories for team j against team i. Further let n be the total number of teams, e.g., eight in the 1954 American League. Then, the head-to-head correction for team i against team j is

   $x_{c,i,j} = x_{i,j} - [(x_i - x_{i,j}) - (y_j - y_{i,j})]/ (n - 2)$.

   Next, consider average corrected head-to-head value for team i against the other n-1 teams. The average × (n-1) is,

   $$\sum_{j \neq i=1}^{n-1} x_{c,i,j} = \sum_{j \neq i=1}^{n-1} x_{i,j} - \{[(n-1)x_i - \sum_{j \neq i=1}^{n-1} x_{i,j}] - [\sum_{j \neq i=1}^{n-1} y_j - \sum_{j \neq i=1}^{n-1} y_{i,j}]\}/(n-2),$$

   where the subscript j is used to designate teams other than team i. Let N equal the number of games two teams play against each other in a season, e.g. 22 games in the 154 season. Next consider the following:

   $$\sum_{j \neq i=1}^{n-1} x_{i,j} = x_i \; ; \; (n-1)nN/2 = \text{total victories for all teams}$$
   in the league or division in a season, and hence,

   $$\sum_{j \neq i=1}^{n-1} y_j = (n-1)nN/2 - x_i \; ;$$

   $$\sum_{j \neq i=1}^{n-1} y_j$$ equals the total number of defeats for team i in a season, and hence the expression is equal to $(n-1)N - x_i$.

   Using these equivalences in the expression for the corrected head-to-head value and collecting terms gives us a value of $(n-1) N/2$. Thus, the average corrected head-to-head victories for a given team over teams in the rest of teams in the league is N/2.
8. The additive nature of the Chi Square distribution allows us to aggregate sums of squared differences as is in the White Sox example over all teams in a season and all seasons for a decade in order to make a comparison to the variance expected by pure luck. The significance test requires the assumption that observations are independent of each other. Because number of victories for one team in a series is inversely related to that for the other, there is a strong dependence between those values. If we hypothetically consider numbers for only one member of each pair, we can make a very conservative calculation by assuming a Chi Square value half as large as the one made for the complete set of values for each decade and use the Chi Square value needed for significance one half as large as that required for significance for all values. This adjustment likely produces an underestimation of the degree of statistical significance.
9. Pete Palmer and Gary Gillette, eds. *The 2005 ESPN Baseball Encyclopedia* (New York: Sterling Publishing Co., Inc., 2005).
10. Pete Palmer, "Why OPS Works." *Baseball Research Journal* 48, no.2 (2019): 43–47.
11. Stanley Rothman, "A New Formula to Predict a Team's Winning Percentage." *Baseball Research Journal* 43, no.2 (2014): 97–105.

Major League Player Ethnicity, Participation, and Fielding Position, 1946–2018[1]

Charles Pavitt

This is a study of the relationship between major league player ethnicity and both overall participation and fielding position—from 1947, Jackie Robinson's debut year, to 2018. I use the term "ethnicity" as an umbrella term encompassing the concept of "race" because the presence of Hispanics as a separate grouping invalidates a simple racial distinction. This is not the forum for a discussion as to whether race is a biological fact or a cultural concept only. In either case, players perceived as "colored," or whatever term was then in fashion, were barred from major league baseball from the 1890s until 1947; Hispanics were only allowed in if, through accident of birth, they were accepted as "white." Even after Jackie Robinson and Larry Doby, teams differed substantially in their willingness to integrate; it took the Red Sox until 1959, when public pressure resulted in Pumpsie Green's call-up from the minors, to become the final major league team to integrate. In baseball there are noticeable associations between ethnicity and position, which for want of a better term I will refer to as "positional differentiation." Baseball has not been alone among team sports with such correlations. In ice hockey, the significant distinction—at least until the influx of players from other countries—had been between English-Canadians and French-Canadians, with fewer of the former at defense and more at goal, while an argument has been made that Aboriginal Canadians have been stereotyped as "enforcers."[2] In football and basketball, the significant distinctions are between Black and White. In American football, Blacks are more prevalent at wide receiver, running back, and defensive back; Whites at quarterback, tight end, and the offensive line.[3] In basketball, Blacks were once more likely to be at forward and center and Whites more often at guard relative to their overall proportions, although these tendencies may have diminished over time.[4] Alone of the major North American team sports, soccer is overall the most diverse of the five, although there is evidence of a small bias toward Blacks at forward and Whites at other positions in the top four divisions of English soccer.[5]

Sociologists have been examining positional differentiation in baseball for about half a century. In an excellent review of work up to that time, Curtis and Loy credited Rosenblatt as beginning academic conversation on this topic, the latter author having noted Blacks to have been underrepresented as pitchers and overrepresented as outfielders in every season from 1953 through 1965.[6,7] Curtis and Loy presented a number of tables summarizing research findings up to that time, including seven previous studies about baseball, encompassing eighteen separate seasons between 1950 and 1975; I am aware of several additional reports since. The data are clearly in support of the claim that positional differentiation has been rampant in professional baseball. Just choosing one study in the set (the others are substantively the same), Loy and Elvogue examined players from 1956 through 1967 and noted that 19.5 percent of major leaguers over that time were Blacks; during that interim, Blacks totaled 5.6 percent of catchers, 9.3 percent of shortstops, 10.3 percent of second basemen, 18 percent of third basemen, 19.4 percent of first basemen, and 32.1 percent of outfielders.[8] Note the similarity between this and both positional centrality (see below) and Bill James's Defensive Spectrum with third base correctly ordered ahead of center field; the only clear difference is the relative preponderance of Black first basemen. If we can accept Loy and Elvogue's interesting assumption that catchers should get assists for their pitchers' strikeouts, it turns out that the rank-ordering of assists per position exactly matched the ranking of Blacks per position just listed.

One problem with some of these studies was the failure to distinguish Hispanics from Black Non-Hispanics and White Non-Hispanics. Loy and Elvogue made the attempt, and although their sample size was too small for clear conclusions, there is a glimpse of the fact that, even then, Hispanics were at least slightly overrepresented in the middle infield.[9] Pattnayak and Leonard also noticed this trend, as (to her surprise) did Gonzalez, discovering that Hispanics have been overrepresented at shortstop since the mid-1950s, at second base since the mid-1960s, and holding their own at catcher.[10,11] The inclusion of Hispanics as a separate category is critical for evaluating the proposed explanations for these disparities, as I will below.

The study reported here is based on a data set Pete Palmer sent me, which he put together with help from Stu Shea and Gary Gillette, categorizing players as either White Non-Hispanic, Black Non-Hispanic, Hispanic, or Other, with the latter mostly First Nation at the beginning but now predominately Asian. For classification, Pete, Stu, and Gary used the 1954 Baseball Register (which at the time included very specific ethnicity information), various Internet sources when ethnicity information was available, and made judgments from photographs when not. Their data set includes the number of game appearances as pitchers, catchers, infielders (including first base), and outfielders for every year between 1946 and 2018. The diagrams included herein were based on the annual data, but labels are only provided for each third year to prevent visual clutter.

ETHNICITY AND TOTAL PARTICIPATION

Figure 1 displays the proportion of game appearances for players within the four ethnicities in the 1946–2018 time frame. In 1946, baseball was almost universally White Non-Hispanic, with 1.1 percent Hispanics considered White and 1.9 percent Other. The proportion of White Non-Hispanics drifted down to about 60 percent in 1970 and has been at about 55 percent since around 2000. The now-well-known rise and fall of Black Non-Hispanic major leaguers is evident, reaching the high-water mark of around 25 percent between 1970 and 1985 and dipping to about 10 percent starting in 2013. Hispanics have taken up most of the slack; climbing to and then leveling off at 13–14 percent between 1967 and 1987 but rising over 34 percent in 2018. The contribution of Others has been above 3 percent only once, in 2008.

In a personal communication, Pete Palmer provided some possible explanations for these patterns with which I agree. For Hispanics, increasing opportunity has led to increased participation, particularly as scouting and player development (for example, the Dominican Summer League) have intensified. For Black Non-Hispanics, the rise was certainly a product of increasing opportunity, with the fall perhaps influenced by the advance of structural racism in inner cities, along with the increasing attraction of football and basketball. An audience member at a presentation of these data at the 2020 annual meeting of the Bob Davids (Greater Washington, DC) SABR chapter proposed the loss of ballfields in inner cities as another possible causal factor.

ETHNICITY AND POSITION

Subsequent diagrams chart the extent of positional differentiation between 1946 and 2018. Figure 2 displays the overall distribution of games played by pitchers, catchers, infielders, and outfielders. Pitchers, although only one of nine positions, has not surprisingly made up a large share of the overall total, and as relievers have become a greater part of the game, this share has increased from about 20 to about 30 percent. In response, the summed four infield positions have dropped from about 40 to 35 percent and three outfield positions from about 30 percent to 26.5. Catching has also declined a tad, from over 10 percent to about 8.

When we classify by ethnicity, the biases become clear. Figure 3 shows proportion of games played per position for White Non-Hispanic Players. As the proportion of other ethnicities entering the major leagues increased during the 1950s and 1960s, the proportion

Figure 2. Proportion of Games Played Per Position—Overall

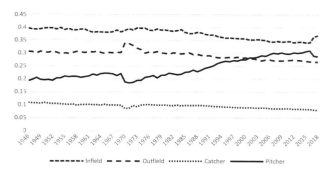

Figure 1. Proportion of Games Played Per Position—Total

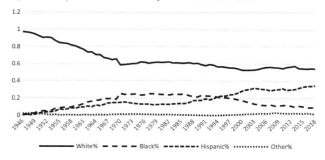

Figure 3. Proportion of Games Played Per Position—Non-Hispanic Whites

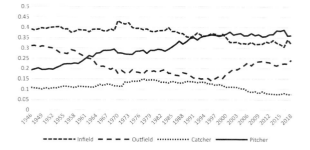

of games for White Non-Hispanic pitchers rose to about 10 percent greater than for pitchers overall, with White Non-Hispanic outfielders falling about the same amount. In the 2000s, the proportion of games for White Non-Hispanic infielders has dipped to noticeably less than the overall proportion.

Figure 4 shows the proportion of games played per position for Black Non-Hispanic players. Simply put, Black Non-Hispanics become outfielders, and are considerably less often found at the other positions.

Figure 5 demonstrates proportion of games played per position for Hispanic players. Again simply put, Hispanics become infielders. Figure 6 makes that clear. Note how in 2018 there were as many games played by Hispanic infielders as White Non-Hispanic infielders, despite the latter's greater overall abundance. Figure 7 reveals another important trend; Hispanics are more and more becoming evident as catchers; their number of games played has almost caught up to those for White Non-Hispanics. In contrast, there are presently no African-American catchers in the major leagues, a situation that has received recent attention.[12]

There have been, and continue to be, too few Others for the related data on positional differentiation to reveal bias or allow us to draw conclusions.

EXPLANATIONS

Sociologists have put considerable work into examining positional differentiation under the concept of "stacking." According to Ball (as cited by Curtis and Loy[13]), stacking is defined as the "assignment of a playing position, an achieved status, on the basis of an ascribed state," with race or ethnicity the ascribed state relevant in sports. Note that this definition works under the assumption that positional assignment is based on ethnicity and not some other factor. The implication is that more "valued" ethnicities are more likely to occupy central positions; in baseball, this means the battery and middle infield. Another contribution of the Curtis and Loy essay is a review of such explanations. Two are based on discrimination. The first is sheer bigotry: based on stereotypes of Blacks as "too dumb" to play a position supposedly requiring smarts, a position argued with no apparent evidence by Smith and Leonard.[14] The second somewhat more subtly proposed that central positions require a lot of communication among players, which allegedly becomes problematic between players of different races; if so, then why not have a totally Black battery or infield?

Two additional explanations do not begin with the presumption of discrimination as such. The first is that

unlike the outfield, the central positions require more expensive training and equipment that the underclass cannot afford (the "economic" hypothesis, favored by Medoff,[15] and by Sack, Singh, and Thiel[16]). The second would be a case of self-fulfilling prophecy: young Blacks acquired players such as Henry Aaron and Willie Mays as role models, and young Hispanics examples

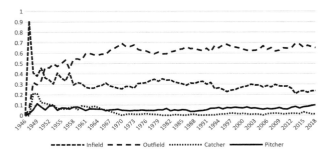

Figure 4. Proportion of Games Played Per Position—Non-Hispanic Blacks

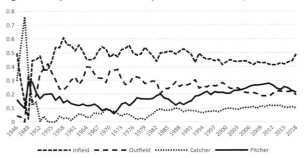

Figure 5. Proportion of Games Played Per Position—Hispanics

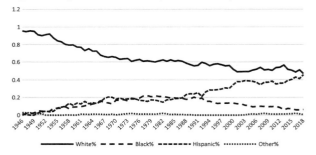

Figure 6. Proportion of Games Played Per Ethnicity—Infielders

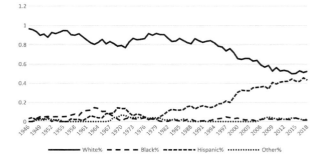

Figure 7. Proportion of Games Played Per Ethnicity—Catchers

such as Luis Aparicio and more recently Ivan Rodriguez and aspired to emulate them all the way down to position. Proposals relying on psychological differences have included the idea that Black people are more prone than White people to be attracted to roles in which they can work independently from others, and the notion that Black people are relatively better at reactive tasks (the outfielder reacts to the flight of the ball) and White people at proactive tasks (pitchers and catchers preplan their strategy). According to the Curtis and Loy review, both of these ideas have some support among the general population, although the second seems to be at least somewhat contradicted by outfielders positioning themselves before the play and catchers having to respond quickly to whatever occurs as plays unfold.[17] One final proposal is that actual physiological differences exist between races such that Black people are better at running and jumping than White people. If there is any evidence of this in the general population, it is irrelevant to the elite grouping from which major leaguers emerge.

Examining just the evidence concerning Black Non-Hispanics versus White Non-Hispanics implies that some sort of racial differentiation is at work. It is hard to evaluate the raw discrimination proposal, although Scully presented some relevant data reprinted from the June 1969 issue of *Ebony* magazine implying that the darker the skin of the Black player, the more likely that he was an outfielder.[18] In an explicit attempt to compare the economic, role model, and either of the discrimination explanations, Guppy looked at ethnic differences in positional changes for players with five years of MLB experience between 1958 and 1973.[19] Forty-seven percent of Black Non-Hispanic infielders were in the outfield five years later versus 26 percent of White Non-Hispanic infielders, whereas 16 percent of White Non-Hispanic outfielders were in the infield five years later versus 7 percent of Black Non-Hispanics. Guppy used the fact that there were no differences in batting average, runs scored, and fielding average between first year Black and White infielders to argue that skill differences did not exist, leaving discrimination as the only viable explanation. However, these performance indicators are mostly irrelevant; positional change is mostly a product of defensive skill, and teams back then probably used their informal observations of ability rather than fielding average as the main basis for their decisions. The issue of defense actually came up in later work by Lavoie and Leonard, based on sociological thinking that discrimination is more likely when there are less certain indicators of performance quality.[20] It follows for the authors that

stacking would be more likely for positions in which defense (which is harder to measure with certainty) is relatively more important. This is clearly true for Black Non-Hispanics, who have historically been underrepresented at catcher and the middle infield.

At the time of Guppy's work, there was reason to believe that Hispanics had status intermediate between White Non-Hispanics and Black Non-Hispanics, as 17 percent moved from the infield to the outfield versus 9 percent in the other direction.[21] Having noticed this trend, Pattnayak and Leonard made just that hypothesis, and also speculated that they might have more success attaining managerial positions upon retirement than Black Non-Hispanics.[22] However, as described above, by the time of Gonzalez's work, it was evident that Hispanics were very well represented in the middle infield and at catcher.[23] This fact certainly contradicts the uncertainty and economic hypotheses, and unless it can be demonstrated that discrimination against Hispanics has decreased over time, spells trouble for proposals relying on it.

Complicating the issue is the work of Margolis and Piliavin, who discovered that, as a group, Black Non-Hispanic players are bigger and Hispanics smaller than White Non-Hispanics.[24] This fits with the assignment of the former to the outfield and the latter to the middle infield, but suggests an additional hypothesis: that positional differentiation could be a product of selective opportunities for players based on size-based stereotypes for the three ethnicities. In support, when combining size with ethnicity in models predicting position centrality, Hispanics were at that time discriminated against in the sense that they were more likely to be assigned non-central positions than White Non-Hispanics of equivalent size. Sack, Singh, and Thiel replicated and extended this discovery, discerning that including indicators of speed (attempted steals) and power (slugging average) decreased although did not eliminate the impact of ethnicity on playing position.[25] As Pete Palmer pointed out to me, the problem with this account is that pitchers tend to be as big as or bigger in both height and weight than players at other positions, and so should feature more Black Non-Hispanics if size differences in ethnicities were relevant.

In conclusion, positional differentiation is a real phenomenon. In my opinion, given the available data, the role modeling process is likely the best overall explanation for positional differentiation, although racism cannot be ruled out, especially in the case of Black Non-Hispanics being stereotyped as less capable of playing the most central positions.[26] ■

Notes

1. Well after completing this manuscript, presenting it at a regional SABR convention, and submitting it for publication, I learned that Mark Armour and Daniel R. Levitt had previously performed an analogous study; Mark Armour and Daniel R. Levitt, "Baseball demographics, 1947–2016," https://sabr.org/bioproj/topic/baseball-demographics-1947-2016.

2. Marc Lavoie, "Stacking, Performance Differentials, and Salary Discrimination in Professional Ice Hockey: A Survey of the Difference," *Sociology of Sport Journal* 6, no. 1: 17–35; John Valentine, New Racism and Old Stereotypes in the National Hockey League: The 'Stacking' of Aboriginal Players into the Role of Enforcer, in *Race and Sport in Canada*, ed. by Danelle Joseph, Simon Darnell and Yuka Nakamura (Toronto: Canada Scholars' Press, 2012): 107–135.

3. J. R. Woodward, "Professional Football Scouts: An Investigation of Racial Stacking," *Sociology of Sport Journal* 21, no. 4 (2004): 356–75; Kyle Siler, "Pipelines of the Gridiron: Player Backgrounds, Opportunity Structures and Racial Stratification in American College Football," *Sociology of Sport Journal* 36, no. 1 (2019): 57–76.

4. Wilbert M. Leonard II, "Stacking in College Basketball: A Neglected Analysis," *Sociology of Sport Journal* 4, no. 4 (1987): 403–09; Rodolphe Perchot, Florent Mangin, Philippe Castel and Marie-Françoise Lacassagne, "For a Socio-Psychological Approach to the Concept of Racial Stacking," *European Journal for Sport and Society* 12, no. 4 (2015): 377–96.

5. Joe A. Maguire, "Race and Position Assignment in English Soccer: A Preliminary Analysis of Ethnicity and Sport in Britain, *Sociology of Sport Journal* 5, no. 3 (1988): 257–69.

6. James E. Curtis and John W. Loy, "Race/Ethnicity and Relative Centrality of Playing Positions in Team Sports," in *Exercise and Sports Sciences Review* Vol. 6, ed. Robert S. Hutton (Philadelphia: Franklin Institute, 1978): 285–313.

7. Aaron Rosenblatt, "Negroes in Baseball: The Failure of Success," *Trans-action* 4, no. 9 (1967): 51–53.

8. John W. Loy and Joseph F. Elvogue, "Racial Segregation in American Sport," International Review of Sport Sociology 5, no. 1 (1970): 5–23.

9. Loy and Elvogue, "Racial Segregation in American Sport."

10. Satya R. Pattnayak and John Leonard, "Racial Segregation in Major League Baseball, 1989," *Sociology and Social Research* 76, no. 1 (1991): 3–9.

11. G. Leticia Gonzalez, "The Stacking of Latinos in Major League Baseball: A Forgotten Minority?," *Journal of Sport and Social Issues* 20, no. 2 (1996): 134–60.

12. Robert Arthur and Daniel R. Epstein, "Why are there no Black catchers?" https://www.baseballprospectus.com/news/article/60634/moonshot-why-are-there-no-black-catchers; Clare Smith. "What happened to the African American catcher?" https://theundefeated.com/features/what-happened-to-the-african-american-catcher.

13. Curtis and Loy, "Race/Ethnicity and Relative Centrality."

14. Earl Smith and Wilbert M. Leonard II, "Twenty-Five Years of Stacking Research in Major League Baseball: An Attempt at Explaining this Re-Occurring Phenomenon," *Sociological Focus* 30, no. 4, (1997): 321–31.

15. Marshall H. Medoff, "Positional Segregation and Professional Baseball," *International Review of Sport Sociology* 12, no. 1 (1977): 49–54.

16. Allen L. Sack, Parbudyal Singh, and Robert Thiel, "Occupational Segregation on the Playing Field: The Case of Major League Baseball," *Journal of Sport Management* 19, no. 3 (2005): 300–18.

17. Curtis and Loy, "Race/Ethnicity and Relative Centrality."

18. Gerald W. Scully, "Discrimination: The Case of Baseball," in *Government and the Sports Business*, ed. Roger G. Noll (Washington, DC: Brookings Institute, 1974): 221–73).

19. N. Guppy, "Positional Centrality and Racial Segregation in Professional Baseball," *International Review of Sport Sociology* 18, no. 4 (1983): 95–109.

20. Marc Lavoie and Wilbert M. Leonard II, "In Search of an Alternative Explanation of Stacking in Baseball: The Uncertainty Hypothesis," *Sociology of Sport Journal* 11, no. 2 (1994): 140–54."

21. Guppy, "Positional Centrality and Racial Segregation."

22. Pattnayak and Leonard, "Racial Segregation in Major League Baseball."

23. Gonzalez, "The Stacking of Latinos in Major League Baseball."

24. Benjamin Margolis and Jane Allyn Piliavin, "Stacking in Major League Baseball: A Multivariate Analysis," *Sociology of Sport Journal* 16, no. 1 (1999): 16–34.

25. Sack, Singh, and Thiel, "Occupational Segregation on the Playing Field."

26. Arthur and Epstein, "Why are there no Black catchers?"

Testing the Koufax Curse

How 18 Jewish Pitchers, 18 Jewish Hitters, and Rod Carew Performed on Yom Kippur

Howard M. Wasserman

Yom Kippur—the Day of Atonement on which Jews fast, seek forgiveness from God and other people, and rehearse their deaths[1]—occupies an iconic space in the annals of baseball and American Jewry. Jewish-American fans regularly contemplate and debate whether Jewish players will and should play on the holy day.[2]

Yom Kippur in the Hebrew Year 5780 (sundown Tuesday, October 8, 2019, through sundown Wednesday, October 9, 2019) offered a unique exhibit in that debate. Three Major League Division Series games began within that 24-hour period. One team in each game featured a Jewish player as star or significant contributor. Each Jewish player appeared in the game. Each team lost.

On Tuesday evening (during *Kol Nidre*, the beginning of the holy day), the Houston Astros lost game four of their best-of-five American League Division Series to the Tampa Bay Rays. Alex Bregman, the Astros star third baseman, played and went 1-for-4. But the Astros allowed three first-inning runs and never were in the game. The loss forced a deciding fifth game, played two days later following an off-day on Yom Kippur.

At 5:02 PM EDT Wednesday (around the start of *Neilah*, the service that closes the holy day), the Atlanta Braves began a deciding game five of their NLDS, surrendering a postseason record 10 first-inning runs in a 13–1 loss. Braves left-hander Max Fried did not start but was pressed into first-inning relief; he surrendered four earned runs in less than two innings of work.

At 5:38 PM PDT Wednesday, before the holy day ended with the blowing of the shofar and breaking of fasts with bagels and kugel, the Los Angeles Dodgers began game five of their NLDS against eventual World Series champion Washington Nationals. Dodgers outfielder Joc Pederson started and hit what appeared to be a first-inning homer, although video review showed the ball traveled through a hole in—rather than over—the fence for a ground-rule double. Pederson scored on a subsequent first-inning homer, so no harm/no foul, except for his statistics. The Dodgers surrendered a two-run lead in the eighth inning and allowed four in the tenth to lose the game and the series.

Journalist Armin Rosen labeled this the "Koufax Curse."[3] It is the curse of the Jewish player who plays on Yom Kippur, rather than following in the footsteps of Dodgers Hall-of-Fame pitcher Sandy Koufax, who did not pitch Game One of the 1965 World Series on Yom Kippur 5726.[4] Koufax is not alone in his actions (or inactions) among Jewish players. Hank Greenberg skipped a Yom Kippur game during a pennant race in September 1934.[5] Shawn Green and Kevin Youkilis earned praise for skipping multiple Yom Kippur games during their careers. But the practice, and thus the curse, remain wedded to Koufax—whether because of his special greatness, that he missed a World Series game, or recency bias.[6]

Rosen acknowledges that "it's a theological stretch to claim that there's some kind of Koufax curse at work whereby *Hashem* punishes teams whose star Jewish players don't sit out on Yom Kippur. That would be an absurd and completely nondisprovable thing to assert. Why would Yom Kippur observance be the determinative factor in a baseball game? Surely *Hashem* isn't that petty."[7]

But correlation does not require causation. There might be a Koufax Curse in the sense of diminished performance by Jewish players and their teams—whether the cause be divine will, Jewish guilt, regression to the mean, or the nature of baseball as a game of failure.

If there is a Koufax Curse, it finds fertile haunting ground in Jewish baseball's new *gilten alter* (golden age).[8] Fifteen Jewish players spent all or part of 2019 in the major leagues.[9] Their ranks included several regulars who contributed significantly to their teams and an All-Star and American League MVP runner-up in Alex Bregman. Thirteen spent all or part of the COVID-19-shortened 2020 season in the majors, including five regulars and a star starting pitcher. The last four World Series have featured at least one Jewish player. The 2017 (Bregman and Pederson), 2018 (Pederson and Ian Kinsler of the Red Sox), and 2020 Series (Pederson and Ryan Sherriff of the Rays) featured one

Jewish player on each team, including the first game in which each team started a Jewish player and the first Series (2017) in which multiple Jewish players homered.[10] Pederson and Bregman have each hit five World Series home runs, most among Jewish players. The two also staged an epic one-on-one contest in the first round of the 2019 Home Run Derby.

This renewal follows a fallow period from the late-1970s to early-1990s, during which the few Jewish players were non-starters.[11] Green arguably launched the renaissance when he emerged as a star outfielder for the Toronto Blue Jays in 1995, the best Jewish player since pitcher Ken Holtzman in the 1970s; the attention on Green included invitations to Bar Mitzvahs in the Toronto area.[12] Numerous Jewish stars and everyday players have followed in the past three decades.

A legacy Jewish press has long covered Jewish athletes wherever they could be found.[13] Jewish-issues publications, such as *The Forward* and *Tablet Magazine*, publish stories on Jewish baseball players.[14] And new sites such as the online Jewish Baseball News, the Jewish Baseball Museum, and the tongue-in-cheek generalist site *Jew or Not Jew,* which includes a section on athletes, have arisen to report on this emerging topic.[15] The result is a perfect confluence—many Jewish baseball players to talk about and many outlets in which to talk about them. And an annual topic remains what Jewish baseball players do or do not do—and should or should not do—on Yom Kippur.[16]

Rosen is correct that *Hashem* is not so petty as to smite Jewish players with poor performance if they play on the holy day.[17] But a correlative question remains: How do Jewish players, and the teams that employ them, perform when they play or choose not to play on Yom Kippur?

This article identifies 36 Jewish players—18 nonpitchers and 18 pitchers—since 1966/5727 (the year after Koufax sat during the World Series). Through box scores from Yom Kippur games for each season of their careers, it explores whether they played on any part of the holy day and charts how they and their teams performed. It conducts the same analysis for Rod Carew, the Hall-of-Famer who is not Jewish but enjoys a unique familial and cultural connection to Judaism-in-baseball. From this, we can draw conclusions about whether players or teams are haunted by the Koufax Curse. And whether Yom Kippur 5780 was an anomaly or reflects a broader historical correlation since 1966.

1. IDENTIFYING THE KOUFAX CURSE
A. The Players
Koufax's 1965 non-start stands as the watershed event in Jewish baseball.[18] This study thus begins in 1966 (Yom Kippur 5727)—the beginning point for any "curse" upon Jewish players who would fail to follow Koufax's lead.

Given the importance of the number 18 in Judaism as the numerical representation of life, that number frames the study.[19] I identify 18 nonpitchers and 18 pitchers since 1966 with at least one Jewish parent and who self-identified to some degree with their Jewish heritage.[20] Players are listed in chronological order from their debuts. (As noted, the 1980s were a fallow period for star Jewish players, leaving a bit of a gap between starters of the 1970s and the revival in the 1990s and early 2000s.)

NONPITCHERS
- Mike Epstein: 1B: 1966–74 (Bal; Was;[21] Oak; Tex; Cal)
- Ron Blomberg: 1B/OF/DH: 1969–78: (NYY, ChW)
- Bob Melvin: C: 1985–94 (Det; SF; Bal; KC; Bos; NYY; ChW)
- Ruben Amaro, Jr.: OF: 1991–98 (Cal; Phi; Cle)
- Brad Ausmus: C: 1993–2010: (SD; Det; Hou; LAD)
- Shawn Green: OF: 1993–2007 (Tor; LAD; Ari; NYM)
- Mike Lieberthal: C: 1994–2007 (Phi; LAD)
- Gabe Kapler: OF: 1998–2010 (Det; Tex; Col; Bos; Mil; Tam)
- Kevin Youkilis: 1B/3B: 2004–13 (Bos; ChW; NYY)
- Ian Kinsler: 2B: 2006–2019 (Tex; Det; LAA; Bos; SD)
- Sam Fuld: OF: 2007–15 (ChC; Tam; Oak; Min)
- Ryan Braun: OF: 2007–Present (Mil)
- Ike Davis: 1B: 2010–16 (NYM; Pit; Oak; NYY)
- Danny Valencia: 3B/1B/OF: 2010–18 (Min; Bos; Bal; KC; Tor; Oak; Sea)
- Kevin Pillar: OF: 2013–Present (Tor; SF; Bos; Col)
- Joc Pederson: OF: 2014–Present (LAD)
- Alex Bregman: 3d: 2016–Present (Hou)
- Rowdy Tellez: 1B/DH: 2018–Present (Tor)

Among nonpitchers, five remain active as everyday players. Most enjoyed at least a few seasons as regular or semi-regular players, appearing in 110 or more games with 400 or more plate appearances. Several enjoyed (or continue to enjoy) lengthy careers.

The best in the group are Green (two-time All Star, third in home runs by a Jewish player); Youkilis (three-time All Star, Gold Glove first baseman, key player on two championship teams); Kinsler (four-time All Star, two-time Gold Glove infielder, played in three World Series); and Braun (six-time All Star, 2007 Rookie of the Year, 2011 MVP, career leader in home runs by a Jewish player with 352[22]). None is likely to make the

Hall of Fame; Green fell off the ballot after receiving two votes in his first year of eligibility, and Youkilis received no votes in his first year of eligibility in 2019.[23] Epstein hit at least 19 home runs in four consecutive seasons, including as the starting first baseman for the 1972 World Series Champion A's. Pederson has topped 24 homers four times, including 36 in 2019, and has hit five World Series home runs. Blomberg claims the historic achievement of being the first designated hitter, drawing a first-inning walk on Opening Day 1973. Bregman could become the best of the group—at 26, he has played five seasons, made two All-Star teams, finished second in the 2019 MVP balloting, and hit five World Series home runs.

PITCHERS

- Ken Holtzman: (S) 1965–79 (ChC; Oak; Bal; NYY)
- Dave Roberts: (S) 1969–81 (SD; Hou; Det; ChC; SF; Pit; Sea; NYM)
- Steve Stone: (S) 1971–81 (SF; ChW; ChC; Bal)
- Ross Baumgarten: (S) 1978–82 (ChW; Pit)
- Jose Bautista: (S/R) 1988–97 (Bal; ChC; SF; Det; St.L)
- Steve Rosenberg: (S/R) 1988–91 (ChW; SDP)
- Scott Radinsky (R) 1990–2001 (ChW; LA; St.L; Cle)
- Andrew Lorraine: (R/S) 1994–2002 (Cal; ChW; Oak; Sea; ChC; Cle; Mil)
- Al Levine: (R) 1996–2005 (ChW; Tex; Ana; Tam; KC; Det; SF)
- Scott Schoeneweis: (R) 1999–2010 (Ana; ChW; Tor; Cin; NYM; Ari; Bos)
- Jason Marquis: (S) 2000–15 (Atl; StL; ChC; Col; Was; Ari; Min; SD; Cin)
- Justin Wayne: (R/S) 2002–04 (Fla)
- John Grabow: (R) 2003–11 (Pit; ChC)
- Craig Breslow: (R): 2005–17: (SD; Bos Cle; Min; Oak; Ari; Mia)
- Scott Feldman: (S/R) 2005–17 (Tex; ChC; Bal; Hou; Tor; Cin)
- Dylan Axelrod: (R) 2011–15 (ChW; Cin)
- Richard Bleier: (R) 2016–Present (NYY; Bal; Mia)
- Max Fried: (S) 2017–Present (Atl)

The pitchers form a less-elite group. Holtzman, Roberts, Stone, Feldman, Marquis, Baumgarten, and Fried spent the majority of their careers as starters; the first five occupy half the spots on the list of top-10 winningest Jewish pitchers. The remainder were spot- and middle-relievers who started the occasional game, some enjoying lengthy careers in this role for multiple teams.[24]

Holtzman pitched two no-hitters, made two All-Star teams, and won 174 games (nine more than Koufax) in fifteen seasons; he was the third starter on the three-time World Series Champion A's of the mid-70s. (He also hit the lone World Series home run by a Jewish player in the long gap between Greenberg in 1945 and

Bregman and Pederson in 2017). Stone won the AL Cy Young Award in 1980 (the only Jewish Cy Young winner other than Koufax), going 25–7. Holtzman (1970) and Roberts (1971) enjoyed better seasons measured by WAR and other metrics. In addition to a decade-plus career as a middle-reliever (including pitching 61 games for the 2013 World Champion Red Sox), Breslow attended Yale and considered becoming a doctor before pursuing a life in baseball.[25]

Two pitchers remain active through the shortened 2020 season. Fried won 17 games with a 4.02 ERA and 173 strikeouts in his first season as a full-time starter in 2019, then went 7–0 with a 2.25 ERA in the COVID-19-shortened 2020. Bleier has been an effective reliever since 2017, sporting a 9-2 lifetime record with four saves.

B. The Jewish Narrative

Many of these players were known among teammates, fans, and media for their Judaism during their careers. Epstein carried the nickname "Super Jew;" one writer described him as "Mickey Mantle bred on blintzes and gefilte fish." Epstein's A's teammate Holtzman became known as "Jew" or "Regular Jew." Following the murder of 11 Israeli athletes at the Munich Olympics in 1972, both sported black fabric strips on their uniforms.[26] As mentioned, Green received invitations to Bar Mitzvahs in the Toronto area.[27] Other players describe invitations to people's homes for Shabbat and High Holy Days.[28] Bregman's Judaism is a flashpoint for a segment vested in his continuing development into greatness.[29]

Using 1966 as the starting point, the story opens with an adjacent game. Yom Kippur fell on Saturday in late September. Koufax pushed his start against the Cubs to Sunday afternoon. His opponent was Holtzman, a rookie left-hander who had pushed his own start back after telling his manager that he observed the holy days. The rookie Jewish pitcher outdueled the greatest Jewish pitcher, pitching a two-hit complete game with eight strikeouts in a 2–1 victory; Koufax gave up four hits and struck out five in his last regular-season loss before retiring following the season.[30] Holtzman's mother had hoped both would earn no-decisions so neither Jewish pitcher would lose.[31]

There is a generational divide among the players. Holtzman never pitched on Yom Kippur. Blomberg sat out *Kol Nidre* games in 1971 and 1974 and made clear early in his career that he could not and would not play on the holy day.[32] Epstein played following the end of Yom Kippur as a late-season call-up in 1966 and sat out a late-season afternoon game in 1971 as the starting first baseman for a division champion after it had clinched the title.

Green's emergence in the mid-90s as the first Jewish star in a quarter century reignited the Yom Kippur debate. The play-or-not question gained strength because it focused on a high-profile star, someone central to his team's success and expected to play every day. Green endured greater scrutiny and criticism on the subject than did his contemporaries; greater pressure to follow earlier stars such as Greenberg, Al Rosen, and Koufax in not playing; and more explicit suggestions that by playing he had failed as a Jew.[33] Green picked his spots. He did not play on *Kol Nidre* 5762 (in 2001), the holy day falling several weeks after 9/11. He split the difference in 2004, playing on *Kol Nidre* and sitting the following afternoon, while doing the converse in 2007.

Youkilis was most consistent among recent players, sitting multiple *Kol Nidre* games, as well as a two-game evening/day combination in 2007. Bautista started a game on *Kol Nidre* during his rookie year but would not attend Yom Kippur games the remainder of his career.[34] Lorraine and Breslow attended games, were in uniform, and were available to pitch. Lorraine attended services in the morning before going to the park.[35] Breslow fasted.[36] Breslow said that appearing at the park "weighed heavily" on him, but he could not shake the belief that as a non-star player he lacked leverage to demand the day off.[37]

But no current player—in particular no current star player—talks about sitting on the holy day. Kinsler played every Yom Kippur on which his team had a game. No news stories raised the prospect of Bregman, Pederson, or Fried not playing or not being available in those 2019 Division Series games and none made an issue of their playing.[38]

This narrative must account for the fact that most of these players—current and past—are not religiously observant, especially the several from mixed marriages. Epstein was unique in this respect, announcing, "I put on tefillin at different shuls in different cities. I was Bar Mitzvahed. I can read Hebrew. I'm a Jew."[39] Game one of the 1973 ALCS between the A's and Orioles fell on Yom Kippur 5734; Holtzman, not scheduled to pitch for the A's, attended synagogue in Baltimore with the Orioles owner.[40] Greenberg attended synagogue in 1934 and received a standing ovation; he described it as one of the times in his life he felt like a hero.[41] Bautista and Holtzman were observant and maintained kosher homes.[42]

Among recent players, many had Bar Mitzvahs (among them Bleier, Bregman, Fried, Lorraine, and Youkilis) and most express deep pride in their Jewish heritage. Green's father said that baseball placed his son in touch with his Judaism.[43] Many have played for Israel in the World Baseball Classic or the Olympics, including Kinsler, who relocated to Israel upon his 2020 retirement.[44]

But not playing on the holy day lacks force for these players, even those raised in the shadow of Koufax and for whom High Holy Day attendance was part of their Jewish upbringing.[45] Kinsler described celebrating Passover and Chanukah with his Jewish father's side of the family and embraced that part of his identity, but did not practice Jewish rituals, including observing the holy days.[46] Explaining his decision to play on *Kol Nidre* in 2004 (a game for which his rookie teammate Youkilis dressed but did not play), Gabe Kapler said it made no sense for him to miss one important game on one day when he was not religiously observant 364 days of the year. While expressing pride in his Jewishness and welcoming the chance to serve as a role model as a Jewish athlete, sitting out the game was not part of that identity.

David Leonard argues that the will-he-play question evolves as Jews gain greater acceptance in US society and anti-Semitism declines.[47] This works in conflicting directions. On one hand, by not playing, Greenberg and Koufax—operating in eras of greater and more explicit anti-Semitism in which Jews occupied a more tenuous space in American society[48]—made it safe to express Jewish identity.[49] On the other, Greenberg and Koufax rendered it unnecessary for current players to demonstrate that identity by not playing; Judaism is part of them and they can move through baseball and American society without calling attention to it. Even recent upticks in anti-Semitism seem unlikely to manifest in widespread criticism of a Jewish player who chooses not to play on Yom Kippur.[50]

2. THE KOUFAX CURSE BY THE NUMBERS

This part turns to the numbers, for teams and players. The sample of players in the study is naturally limited. The number of Jewish major leaguers is small, which is why it is the subject of many books.[51] Howard Megdal wrote that, as of 2008, fewer than 160 Jews, broadly defined, have played in the majors, representing less than one percent of players in MLB history. Focusing on a subset of 18 nonpitchers and 18 pitchers—rather than looking at every Jewish-identifying player—further shrinks the sample, while centering it on players more likely to play in a typical game.

The sample of games also is naturally limited. Jewish holy days run from sundown to sundown, so the study focuses on two days and, at most, two games each season. Teams may have no games scheduled on Yom Kippur.

Following the Hebrew calendar, I treat three categories of games as "on" Yom Kippur: 1) evening, when *Kol Nidre* and the fast have begun; 2) during daylight the following day, which I define as beginning before 6:00 PM; and 3) first pitch between 6:00 PM and 8:00 PM the following evening, beginning as the holy day is ending for some number of Jews but finishing after its conclusion.

A. Team Records

The first consideration is team success when Jewish players play. The events of 2019 were striking less because of the performance of three Jewish players than for the fact that all teams lost, two of them series-deciding games.[52]

Table 1 shows team performance when Jewish players play, broken by three classes of Yom Kippur games and all holy-day games. In the "Team W-L" column, the larger record is for all players, while parentheses show records when the Jewish player is a pitcher.

In 120 games, teams are 53–67 when a Jewish player plays at any point on Yom Kippur, 14 games below .500—ten games under on *Kol Nidre*, five games under before sundown the following day, and one game over in games played as or after the holy day is ending. This is a .442 winning average, projecting to a 71–91 record in a 162-game season. Teams won six of 23 games in which the Jewish player is a pitcher, a .261 winning average.

Teams had a –114 run differential when Jewish players played, including a –61 differential on *Kol Nidre* and a –40 differential at the end of the holy day. Interestingly, teams outperformed that run differential. A team with those numbers of runs scored and allowed expects to win 47 of 120 games (.392 winning average), six fewer than teams won.

Table 2 shows team records when Jewish non-pitchers (excluding pitchers) do not play on Yom Kippur, whether for religious or other reasons.

Teams remain two games below .500 on *Kol Nidre* and one game below during Yom Kippur day. But the record jumps to ten games above .500 in after-holy-day evening games. This produces a total of seven games over .500 in about half the number of games.

B. Nonpitchers

1. Total Statistics

Table 3 shows combined performance for the 18 non-pitchers in the study, again broken by three categories of games, all holy-day games, and careers.

As a group, nonpitchers match combined career batting average and OPS for all holy-day games. They significantly out-perform on *Kol Nidre*—surprising, given team records in those games. Only in Yom Kippur day games, the smallest of the three categories, do they under-perform career numbers to a significant degree. Power and run-production numbers are not great, but the sample size is small.

Table 1. Team Performance With Jewish Players

	Games	Team W–L	Winning Average	Projected	Run Differential	Expected Record
Kol Nidre	56	23–33 (4–10)	.410	66–96	180–241 (-61)	21–35
Yom Kippur (D)	19	7–12 (1–1)	.368	60–102	66–77 (-11)	8–10
Yom Kippur (E)	45	23–22 (1–6)	.511	83–79	190–232 (-42)	19–27
All Yom Kippur	120	53–67 (6–17)	.442	71–91	436–550 (-114)	47–73

Table 2. Team Performance Without Jewish Players (Nonpitchers Only)

	Games	Team W–L
Kol Nidre	30	14–16
Yom Kippur (D)	11	5–6
Yom Kippur (E)	18	14–4
All Yom Kippur	59	33–26

Table 3. Nonpitcher Performance

	G	AB	R	H	2B	3B	HR	RBI	BB	K	Avg	OPS
Kol Nidre	42	117	19	34	6	1	4	15	17	24	.299	0.858
Yom Kippur (D)	17	47	3	9	3	1	1	6	1	9	.191	0.570
Yom Kippur (E)	38	106	19	29	4	0	5	14	14	14	.273	0.811
All Yom Kippur	97	270	41	72	13	2	10	35	32	47	.267	0.777
Career Totals	18006	59852	8624	15984	3347	306	2171	8150	6035	10857	.267	0.777

Ninety-seven games represent 59.9 % of one season. Imagining these as the statistics for one Jewish non-pitcher (call him "Moses"), Table 4 projects Yom Kippur performance for a 162-game season.

Moses finishes a full season with a .267 average, .776 OPS, with 120 hits, a modest 17 home runs, 58 RBI, a slash line of .267/.343/.433, and more strike-outs than walks.

2. Individual Statistics

Appendix A shows career performance for the 18 non-pitchers, listed in chronological order of MLB debut. For each player, it lists performance in the three categories of games, all holy-day games, and career.

Kinsler (15), Ausmus (12), and Braun (10) have played the most games, a reminder of the small sample size. Ausmus significantly outperformed his career stats on *Kol Nidre*. Kinsler hit well in eight end-of-holy-day games, but otherwise under-performed his career numbers for the full holy day.

Youkilis never played on *Kol Nidre* or during the day, but went 2-for-3 with two home runs and 3 RBIs in a 2009 post-fast loss. Pillar provides the stand-out game, going 3-for-3 with a solo home run in 2015 (*Kol Nidre* 5776) in a loss. Epstein played at the end of the holy day as a late-season call-up in 1966, going 2-for-4 with a triple and 3 RBIs.

In 2004, Green played on *Kol Nidre* 5765 so he could sit the following afternoon; he went 1-for-3 with a two-run home run in an important late-season victory. Bregman played two Yom Kippur games in 2017. On *Kol Nidre*, he went 3-for-4 with a home run and 3 RBIs in a late-season 3–2 win; the following afternoon he went 0-for-4 in a loss.

As a rookie in 2010 (5771), Valencia enjoyed the best overall Yom Kippur. On *Kol Nidre*, he went 2-for-3 with a solo home run, the lone run for his Twins in a loss. The following afternoon, he went 2-for-4 with a home run, driving in three of the team's four runs in a victory. Valencia arguably enjoyed the best Yom Kippur

career, with eight hits, including two home runs, five walks, and seven runs batted in in eight games.

C. Pitchers
1. Total Statistics
Table 5 shows combined performance for the eighteen pitchers in the study.

Pitchers provide a smaller sample than nonpitchers, with fewer games and fewer innings pitched. Eighteen of 23 Yom Kippur appearances were in relief, the average appearance lasting two innings. A Jewish pitcher earned a decision in five games in which any Jewish pitcher appeared, going 2–3; the win or loss was charged to a different, non-Jewish pitcher in 18 games. There was one save earned.

The sample size for pitchers is too small to extrapolate over a full season.

2. Individual Statistics
Appendix B shows career performance for the 18 pitchers, listed in chronological order of MLB debut. The first parenthetical indicates whether he threw lefty or righty; the second indicates starter, reliever, or both.

Breslow made the most appearances with four, all in relief, followed by three for Marquis (two starts) and for Roberts (all in relief). Four players on the list never appeared on the holy day, although only Holtzman appears to have done so as a religious decision, as opposed to not being needed.

The best combined pitching performance occurred in 1980 (Yom Kippur 5741). On *Kol Nidre*, Baumgarten surrendered one earned run on five hits with four strikeouts in seven innings and left with a 3–2 lead; he earned no decision when the bullpen surrendered the lead. As the holy day ended 24 hours later, Stone surrendered one run on six hits in eight innings, striking out five in a win, continuing his dream season.

Marquis earned the other win in 2001 (*Kol Nidre* 5762), allowing one run on five hits in six innings. Schoeneweis earned the lone save in the study, striking

Table 4. Projected Season Performance for "Moses"

G	AB	R	H	2B	3B	HR	RBI	BB	K	Avg	OPS
162	450	68	120	22	1	17	58	53	78	.267	.776

Table 5. Pitcher Performance

	G	GS	CG	IP	H	R	ER	BB	K	ERA	W–L
Kol Nidre	14	4	0	32.1	41	23	22	21	23	6.12	1–2
Yom Kippur (D)	2	0	0	2.1	4	4	4	1	2	15.43	0–0
Yom Kippur (E)	7	1	0	12.1	11	6	5	6	12	3.65	1–1
All	23	5	0	47	56	33	31	28	37	5.94	2–3
Career	5407	1832	278	15553.2	15637	7824	6929	5493	8158	4.01	856–763

out three of the four batters he faced to preserve a 2007 (*Kol Nidre* 5768) win. Breslow never allowed a run and struck out five of his seven outs—impressive performance considering he fasted.

The three losses reflect poor outings. Marquis surrendered six runs on six hits in $\frac{1}{3}$ of an inning in a 2010 (*Kol Nidre* 5771) loss. Levine surrendered the winning run on three hits in the bottom of the ninth in relief in a 2002 end-of-holy-day game (Yom Kippur 5763). Bautista lost the only Yom Kippur game he pitched in 1988 (*Kol Nidre* 5749), allowing five runs on seven hits in $4\frac{2}{3}$ innings.

Several poor relief performances have come in games in which the team trailed, resulting in a team loss but no decision. Fried surrendered four runs on four hits in $1\frac{2}{3}$ innings in his 2019 playoff game, but the Braves trailed, 4–0, before Fried entered in the first inning of an eventual 13–1 loss. Radinsky surrendered two hits, three walks, and four earned runs in less than one inning in 1990, but his White Sox trailed, 7–4, on the way to a 13–4 loss.

D. The Special Case of Rod Carew

Preliminary discussions with colleagues about this article and the players to include in the study precipitated a miniature debate: What of Rod Carew, the Hall-of-Fame infielder for the Minnesota Twins and California Angels from 1967–85? Carew occupies a unique space in the conversation about Jews and baseball, earning him a unique space in this study.

Were Carew Jewish, he would be on the Mount Rushmore of Jewish players (Mount Sinai?) with Koufax and Greenberg, while perhaps waiting for Bregman to fulfill his potential and form a quartet. Although he lacked power, Carew was among the best hitters of his generation. He had more than 3000 career hits, ranking ninth all-time in singles; a career batting average of .328; and a career OPS of .822. He was an 18-time All Star; won 1967 American League Rookie-of-the-Year; and won 1977 American League Most Valuable Player, when he batted .388 (second-highest batting average since 1931 by a player not named Ted Williams) with an OPS of 1.019. He was elected to the Hall of Fame on the first ballot in 1991. And MLB placed his name on the AL batting champion award in 2016.[53]

Carew was born to an African American father and Panamanian mother with West Indian roots. He was married to a Jewish woman during his playing career and raised three Jewish daughters.[54] Carew appeared on the covers of *Time* and *Sports Illustrated* in 1977 wearing his Twins uniform and a chai (a pendant spelling the Hebrew word "life") that he wore on the

Sandy Koufax set a precedent when he did not pitch Game One of the 1965 World Series on Yom Kippur 5726.

field. He spoke during his playing career about converting to Judaism.[55] Baseball writer Thomas Boswell described him in an essay titled "The Zen of Rod Carew" as a "Jewish convert."[56] Most famously, comedian Adam Sandler included Carew in his first Chanukah Song, including Sandler's vocal aside: "He converted."[57] But Carew never converted, which he explained in a phone call to Sandler.[58] Although he took preliminary steps, he never completed the process. Carew's connection to Judaism made news when his youngest daughter died of a rare form of leukemia in 1996; her mix of African, West Indian, and Panamanian ancestry on her father's side and Eastern-European Jewish ancestry on her mother's made finding a bone marrow donor difficult.[59] Stories did not mention Carew having converted.

Nevertheless, Carew skipped Yom Kippur games five times.[60] In 1980, after missing a *Kol Nidre* evening game, he did not enter the following evening game until the ninth inning, well after the shofar had sounded and the fast had ended. In 1982, he played in a late-afternoon game prior to *Kol Nidre*, intending to leave had the game run past eight o'clock.[61] In 1977, while Carew's Twins played in Kansas City on *Kol Nidre*, Carew was home in Minneapolis; news reports conflicted about whether he went to seek medical attention for an ailing arm or whether he had planned to be home to observe the holy day with his family.[62]

Non-conversion makes Carew not Jewish for inclusion with the 18 Jewish nonpitchers.[63] But his connection to Judaism and his intentional avoidance of playing on Yom Kippur compel his consideration in the study.

Table 6 shows Carew's individual performance in nine games—two on *Kol Nidre*, none during Yom Kippur day, and seven in the late-afternoon or evening following the end of the holy day—while Table 7 shows team records in those ten games.

Carew's Yom Kippur experience mirrors that of the Jewish players in the study. He performed well, with numbers (in a small sample size of nine games and 34 plate appearances) outstripping even his Hall-of-Fame career numbers. And his team lost more than it won, although they at least broke even when he played on *Kol Nidre*.

III. A KOUFAX CURSE?

We conclude with the question that begat this paper: does the Koufax Curse exist, even as a correlative matter?

At the individual level, the answer appears to be no. As a group, Yom Kippur hitting numbers for non-pitchers match their career batting average and OPS, if limited power and run production, with higher numbers on *Kol Nidre* than in games during the following afternoon or evening. Pitcher performances have been mixed, with several good starts and relief appearances balanced against some poor games.

At the team level, however, something strange happens. Teams are 14 games under .500 in all Yom Kippur games, including ten games under on *Kol Nidre*. When a Jewish player plays on Yom Kippur, their teams are the equivalent of a 71–91 team. And they project to a worse record.

The events of October 2019 (Yom Kippur 5780), with which the article began, reflect this trend. Neither Bregman nor Pederson played poorly. Bregman had one hit in four at-bats and made some plays in the field, but the Astros surrendered three runs in the first inning. Pederson had two hits, including a double that

was initially ruled a home run, scored one run, and made two plays in the outfield, but the bullpen blew a late lead. Fried pitched poorly in surrendering four runs in an inning-plus of work, but the game was lost before he entered.

In other words, any curse appears to target not Jewish players, but their non-Jewish teammates, with consequences befalling the whole team. Perhaps this warrants a new approach to Yom Kippur—teams should welcome and encourage Jewish players to sit these games. The media can retire the historic narrative of a dilemma between team and faith or of a player letting his teammates down by missing one game that could decide the season.[64,65] The story becomes that the Jewish player helps his team and supports his teammates by not playing, at least for one or two games. The player becomes a hero to Jewish fans, offers the team an ironically better chance at victory, and perhaps appeases *Hashem*.

This revised narrative recalls the biblical story of Jonah, fittingly read and studied on Yom Kippur.[66] God's anger at Jonah causes a storm certain to wreck the boat and kill everyone on board, so Jonah urges his shipmates to throw him overboard. The crew reluctantly does so, after which the "sea ceased from its raging."[67] Perhaps by casting their Jewish teammates into the sea of a day off, the storm of defeat will cease from raging that day.

On the other hand, overall team record is better than it should be, given performance. While teams won 53 games with a Jewish player, their run differential reflects a team that should have won 47 games. Perhaps winning six more games than expected reflects *Hashem* smiling upon these teams and their Jewish players.

On a third hand (invoking the oft-repeated phrase "two Jews, three opinions"[68]), teams do not win when

Table 6. Carew Performance

	G	AB	R	H	2B	3B	HR	RBI	BB	K	Avg	OPS
Kol Nidre	2	7	0	3	0	0	0	1	3	0	.429	1.029
Yom Kippur (D)	–	–	–	–	–	–	–	–	–	–		
Yom Kippur (E)	7	21	3	10	1	0	0	1	3	4	.476	1.065
All	9	28	3	13	1	0	0	2	6	4	.464	1.059
Career	2469	9315	1424	3053	445	112	92	1015	1018	1028	0.328	0.822

Table 7. Team Performance With Carew

	G	REC
Kol Nidre	2	1–1
Yom Kippur (D)	0	0–0
Yom Kippur (E)	7	2–5
All	9	3–6

their Jewish players rest on *Kol Nidre* or during the following day, finishing a combined three games below .500. The foundational events that beget any curse reflect this. With Greenberg sitting during Yom Kippur day in 1934, the Tigers lost—although they had built a lead in the pennant race thanks in part to Greenberg hitting two home runs in a Rosh Hashanah win nine days earlier.[69] With Koufax sitting in a Minneapolis hotel room, the Dodgers lost game one of the 1965 World Series, with future Hall-of-Famer Don Drysdale surrendering 7 hits (2 home runs) and 7 runs (3 earned) in 2⅔ innings. The story is that when Dodger manager Walter Alston pulled him from the game, Drysdale said, "I bet you wish I was Jewish today, too."[70] Team records without Jewish players improve in evening games, as or after the sounding of the shofar and breaking of the fast.

Perhaps the solution is that no one should play on Yom Kippur, at least not teams with Jewish players. Like public schools or the Supreme Court, everyone should benefit from the off day that the Hebrew calendar and a Jewish population provides.[71] Jews can recommit to their faith. And everyone can be ready to play the following day.

I make both suggestions with tongue in cheek, of course. MLB should not stop playing on Yom Kippur, nor should it urge Jewish players not to play. But these numbers might relieve Jewish players of the belief, expressed by Breslow, that they lack the leverage to request the day off. ■

Acknowledgments

Thanks to David Fontana, Michael Helfand, Roberta Kwall, David Leonard, Peter Oh, Howard Simon, and Spencer Weber Waller for help and comments. Thanks to Alexis de la Rosa, Jesse Goldblum, Jordan Roth, Carlos San Jose, and Jesse Stolow for research assistance.

Source

Unless otherwise stated, all game, season, and career statistics were found on player biography pages on Baseball-Reference.com. All scores and details were found on box scores for the relevant games on Baseball-Reference.com.

Notes

1. 16 Leviticus 1–34; 58 Isaiah 3–6; Irving Greenberg, *The Jewish Way: Living the Holidays* (New York: Touchstone, 1993) 184–85.
2. Edward Sherman, "L'dor v'dor: The annual re-telling of the Sandy Koufax Yom Kippur story," *Jewish Baseball Museum*. Oct. 10, 2016, http://jewishbaseballmuseum.com/spotlight-story/tradition-annual-re-telling-sandy-koufax-yomkippur-story.
3. Armin Rosen, "The Koufax Curse," *Tablet Magazine*, Oct. 10, 2019, https://www.tabletmag.com/sections/sports/articles/the-koufax-curse.
4. Jane Leavy, *Sandy Koufax: A Lefty's Legacy* (New York: HarperCollins, 2002), 170–71, 183–84; Larry Ruttman, *American Jews & America's Game: Voices of a Growing Legacy in Baseball* (Lincoln: University of Nebraska Press, 2013), 129; David J. Leonard. "To Play or Pray? Shawn Green and His Choice Over Atonement," *Shofar* 25, no.4 (2007): 159 & n.25; Matt Rothenberg, "Sandy Koufax Responded to a Higher Calling on Yom Kippur in 1965," *National Baseball Hall of Fame*, https://baseballhall.org/discover/sandy-koufax-sits-out-game-one.
5. Mark Kurlansky, *Hank Greenberg: The Hero Who Didn't Want to Be One* (New Haven: Yale University Press, 2011); Leonard, "To Play or Pray," 157-58; Howard M. Wasserman, "When They Were Kings: Greenberg and Koufax Sit on Yom Kippur." *Tablet Magazine*, Oct. 11, 2016, https://www.tabletmag.com/sections/news/articles/when-they-were-kingsgreenberg-and-koufax-sit-on-yom-kippur.
6. Leavy, *Sandy Koufax*, 171.
7. Rosen, "The Koufax Curse." *Hashem* ("the name") is one of the names Jews use to speak of God.
8. David Fontana, "The Return of the Jewish Athlete." Huffington Post, Dec. 6, 2017, https://www.huffpost.com/entry/the-return-of-the-jewish-_b_4601775.
9. Jewish Baseball News, http://www.jewishbaseballnews.com.
10. The Oakland A's starting lineup for Games one and four of the 1972 World Series included pitcher Ken Holtzman and first baseman Mike Epstein.
11. In Howard Megdal's ranking of the top Jewish players by position, no top-five non-pitcher played the bulk of his career during the 1980s and the only player on his All-Time Jewish team who played the bulk of his career in the '80s is a relief pitcher. Howard Megdal, *The Baseball Talmud: The Definitive Position-by-Position Ranking of Baseball's Chosen Players* (New York: HarperCollins, 2009), 287–88.
12. Steve Wulf, "The bat belongs to Shawn Green, the Mitzvah is his breakout for the Blue Jays." ESPN.com, July 10, 2012, https://www.espn.com/espn/magazine/archives/news/story?page=magazine-19990614-article43.
13. Robert L. Cohen, "How the Jewish Baseball Superstars Have Handled the High Holiday Conflict," *St. Louis Jewish Light*, Sept. 26, 1984, 3.
14. Jesse Bernstein, "The Greatest Jewish Baseball Players of All Time, By Position," *Tablet Magazine*, July 29, 2016, https://www.tabletmag.com/sections/news/articles/the-greatest-jewish-baseball-players-of-all-time-by-position; David Hazony, "Why Israel's Sudden Baseball Prowess Actually Means Something." *The Forward*, Mar. 10, 2017, https://forward.com/opinion/365646/why-israels-sudden-baseball-prowess-actually-means-something.
15. Leonard, "To Play or Pray?", 151, 160–61; http://www.jewishbaseball-news.com/; http://jewishbaseballmuseum.com; http://www.jewornotjew.com/category.jsp?CAT=Athletes%20and%20Coaches.
16. Leonard, "To Play or Pray?", 151; Sherman, "L'dor v'dor."
17. Rosen, "The Koufax Curse."
18. No World Series game has been played on Yom Kippur since game one in 1978 fell on *Kol Nidre*. No Jewish player has missed a World Series game since Koufax. And none will repeat that feat, as Yom Kippur and the World Series no longer overlap. Under the current (and expanding) post-season format, the World Series never will begin earlier than October 20, while Yom Kippur cannot fall later than October 14. This adds to Koufax's legend.
19. The Hebrew word for life is *chai*. It is spelled in Hebrew with two letters, the 8th and 10th in the alphabet. This gives the word a numerical value of 18.
20. Traditional Judaism is matrilineal. Observant Jews would not recognize as Jewish a person with a Jewish father and non-Jewish mother, unless the person converted. Reform and more liberal Judaism recognize patrilineal descent.
21. The second iteration of the Washington Senators, that played from 1961–72 before relocating to Dallas-Fort Worth and becoming the Texas Rangers.
22. *Jewish Baseball Museum*, http://jewishbaseballmuseum.com/stats.

23. Braun's early-career numbers might have been Hall-worthy, Megdal, *The Baseball Talmud*, 130, but he has not maintained the pace. His candidacy also may be hurt by his 65-game suspension in 2013 for using performance-enhancing drugs during that MVP season, including defending himself by impugning the integrity of the lab technician who collected his sample. Bernstein, "The Greatest Jewish Baseball Players." Hall voters have been unforgiving of PED users, and Braun's response to being caught may not help. David Sheinin, "The key changes that could finally put PED users into the Baseball Hall of Fame," *Washington Post*, Jan. 17, 2017.

24. In his position-by-position rankings, Megdal identified 20 Jewish starting pitchers (7 lefty, 13 righty) and 47 Jewish relief pitchers (21 lefty, 26 righty). Megdal, *The Baseball Talmud*, 181–285.

25. Megdal, *The Baseball Talmud*, 225; Ruttman, *American Jews*, 424–25; "Red Sox Reliever Craig Breslow Brings Brains and Jewish Faith to Mound." *Haaretz*, Oct. 23, 2014, https://www.haaretz.com/jewish/red-sox-s-breslow-brings-judaismto-mound-1.5278574.

26. Jason Turbow, *Dynastic, Bombastic, Fantastic: Reggie, Rollie, Catfish, and Charlie Finley's Swingin' A's* (Boston: Mariner Books, 2017), 48–61.

27. Wulf, "The bat belongs to Shawn Green."

28. Ira Gewanter, "Seven Questions for a Pair of Jewish Birds," *JMore: Jewish Baltimore Living*, May 16, 2018, https://www.jmoreliving.com/2018/05/16/seven-questions-for-a-pair-of-jewish-birds.

29. Armin Rosen, "Is Alex Bregman Having the Best Season Ever By a Jewish Baseball Player?" *Tablet Magazine*, Sept. 27, 2019, https://www.tabletmag.com/sections/news/articles/is-alex-bregman-having-the-best-season-ever-by-ajewish-baseball-player; Dave Sheinin, "Alex Bregman nears MLB greatness set in motion generations ago in D.C. sandlots and boardrooms," *Washington Post*, Oct. 4, 2018.

30. Ruttman, *American Jews*, 214–15.

31. *Ibid.* at 215.

32. "Yankees Edge Bengals." *New York Daily News*, Sept. 27, 1971.

33. Leonard, "To Play or Pray?", 150–51, 160–61.

34. Horvitz & Horvitz, *The Big Book of Jewish Baseball*, 25–26.

35. George Castle, "A Jewish Lefty: Lefty Lorraine continues tradition." *Jewish World Review*, Sept. 22, 1999. http://www.jewishworldreview.com/0999/lorraine.html.

36. "Red Sox Reliever Craig Breslow."

37. Ruttman, *American Jews*, 424.

38. Jonathan S. Tobin, "Did we need another Sandy Koufax?" Jewish News Syndicate, Oct 11, 2019, https://wwwjns.org/opinion/did-we-need-another-sandy-koufax.

39. Turbow, *Dynastic, Bombastic, Fantastic*, 49.

40. Ruttman, *American Jews*, 221–22; "A's, Orioles Call 1st Playoff Game 'Vital'," *Sacramento Bee*, Oct. 6, 1973.

41. Kurlansky, *Hank Greenberg*, 10.

42. Horvitz & Horvitz, *The Big Book of Jewish Baseball*, 26; Ruttman, *American Jews*, 213.

43. Wulf, "The bat belongs to Shawn Green."

44. Referred to as "Making *Aliyah*," or the "act of going up to Jerusalem."

45. David R. Cohen, "Max Fried's Birthright from Israel to SunTrust Park," *Atlanta Jewish Times*, Aug. 25, 2017, https://atlantajewishtimes.time-sofisrael.com/fried-is-working-to-fill-koufaxs-shoes; Gewanter, "Seven Questions."

46. Ruttman, *American Jews*, 488-90; Jackie Headopohl, "Kinsler and Ausmus connect with their family roots," *The Jewish News*, June 8, 2017, https://thejewishnews.com/2017/06/08/kinsler-ausmus-connect-family-roots.

47. Leonard, "To Play or Pray?", 162.

48. *Id.* at 159–60; Wasserman, "When They Were Kings."

49. Leonard, "To Play or Pray?", 162, 165.

50. Jonathan Weisman, *(((Semitism))): Being Jewish in America in the Age of Trump* (New York: St. Martin's Press, 2018), 11–14, 31.

51. Horvitz & Horvitz, *The Big Book of Jewish Baseball*; Megdal, *The Baseball Talmud*; Ruttman, *American Jews*.

52. Rosen, "The Koufax Curse."

53. Snyder, "MLB All-Star Game."

54. Mike Digiovanna, "A Father's Prayer: 'Give Her More Time': Rod Carew's Daughter Michelle, in a Battle for Life, Waits for a Bone-Marrow Transplant," *Los Angeles Times*, Mar. 3, 1996.

55. Steve Lipman, "Carew Heading Home to Judaism," *The Journal News*, Sept. 29, 1977,16B

56. Thomas Boswell, "The Zen of Rod Carew," in *How Life Imitates the World Series* (New York: Penguin Sports Library, 1982).

57. Carly Mallenbaum, "Adam Sandler's 'Chanukah Song': Are of those celebs in the song actually Jewish?" *USA Today*, Dec. 23, 2019, https://www.usatoday.com/story/life/music/2018/11/29/adam-sandler-chanukah-lyrics/2133567002.

58. "Hall of Famer Rod Carew Ruins Adam Sandler's Hanukkah Song by Admitting He Isn't Jewish." *NESN*. Last modified Aug. 6, 2012. https://nesn.com/2012/08/hall-of-famer-rod-carew-ruins-adam-sandlers-hanukkah-song-byadmitting-he-isnt-jewish.

59. Ron Lesko. "Michelle Carew: 'She Was the Light of the World.'" Associated Press, Apr. 21, 1996.

60. R. Cohen, "How the Jewish Baseball Superstars," 3.

61. "Angels," 13.

62. Lipman, "Carew Heading Home to Judaism," 16B; "Arm Injury."

63. Megdal, *The Baseball Talmud*, 67.

64. Leonard, "To Play or Pray?", 153–54; R. Cohen, "How the Jewish Baseball Superstars," 3; Sherman, "L'dor v'dor."

65. Leonard, "To Play or Pray?," 158, 163; Tobin, "Did we need another Sandy Koufax?"; Wolpe, "A Rabbi's Advice for Shawn Green," BeliefNet, Sept. 24, 2004, https://wwwquestia.com/library/journal/1Ps-1318031171/to-play-or-pray-shawn-green-and-his-choice-over-atonement; Marc Tracy, "Marquis to Pitch on Kol Nidre," Tablet Magazine, Sept 14, 2010, https://www.tabletmag.com/sections/news/articles/marquis-to-pitch-on-kol-nidre.

66. Greenberg, *The Jewish Way*, 213.

67. 1 Jonah 12–16.

68. Sandee Brawarsky & Deborah Mark, *Two Jews, Three Opinions: A Collection of Twentieth-century Jewish Quotations* (New York: Pedigree Books, 1998).

69. Kurlansky, *Hank Greenberg*; Leonard, "To Play or Pray?," 157–58; Wasserman, "When They Were Kings."

70. Leavy, *Sandy Koufax*, 184–85.

71. Nathaniel Lewin, "When Jewish justices got the Supreme Court to shut down on Yom Kippur," *Jewish Telegraphic Agency*, Sept. 29, 2017, https://www.jta.org/2017/09/29/opinion/when-jewish-justices-got-the-supreme-court-to-shutdown-on-yom-kippur.

Appendix A. (Nonpitchers)

PLAYER		G	AB	R	H	2B	3B	HR	RBI	BB	K	Avg	OPS
Mike Epstein (1B)	Kol Nidre	-	-	-	-	-	-	-	-	-	-	-	
	Yom Kippur (D)	-	-	-	-	-	-	-	-	-	-	-	
1966-74	Yom Kippur (E)	1	4	1	2	0	1	0	3	0	1	.500	1.500
Bal; Was; Tex; LAA	All	1	4	1	2	0	1	0	3	0	1	.500	1.500
	Career	907	2854	362	695	93	16	130	380	448	645	0244	.782
Ron Blomberg	Kol Nidre	-	-	-	-	-	-	-	-	-	-	-	-
(1B/OF/DH)	Yom Kippur (D)	-	-	-	-	-	-	-	-	-	-	-	-
1969-78	Yom Kippur (E)	-	-	-	-	-	-	-	-	-	-	-	-
NYY; ChW	All	-	-	-	-	-	-	-	-	-	-	-	-
	Career	461	1333	184	391	67	8	52	224	140	134	.293	0.832
Bob Melvin (C)	Kol Nidre	3	4	0	0	0	0	0	0	1	1	.000	.200
1985-94	Yom Kippur (D)	1	4	0	0	0	0	0	0	0	0	.000	.000
SF; Bal; KC; Bos;	Yom Kippur (E)	3	6	0	2	1	0	0	0	0	0	.333	.833
NYY; ChW	All	7	14	0	2	1	0	0	0	1	1	.142	.414
	Career	692	1955	174	456	85	6	35	212	98	396	0233	0604
Ruben Amaro, Jr. (OF)	Kol Nidre	-	-	-	-	-	-	-	-	-	-	-	-
1991-98	Yom Kippur (D)	-	-	-	-	-	-	-	-	-	-	-	-
Cal; Phi; Cle	Yom Kippur (E)	1	4	0	2	0	0	0	1	0	1	.500	1.000
	All	1	4	2	2	0	0	0	1	0	1	.500	1.000
	Career	485	927	99	218	43	9	16	100	88	128	.235	.663

PLAYER		G	AB	R	H	2B	3B	HR	RBI	BB	K	Avg	OPS
Brad Ausmus (C)	Kol Nidre	5	17	1	7	0	0	0	1	1	5	.411	.832
1993-2010	Yom Kippur (D)	3	8	0	0	0	0	0	0	0	2	.000	.000
SD; Det; Hou	Yom Kippur (E)	4	11	2	3	1	0	0	0	2	3	.157	.437
	All	12	36	3	10	1	0	0	1	3	10	.277	.666
	Career	1971	6279	718	1579	270	34	80	607	634	1034	.251	.669
Shawn Green (OF)	Kol Nidre	2	6	3	1	0	0	1	2	2	1	0.167	1.042
1993-2007	Yom Kippur (D)	1	3	1	1	0	0	0	0	1	1	.333	.833
Tor; LAD; Ari; NYM	Yom Kippur (E)	1	3	2	2	0	0	0	0	2	0	0.5	1.167
	All	4	12	6	4	0	0	1	2	5	2	.333	1.112
	Career	1951	7082	1129	2003	445	35	328	1070	744	1315	.283	.850
Mike Lieberthal (C)	Kol Nidre	1	3	0	2	1	0	0	0	0	0	.667	1.267
1994-2007	Yom Kippur (D)	-	-	-	-	-	-	-	-	-	-	-	-
Phi; LAD	Yom Kippur (E)	3	13	1	5	0	0	0	1	0	0	.384	.768
	All	4	16	1	7	1	0	0	1	0	0	.438	.973
	Career	1212	4218	534	1155	257	10	150	610	335	571	.274	.783
Gabe Kapler (OF)	Kol Nidre	2	3	0	1	1	0	0	3	0	0	.333	1.000
1998-2010	Yom Kippur (D)	1	0	0	0	0	0	0	0	0	0	.000	.000
Det; Tex; Col; Bos	Yom Kippur (E)	3	5	2	1	0	0	1	1	1	2	.200	1.113
Mil; Tam	All	6	8	2	2	1	0	1	4	1	2	.250	1.083
	Career	1104	2983	443	799	176	16	82	386	269	480	.268	.749

PLAYER		G	AB	R	H	2B	3B	HR	RBI	BB	K	Avg	OPS
Kevin Youkilis (1B/3B)	**Kol Nidre**	-	-	-	-	-	-	-	-	-	-	-	-
2004-13	**Yom Kippur (D)**	-	-	-	-	-	-	-	-	-	-	-	-
Bos; ChW; NYY	**Yom Kippur (E)**	2	8	3	3	0	0	2	3	0	0	.375	1.375
	All	2	8	3	3	0	0	2	3	0	0	.375	1.375
	Career	1061	3749	653	1053	254	18	150	618	539	828	.281	.861
Ian Kinsler (2B)	**Kol Nidre**	6	20	5	3	0	0	0	1	7	4	.150	.520
2006-2019	**Yom Kippur (D)**	1	4	0	2	0	0	0	0	0	0	.500	1.000
Tex; Det; LAA: Bos; SD	**Yom Kippur (E)**	8	24	6	7	1	0	1	5	7	2	.321	.921
	All	15	48	11	12	1	0	1	6	14	6	.250	.753
	Career	1888	7423	1243	1999	416	41	257	909	693	1046	.269	.777
Sam Fuld (OF)	**Kol Nidre**	2	0	0	0	0	0	0	0	0	0	.000	.000
2007-15	**Yom Kippur (D)**	1	0	0	0	0	0	0	0	1	0	.000	1.000
ChC; Tam; Oak; Min	**Yom Kippur (E)**	2	1	0	0	0	0	0	0	0	0	.000	.000
	All	5	1	0	0	0	0	0	0	1	0	.000	.500
	Career	598	1354	177	308	60	18	12	112	153	227	.227	.632
Ryan Braun (OF)	**Kol Nidre**	6	21	4	8	2	0	0	0	1	5	.380	.885
2007-Present	**Yom Kippur (D)**	2	9	1	2	2	0	0	1	0	1	.222	.666
Mil	**Yom Kippur (E)**	5	9	2	2	1	0	1	2	0	0	.222	.610
	All	10	39	7	12	5	0	1	2	1	6	.307	.837
	Career	1766	6622	1080	1963	408	49	352	1154	586	1363	.296	.891

PLAYER		G	AB	R	H	2B	3B	HR	RBI	BB	K	Avg	OPS
Ike Davis (1B)	Kol Nidre	2	6	1	0	0	0	0	0	2	3	.000	.250
2010-16	Yom Kippur (D)	1	4	0	0	0	0	0	0	0	3	.000	.000
NYM; Pit; Oak; NYY	Yom Kippur	1	3	0	0	0	0	0	0	1	2	.000	.250
	All	4	13	1	0	0	0	0	0	3	8	.000	.187
	Career	665	2076	260	496	117	2	81	291	294	538	.239	.746
Danny Valencia	Kol Nidre	5	16	2	5	0	0	1	4	4	4	.312	.950
(3B; 1B; OF)	Yom Kippur (D)	2	7	1	2	0	0	1	3	0	3	.285	.999
2010-18	Yom Kippur (E)	1	3	0	1	0	0	0	0	1	1	.333	.833
Min; Bos; Bal; KC; Tor;	All	8	26	3	8	0	0	2	7	5	8	.308	.803
Oak; Sea;	Career	864	2963	360	795	154	12	96	397	217	651	.268	.742
Kevin Pillar (OF)	Kol Nidre	2	3	1	3	1	0	1	1	1	0	1.000	3.333
2013-Present	Yom Kippur (D)	-	-	-	-	-	-	-	-	-	-	-	-
Tor; SF; Bos; Col	Yom Kippur (E)	2	7	0	1	0	0	0	1	0	2	.142	.284
	All	4	10	1	4	1	0	1	2	1	2	.400	1.354
	Career	905	3270	419	858	205	13	82	344	142	555	.262	.707
Joc Pederson (OF)	Kol Nidre	2	2	0	0	0	0	0	0	0	1	.000	0
2014-Present	Yom Kippur (D)	-	-	-	-	-	-	-	-	-	-	-	-
LA	Yom Kippur (E)	4*	9	1	2	1	0	0	0	0	2	.222	.555
	All	6	11	1	2	1	0	0	0	0	3	.181	.453
	Career	748	2153	345	496	112	7	130	303	304	609	.230	.806

* Includes 2019 game that began at 6:15 p.m.

PLAYER		G	AB	R	H	2B	3B	HR	RBI	BB	K	Avg	OPS
Alex Bregman (3B)	**Kol Nidre**	3	12	1	4	1	0	1	3	0	2	.333	.749
2016-Present	**Yom Kippur (D)**	1	4	0	0	0	0	0	0	0	1	.000	.000
Hou	**Yom Kippur**	1	2	0	0	0	0	0	0	1	0	.000	.333
	All	5	18	1	4	1	0	1	3	1	3	.222	.707
	Career	559	2058	365	582	152	12	105	342	309	343	0283	.902
Rowdy Tellez	**Kol Nidre**	1	4	1	1	0	0	0	0	0	1	.250	.500
(1B/DH)	**Yom Kippur (D)**	-	-	-	-	-	-	-	-	-	-	-	-
2018-Present	**Yom Kippur (E)**	1	1	0	0	0	0	0	0	0	0	.000	.000
Tor	**All**	2	5	1	1	0	0	0	0	0	1	.200	.400
	Career	169	553	79	138	33	0	33	91	42	157	.250	0.797

Appendix B. (Pitchers)

PLAYER		G	GS	CG	IP	H	R	ER	BB	K	ERA	W-L
Ken Holtzman (L) (S)	**Kol Nidre**	-	-	-	-	-	-	-	-	-	-	-
1965-79	**Yom Kippur (D)**	-	-	-	-	-	-	-	-	-	-	-
ChC; Oak; Bal; NYY	**Yom Kippur (E)**	-	-	-	-	-	-	-	-	-	-	-
	All	-	-	-	-	-	-	-	-	-	-	-
	Career	451	410	127	2867	2787	1273	1111	910	1601	3.49	174-150
Dave Roberts (R) (S)	**Kol Nidre**	1	0	0	3.1	4	0	0	0	1	0.00	
1969-81	**Yom Kippur (D)**	1*	0	0	0.2	0	0	0	0	0	0.00	
SD; Hou; Det; ChC; SF	**Yom Kippur (E)**	1	0	0	0.1	0	2	0	1	1	0.00	
Pit; Sea; NYM	**All**	3	0	0	4.1	4	2	0	1	2	0.00	
	Career	445	277	77	2099	2188	979	882	615	80	3.78	103-125
Steve Stone (R) (S)	**Kol Nidre**	-	-	-	-	-	-	-	-	-	-	-
	Yom Kippur (D)	-	-	-	-	-	-	-	-	-	-	
1971-81	**Yom Kippur (E)**	1	1	0	8	6	1	1	3	5	3.05	1–0
SF; ChW; ChC; Bal	**All**	1	1	0	8	6	1	1	3	5	3.05	1–0
	Career	320	269	15	1788	1707	880	788	716	1065	3.97	107-93
Ross Baumgarten (L) (S)	**Kol Nidre**	1	1	0	7	5	2	1	3	4	1.28	0–0
1978-82	**Yom Kippur (D)**	-	-	-	-	-	-	-	-	-		
ChW; Pit;	**Yom Kippur (E)**	-	-	-	-	-	-	-	-	-		
	All	1	1	0	7	5	2	1	3	4	1.28	0–0
	Career	90	84	10	495.1	492	246	220	211	222	4.00	22-36

*Game began at 5 p.m and was coded as a day game.

PLAYER		G	GS	CG	IP	H	R	ER	BB	K	ERA	W-L
Jose Bautista (R) (R/S)	**Kol Nidre**	1	1	0	4.2	7	5	5	3	2	10.71	0—1
1988-97	**Yom Kippur (D)**	-	-	-	-	-	-	-	-	-		
Bal; ChC; SF; Det; St.L	**Yom Kippur (E)**	-	-	-	-	-	-	-	-	-		
	All	1	1	0	4.2	7	5	5	3	2	10.71	0-1
	Career	312	49	4	685.2	732	376	352	171	328	4.62	32-42
Scott Radinsky (L) (R)	**Kol Nidre**	1	0	0	0.2	2	4	4	3	0	53.73	
1990-2001	**Yom Kippur**		-	-	-	-	-	-	-	-	-	
ChW; LA; St.L; Cle	**Yom Kippur**		-	-	-	-	-	-	-	-	-	
	All	1	0	0	0.2	0.2	2	4	4	3	53.73	
	Career	557	0	0	481.2	461	261	184	209	358	3.44	42-25
Steve Rosenberg (R) (R/S)	**Kol Nidre**	2	0	0	1.2	3	2	2	2-	2	15.00	
1991-92	**Yom Kippur (D)**	-	-	-	-	-	-	-	-	-		
Tex	**Yom Kippur (E)**	-	-	-	-	-	-	-	-	-		
	All	2	0	0	1.2	3	2	2	2	2	15.00	
	Career	87	21	2	209.2	222	129	114	87	114	4.94	6-15
Andrew Lorraine (L) (R)	**Kol Nidre**	-	-	-	-	-	-	-	-	-		
1994-2002	**Yom Kippur (D)**	-	-	-	-	-	-	-	-	-		
Cal; ChW; Oak; Sea;	**Yom Kippur (E)**	-	-	-	-	-	-	-	-			
ChC; Cle; Mil	**All**	-	-	-	-	-	-	-	-	-		
	Career	59	26	2	175	218	138	127	83	113	6.53	6—11

PLAYER		G	GS	CG	IP	H	R	ER	BB	K	ERA	W-L
Al Levine (L) (R)	**Kol Nidre**	-	-	-	-	-	-	-	-	-		
1996-2005	**Yom Kippur (D)**	-	-	-	-	-	-	-	-			
ChW; Tex; Ana; Tam;	**Yom Kippur (E)**	1	0	0	0.1	3	1	1	0	0	27.27	0--1
KC; Det; SF	**All**	1	0	0	0.1	3	1	1	0	0	27.27	
	Career	416	7	0	575.1	597	287	253	236	278	3.96	24-33
Scott Schoeneweis (R) (R/S)	**Kol Nidre**	1	0	0	1.1	0	0	0	0	3	0.00	S
1999-2010	**Yom Kippur (D)**	-	-	-	-	-	-	-	-	-		
Ana; ChW; Tor; Cin	**Yom Kippur (E)**	1	0	0	0	1	1	1	1	0	*	
NYM; Ari; Bos	**All**	2	0	0	1.1	1	1	1	1	3	8.18	
	Career	577	93	2	972	1035	580	541	398	568	5.01	47-57
Jason Marquis (R)(S)	**Kol Nidre**	2	2	0	6.1	11	7	7	4	3	9.95	1--1
2000-15	**Yom Kippur (D)**	-	-	-	-	-	-	-	-	-	-	
Atl; StL; ChC; Col;	**Yom Kippur (E)**	1	0	0	1	0	0	0	0	2	0.00	0-0
Was; Ari; Min; SD	**All**	3	2	0	7.1	11	7	7	4	5	8.59	1--1
	Career	377	318	8	1968.1	2079	1114	1008	769	1174	4.61	124-118
Justin Wayne (R) (R)	**Kol Nidre**	-	-	-	-	-	-	-	-	-	-	
2002-04	**Yom Kippur (D)**	-	-	-	-	-	-	-	-	-	-	
Mia	**Yom Kippur (E)**	-	-	-	-	-	-	-	-	-	-	
	All	-	-	-	-	-	-	-	-	-	-	
	Career	26	8	0	61.2	66	47	42	36	37	6.13	5--8

PLAYER			G	GS	CG	IP	H	R	ER	BB	K	ERA	W-L
John Grabow (L) (R)	Kol Nidre		1	0	0	2	3	1	1	1	1	4.50	
2003-11	Yom Kippur (D)		-	-	-	-	-	-	-	-	-		
Pit; ChC	Yom Kippur (E)		-	-	-	-	-	-	-	-	-		
	All		1	0	0	2	3	1	1	1	1	4.50	
	Career		506	0	0	476.1	481	250	228	220	400	4.31	24-19
Craig Breslow (L) (R)	Kol Nidre		3	0	0	1.1	2	0	0	2	2	0	0-0
2005-17	Yom Kippur (D)		-	-	-	-	-	-	-	-	-	-	-
SD; Bos; Cle; Min;	Yom Kippur (E)		1	0	0	1	0	0	0	1	3	0	0-0
Oak; Ari; Mia	All		4	0	0	2.1	2	0	0	3	5	0	0-0
	Career		576	2	0	570.2	536	250	219	226	442	3.45	23-30
Scott Feldman (R) (S/R)	Kol Nidre		1	1	0	4	4	2	2	3	5	4.50	0-0
2005-17	Yom Kippur (D)		-	-	-	-	-	-	-	-	-	-	
Tex; ChC; Bal;	Yom Kippur (E)		-	-	-	-	-	-	-	-	-	-	
Hou; Tor; Cin	All		1	1	0	4	4	2	2	3	5	4.50	0-0
	Career		342	204	5	1386	1441	753	682	439	882	4.43	78-84
Dylan Axelrod (R) (R)	Kol Nidre		-	-	-	-	-	-	-	-	-	-	-
2011-15	Yom Kippur (D)		-	-	-	-	-	-	-	-	-	-	-
ChW; Cin	Yom Kippur (E)		-	-	-	-	-	-	-	-	-	-	-
	All		-	-	-	-	-	-	-	-	-	-	-
	Career		59	34	17	228.2	269	146	134	85	164	5.27	9-15

PLAYER		G	GS	CG	IP	H	R	ER	BB	K	ERA	W-L
Richard Bleier (L) (R)	**Kol Nidre**	-	-	-	-	-	-	-	-	-		
2016-Present	**Yom Kippur (D)**	-	-	-	-	-	-	-	-	-		
NYY; Bal	**Yom Kippur (E)**	1**			1.2	1	0	0	0	1	0.00	
	All	1			1.2	1	0	0	0	1	0.00	
	Career	185	1	0	191	197	76	63	33	95	2.97	9-2
Max Fried (L) (S)	**Kol Nidre**	-	-	-	-	-	-	-	-	-	-	-
2017-Present	**Yom Kippur (D)**	1	0	0	1.2	4	4	4	1	2	27.69	0-0
	Yom Kippur (E)	-										
Atl	**All**	1	0	0	1.2	4	4	4	1	2	27.69	0-0
	Career	67	50	1	281.1	272	121	110	98	289	3.52	26-11

**Game began at 6 p.m. and was coded as an evening game.

Day-In/Day-Out Double-Duty Diamondeers, 1946–60

Missing in the Majors… Many in the Minors

Herm Krabbenhoft

A few days after Shohei Ohtani made his major league debut (March 29, 2018), Jay Jaffe wrote, "Ohtani is doing things that haven't been done at the major league level in nearly a century. … and not since 1919 has a player served as both a starting pitcher and a position player with any kind of regularity."[1] Jaffe also included a chart to illustrate his point. The salient aspects of Jaffe's chart plus some additional information (such as Ohtani's full-season statistics for 2018) are shown in Table 1.

The six left-most columns are taken as-is from Jaffe's chart with the number of games played per team added (in parentheses). The next two columns—Innings Pitched (IP) and Plate Appearances (PA)—are presented to provide additional perspective. The final two columns (IP% and PA%) show to what extent the player was a full-time performer as a pitcher and as a batter, according to the official rules of Major League Baseball.[2] IP% and PA% are defined as follows:

IP% = [Innings Pitched (Player) / Games Played (Team)] x 100

PA% = [Plate Appearances (Player)) / 3.1 x Games Played (Team)] x 100

IP% is simply a player's Innings Pitched divided by the number of games his team played. Similarly, PA% is a player's plate appearances divided by the product of 3.1 times the number of games his team played. Thus, for a pitcher to be considered a full-time performer—i.e., to qualify for the earned run average title—he must have accumulated at least one inning pitched per game played by his team. Therefore his IP% must be equal to or greater than 100. Similarly, for a batter to be considered a full-time performer—i.e., to qualify for the batting average championship—he must have accumulated at least 3.1 plate appearances per game played by his team. His PA% must be equal to or greater than 100. For example, in 1918, Ray Caldwell amassed 177 innings pitched, which are 51 IP greater than the 126 IP needed to qualify for the ERA crown (i.e., IP% = 140%); and he accumulated a total of 169 plate appearances, which are 222 PA fewer than the 391 PA needed to qualify for the batting crown (i.e., PA% = 43%). [NOTE: Appendix One on page 99 presents a chronological summary of the official qualifications required for the earned run average and batting average crowns for the 1946–60 period.]

Jaffe's criteria for inclusion in his list of double-duty players are that the player "pitched at least 15 times in a season and played a(nother) position …at least 15 times as well." Thus, for the 100-year period from 1918 through 2017, Jaffe identified seven players as double-duty major-league players—Ray Caldwell, George Cunningham, Babe Ruth, Johnny Cooney, Ossie Orwoll, Earl Naylor, and Willie Smith. However, as shown in the four right-most columns of Table 1, none of these players—including Babe Ruth—were simultaneously truly full-time pitchers and truly full-time batters. There were only four instances where a pitcher

Table 1. Additional Information on Double-Duty Players (1918–2017)

Player	Year	Team (Games)	G (Pitch)	G (Total)	Nonpitching Position	IP	PA	IP %	PA %
Ray Caldwell	1918	Yankees (126)	24	65	OF	177	169	140	43
George Cunningham	1918	Tigers (128)	27	56	RF	140	131	109	33
Babe Ruth	1918	Red Sox (126)	20	95	LF	166	380	132	97
Babe Ruth	1919	Red Sox (138)	17	130	LF	133	542	96	127
Johnny Cooney	1924	Braves (154)	34	55	CF	181	144	118	30
Johnny Cooney	1926	Braves (153)	19	64	1B	83	147	54	31
Ossie Orwoll	1928	Athletics (158)	27	64	1B	106	191	69	40
Earl Naylor	1942	Phillies (151)	20	76	CF	60	182	40	39
Willie Smith	1964	Angels (162)	15	118	LF/RF	32	370	19	74
Shohei Ohtani	2018	Angels (162)	10	114	DH	52	365	31	73

achieved at least the minimum number of innings pitched—Caldwell, Cunningham, Ruth (1918), and Cooney (1924); and there was only one occurrence where a pitcher accumulated at least the minimum number of plate appearances—Ruth (1919). Table 1 shows that going back to 1918 there has not been even one player in the major leagues who was both a full-time pitcher and a full-time batter in the same season. But what about the minor leagues? In this article I present the results of my research to address this question.

RESEARCH PROCEDURE

As shown in Table 1, no player—not even Babe Ruth—was technically a full-time pitcher and a full-time batter in the same season. In order to not be so restrictive, I have chosen to moderate the qualifications and have reduced the official requirements by ten percent. Thus, to be regarded as a full-time pitcher for purposes of this article, the player had to have amassed at least 0.9 IP per game played by his team (IP% ≥ 90). Likewise, to be regarded as a full-time batter, the player had to have accumulated at least 2.8 PA per game played by his team (PA% ≥ 90). I have chosen to research 1946

through 1960. The 1946 season was the first after the conclusion of World War II, while the 1960 season was the last before the American League expanded in 1961. Significantly, the 1946–60 period includes the so-called "Golden Age" of minor league baseball (1946–51).[3] All teams in all leagues from classifications AAA through D were included. Using the annual *Official Baseball Guide and Record Book* (published by *The Sporting News*) as the source for the statistics, I first ascertained which players qualified as full-time pitchers. Then I ascertained which of them on that list also qualified as full-time batters.

RESULTS

According to my research, during the 1946–60 seasons there were 59 players who were day-in/day-out double-duty diamondeers for at least one campaign in the minor leagues. All together, there were 75 day-in/day-out double-duty player-seasons; see Table 2 for pertinent information for each of these player-seasons. The main focus of this article is on those day-in/day-out double-duty diamondeers who were top performers as either pitchers or hitters—and a few

Table 2. Selected Statistics for Day-In/Day-Out Double-Duty Diamondeers (1946-1960)

Player (1946)	Team [League (Level)]	IP (%)	W-L (ave)	SO	ERA	PA (%)	BA/OBA/SLG	HR	POS (G)	FA
* Bob Borkowski *	Elizabethton [Appalachian (D)]	208	18-9 (.667)	183	3.46	432	.384/.417/.589	12	OF (86)	**.982**
Stan Karpinski	St. Augustine [Florida State (D)]	144	7-11 (.389)	107	4.12	475	.324/.394/.438	3	OF (87)	.984
Herb Moore	Albany [Georgia-Florida (D)]	175	15-3 (**.833**)	214	**1.44**	436	.323/.419/.430	2	OF (68)	.955
Player (1947)	**Team [League (Level)]**	**IP (%)**	**W-L (ave)**	**SO**	**ERA**	**PA (%)**	**BA/OBA/SLG**	**HR**	**POS (G)**	**FA**
Al Barillari	Port Chester [Colonial (B)]	119 (98)	7-7 (.500)	59	3.86	344 (91)	.261/.320/.358	4	SS (25)	.899
Woody Wheaton	Moline [Central Association (C)] Martinsville [Carolina (C)]	185	11-9 (.550)	94	3.70	380 (92)	.299/.385/.372	1	OF (72)	.975
George Biershenk	Lakeland [Florida International (C)]	144 (95)	8-9 (.471)	46	3.88	529	.265/.329/.381	7	3B (59)	.923
* *Hack Miller* *	Tyler [Lone Star (C)]	145	10-4 (.714)	48	3.79	535	.284/.384/.411	6	C (110)	**.990**
Bob Bailey	Pampa [West Texas-New Mexico (C)]	146	7-7 (.500)	78	7.09	594	.316/.425/.463	8	1B (117)	.981
* *Bob Benish* *	Troy [Alabama State (D)]	153	11-7 (.611)	60	3.47	520	.287/.361/.426	8	1B (100)	**.991**
* *Charles Allen* *	Kingsport [Appalachian (D)]	132	9-6 (.600)	70	**2.80**	460	.268/.366/.418	13	OF (89)	.992
Harold Livingstone	Radford [Blue Ridge (D)]	128	9-7 (.563)	122	4.57	325 (91)	.331/.368/.492	2	OF (56)	.948
* *Paul Bruno* *	Hammond [Evangeline (D)]	253	**25**-5 (.833)	**260**	**1.96**	459	.332/.434/**.563**	18	1B (89)	.987
George Washburn	Houma [Evangeline (D)]	171	12-11 (.522)	153	3.89	386 (90)	.327/.375/.537	12	OF (40)	.978
Buddy Lake	Sanford [Florida State (D)]	156	8-9 (.471)	69	1.91	556	.281/.406/.379	1	3B (62)	.858
* *Myril Hoag* *	Gainesville [Florida State (D)]	173	17-3 (**.850**)	115	**1.82**	377 (89)	**.350**/.437/.474	4	OF (64)	.947
Player (1948)	**Team [League (Level)]**	**IP (%)**	**W-L (ave)**	**SO**	**ERA**	**PA (%)**	**BA/OBA/SLG**	**HR**	**POS (G)**	**FA**
Manuel Fortes	Juarez [Arizona-Texas (C)]	194	14-13 (.519)	84	4.36	527	.316/.465/.513	8	OF (95)	.907
Louis Palmisiano	Pittsfield [Canadian-American (C)]	137	13-5 (.722)	41	3.61	459	.289/.399/.391	4	OF (94)	.975
Woody Wheaton	Welch [Appalachian (D)]	191	14-6 (.700)	132	3.53	429	.357/.448/.484	2	OF (75)	.958
* Roy Sanner *	Houma [Evangeline (D)]	199	21-2 (**.913**)	251	2.58	553	**.386**/.454/**.669**	**34**	OF (103)	.955
* *Paul Bruno* *	Hammond [Evangeline (D)]	248	**22**-5 (.815)	228	2.87	404 (95)	.337/.479/.546	16	IB (87)	.987
Edward Bowles	Hammond [Evangeline (D)]	170	11-9 (.550)	87	5.40	397 (93)	.284/.338/.339	0	1B (42)	.970
* Fred Campbell *	Griffin [Georgia-Alabama (D)]	122 (97)	8-5 (.615)	99	3.69	540	**.357**/.435/.473	3	SS (96)	.905
John Farkas	Matoon [Illinois State (D)]	115 (97)	9-6 (.600)	41	3.29	349 (95)	.273/.352/.370	5	C (48)	.970
Robert Keane	Sanford [Tobacco State (D)]	128 (94)	7-8 (.467)	78	4.99	571	.303/.385/.364	1	SS (99)	.914
* Robert McGimsey *	Morgantown [Western Carolina (D)]	153	12-6 (.667)	117	**2.76**	342	.355/.419/.557	8	1B (59)	.972

Player (1949)	Team [League (Level)]	IP (%)	W-L (ave)	SO	ERA	PA (%)	BA/OBA/SLG	HR	POS (G)	FA
Stanley Goletz	Bryon [East Texas (C)]	138 (99)	10-5 (.667)	86	3.07	496	.332/.438/.469	7	1B (91)	.990
George Washburn	Houma [Evangeline (C)]	138 (99)	7-9 (.437)	79	2.47	464	.331/.389/.555	17	OF (102)	.935
Edward Bowles	Hammond [Evangeline (C)]	142	8-7 (.533)	45	4.63	404 (94)	.272/.309/.337	3	1B (69)	.970
* Roy Parker *	Pampa [West Texas-New Mexico (C)]	263	**23**-10 (.697)	**235**	4.86	453	.296/.396/.582	24	OF (77)	.859
* Louis Bevil *	Daytona Beach [Florida State (D)]	251	19-11 (.633)	180	2.39	529	.291/.423/.493	**18**	LF (95)	.964
Benjamin Fasano	Baxley-Hazlehurst [Georgia State (D)]	155	7-10 (.413)	72	4.65	449	.237/.320/.333	4	OF (104)	.946
Al Gardella	Peekskill [North Atlantic (D)]	135 (97)	8-7 (.533)	63	6.40	597	.272/.401/.352	3	1B (131)	.984
* Joe Roseberry *	Fayetteville [Tobacco State (D)]	125 (91)	7-7 (.500)	69	4.03	509	**.409/.512**/.555	6	OF (98)	.944
Player (1950)	**Team [League (Level)]**	**IP (%)**	**W-L (ave)**	**SO**	**ERA**	**PA (%)**	**BA/OBA/SLG**	**HR**	**POS (G)**	**FA**
Julio Gomez	Henderson [East Texas (C)]	148	13-6 (.684)	67	3.95	551	.286/.389/.398	3	OF (80)	.932
Red Murff	Baton Rouge [Evangeline (C)]	176	17-4 (.810)	139	2.96	436	.332/.371/.423	3	OF (74)	.955
* Edwin Carnett *	Borger [West Texas-New Mexico (C)]	137 (95)	13-6 (.684)	81	**3.15**	623	.361/.445/.604	24	CF (76)	.957
Perry Roberts	DeLand/Gainesville [Florida State (D)]	159	12-6 (.667)	57	4.35	533	.345/.380/.482	3	RF (123)	.945
Henry Clifton	Dublin [Georgia State (D)]	169	13-7 (.650)	107	3.83	406 (93)	.267/.364/.356	4	1B (69)	.975
Robert Pugh	Rockingham [Tobacco State (D)]	196	11-11 (.500)	47	3.99	381 (94)	.254/.381/.402	5	OF (56)	.926
Robert McGimsey	Lincolnton/Morgantown [W. Carolina (D)]	158	13-5 (.722)	116	4.27	409	.273/.394/.407	7	OF (49)	.937
Player (1951)	**Team [League (Level)]**	**IP (%)**	**W-L (ave)**	**SO**	**ERA**	**PA (%)**	**BA/OBA/SLG**	**HR**	**POS (G)**	**FA**
Roy Parker	Sherman-Denison [Big State (B)]	156	11-10 (.524)	110	4.55	532	.345/.408/.559	18	OF (101)	.942
Ray Mink	Corpus Christi [Gulf Coast (B)]	191	14-7 (.667)	68	3.48	498	.339/.388/.424	1	OF (78)	.975
Thomas Warren	Miami [Kansas-Oklahoma-Missouri (D)]	213	14-13 (.519)	136	2.66	394	.320/.429/.480	8	OF (72)	.935
* Lee Tunnison *	Centralia [Mississippi-Ohio Valley (D)]	205	**20**-8 (.714)	**170**	**3.12**	383	.272/.318/.429	8	1B (38)	.971
Player (1952)	**Team [League (Level)]**	**IP (%)**	**W-L (ave)**	**SO**	**ERA**	**PA (%)**	**BA/OBA/SLG**	**HR**	**POS (G)**	**FA**
Edward Graham	Phoenix [Arizona-Texas (C)]	204	13-10 (.565)	88	4.94	429 (99)	.317/.364/.620	29	OF (66)	.944
John Karpinski	Houma [Evangeline (C)]	217	15-9 (.625)	105	5.13	560	.297/.360/.503	25	OF (79)	.976
Billy Russell	San Angelo [Longhorn (C)]	149	10-8 (.556)	78	4.35	405 (93)	.244/.386/.380	10	1B (51)	.974
* Bob Trice *	St. Hyacinthe [Provincial (C)]	152	**16**-3 (**.842**)	68	3.49	357 (89)	.297/.399/.383	1	OF (62)	.963
Eddie Carnett	Borger [West Texas-New Mexico (C)]	135 (96)	10-6 (.625)	42	4.00	526	.318/.384/.499	16	1B (98)	.988
* Perry Roberts *	DeLand [Florida State (D)]	153	15-2 (**.882**)	49	**1.94**	600	.356/.403/.502	5	1B (107)	.984
James Warren	Jesup [Georgia State (D)]	130	6-11 (.353)	77	5.26	571	.314/.368/.510	23	OF (116)	.918
* Wilbur Caldwell *	Eastman [Georgia State (D)]	125	9-7 (.563)	84	3.67	554	.300/.424/.466	13	3B (107)	**.950**
Sam Lamitina	Fulton [Kitty (D)]	125	9-6 (.600)	71	2.95	419	.284/.404/.447	7	C (56)	.981
John Bohna	Union City [Kitty (D)]	126	11-6 (.647)	88	4.06	409	.296/.423/.467	9	OF (76)	.960
Robert Signaigo	Mt. Vernon [Mississippi-Ohio Valley (D)]	107 (91)	5-7 (.417)	76	6.64	448	.293/.399/.409	4	OF (39)	.949
Robert McGimsey	Morgantown/Marion [W. Carolina (D)]	152	12-6 (.667)	82	3.73	444	.299/.394/.516	17	1B (88)	.989
Player (1953)	**Team [League (Level)]**	**IP (%)**	**W-L (ave)**	**SO**	**ERA**	**PA (%)**	**BA/OBA/SLG**	**HR**	**POS (G)**	**FA**
John Karpinski	Baton Rouge [Evangeline (C)]	180	12-10 (.545)	83	4.19	440	.249/.313/.413	16	OF (47)	.958
Roy Parker	Clovis [West Texas-New Mexico (C)]	182	12-11 (.522)	102	4.94	651	.353/.451/.690	41	OF (119)	.941
Roy Sinquefield	Andalusia [Alabama-Florida (D)]	152	14-4 (.778)	121	1.89	386	.346/.426/.512	11	OF (74)	.961
Jessie Cade	DeLand [Florida State (D)]	131 (98)	10-3 (.769)	65	2.68	604	.351/.454/.483	4	3B (105)	.912
Bama Rowell	Cocoa [Florida State (D)]	128 (93)	11-8 (.579)	52	2.95	568	.345/.426/.490	12	2B (113)	.952
Wilbur Caldwell	Eastman [Georgia State (D)]	136	13-6 (.684)	61	4.43	583	.297/.410/.432	7	3B (96)	.931
Player (1954)	**Team [League (Level)]**	**IP (%)**	**W-L (ave)**	**SO**	**ERA**	**PA (%)**	**BA/OBA/SLG**	**HR**	**POS (G)**	**FA**
Paul Pettit	Salinas [California (C)]	132 (94)	8-7 (.533)	68	3.60	488	.324/.493/.573	20	OF (65)	.952
John Karpinski	Baton Rouge [Evangeline (C)]	228	14-14 (.500)	106	5.53	581	.248/.323/.409	21	OF (105)	.964
Juan Izaguirre	Crowley [Evangeline (C)]	131 (93)	14-5 (.737)	60	3.02	616	.322/.367/.470	16	OF (119)	.980
Eddie Locke	Amarillo [West Texas-New Mexico (C)]	267	24-15 (.615)	211	4.79	399 (96)	.311/.369/.493	12	OF (71)	.940
Donald Tierney	Pampa/Plainview [W. Texas-N. Mex. (C)]	125 (93)	7-5 (.583)	108	5.40	481	.365/.428/.616	24	OF (97)	.932
* James Warren *	Statesboro [Georgia State (D)]	178	15-7 (.682)	169	3.19	400 (99)	.332/.376/**.620**	30	OF (80)	.887
Player (1955)	**Team [League (Level)]**	**IP (%)**	**W-L (ave)**	**SO**	**ERA**	**PA (%)**	**BA/OBA/SLG**	**HR**	**POS (G)**	**FA**
* Dick Hall *	Lincoln [Western (A)]	153	12-5 (.706)	137	**2.24**	393 (84)	.302/.395/.508	13	OF (73)	.992
Juan Izaguirre	Crowley [Evangeline (C)]	159	10-8 (.556)	60	3.28	591	.300/.345/.409	10	OF (70)	.991
Wilbur Caldwell	Douglas [Georgia State (D)]	102 (94)	7-4 (.636)	88	2.03	401	.251/.361/.346	4	3B (54)	.939
Ronald Foster	Fulton [Kitty (D)]	117	8-8 (.500)	80	5.54	329 (97)	.315/.405/.401	1	OF (63)	.931

Player (1956)	Team [League (Level)]	IP (%)	W-L (ave)	SO	ERA	PA (%)	BA/OBA/SLG	HR	POS (G)	FA
Harold Hacker	Tucson [Arizona-Mexico (C)]	153	8-10 (.444)	68	5.00	404	.288/.336/.457	14	3B (82)	.898
Player (1957)	**Team [League (Level)]**	**IP (%)**	**W-L (ave)**	**SO**	**ERA**	**PA (%)**	**BA/OBA/SLG**	**HR**	**POS (G)**	**FA**
Curtis Johnson	St. Petersburg [Florida State (D)]	224	16-13 (.552)	114	3.18	385 (89)	.273/.351/.315	0	CF (67)	.967
Player (1959)	**Team [League (Level)]**	**IP (%)**	**W-L (ave)**	**SO**	**ERA**	**PA (%)**	**BA/OBA/SLG**	**HR**	**POS (G)**	**FA**
Von McDaniel	Daytona Beach [Florida State (D)]	147	13-5 (.722)	84	3.49	372 (90)	.313/.361/.442	10	1B (22)	.982

NOTES

[1] When a player's name is shown in boldface and bracketed with *asterisks* it indicates that the player led his league in one or more of the statistical categories shown; the league-leading number is shown in underscored boldface.

[2] When a player's name is shown in underscored italics it indicates that the player was his team's full-season player-manager.

[3] For the IP (%) and PA (%) columns, the former gives the Innings Pitched by the player and the latter gives the number of Plate Appearances the player had. If the player had fewer innings pitched than 100% of the games played by his team(s), then that percentage is shown (in parentheses); if the player's number of innings pitched is equal to or greater than the number of games played by his team(s) (e.g., 100% or 123%), then the percentage is not shown. Likewise for the PA (%) column—if the player's number of plate appearances is less than 3.1 times the number of games played by his team(s), then the percentage of plate appearances is shown (in parentheses); if the player's number of plate appearances is equal to or greater than 3.1 times the number of games played by his team(s) (e.g., 100% or 145%), then the percentage is not shown.

[4] Plate Appearances (PA) were calculated by adding the player's number of At Bats (AB), Bases on Balls (BB), Hit by Pitched balls (HP), and Sacrifice Hits (SH) as given in the Official Baseball Guide and Record Book (published annually by *The Sporting News*).

[5] The entries in the columns W–L (pct), SO, ERA, HR, POS (G), and F% are taken directly from the *Official Baseball Guide and Record Book* (published annually by *The Sporting News*); likewise the BA entry.

[6] The entry for OBA was calculated as follows: [H + BB + HP] / [AB + BB + HP]; the values for H, BB, HP, and AB were taken directly from the *Official Baseball Guide and Record Book* (published annually by *The Sporting News*).

[7] The entry for SLG was calculated as follows: TB / AB; the values for TB and AB were taken directly from the *Official Baseball Guide and Record Book* (published annually by *The Sporting News*).

[8] The POS (G) column provides the principal fielding position, POS, of the player; the games player played at that position are given (in parentheses) and were taken directly from the *Official Baseball Guide and Record Book* (published annually by *The Sporting News*).

[9] The F% column provides the fielding percentage the player accomplished in his principal fielding position; the F% was taken directly from the *Official Baseball Guide and Record Book* (published annually by *The Sporting News*).

were top performers both on the slab and at the plate. Six topics are covered:

1. Top Pitchers
2. Top Batters
3. A Composite All-Star Lineup
4. Playing-Managers
   (i.e., Triple-Duty Diamondeers)
5. Players with Multiple Day-In/Day-Out Double-Duty seasons
6. Minor League Double-Duty Players Who Played in the Major Leagues

1. Top Pitchers Among Day-In/Day-Out Double-Duty Diamondeers

There were nine day-in/day-out double-duty diamondeers who compiled the lowest ERA in their respective leagues—Herb Moore (1946), Charles Allen (1947), Paul Bruno (1947), Myril Hoag (1947), Robert McGimsey (1948), Eddie Carnett (1950), Lee Tunnison (1951), Perry Roberts (1952), and Dick Hall (1955). All but one of the players achieved his ERA crown in a class D or C minor league. The lone exception was Dick Hall of the 1955 Lincoln Chiefs of the Class A Western League. Hall did not technically achieve full-time batter status—his PA% was "only" 84 (instead of the specified 90%; he had 393 PA of the required 468 PA). But Hall also spent time with Pittsburgh in the National League—21

games with 47 PA. Including those 47 PA affords a composite total of 440 PA, which yields a PA% of 94.

Two of the double-duty diamondeers who claimed ERA thrones also led in wins and strikeouts. Both Paul Bruno and Lee Tunnison emerged with the most wins (25 and 20, respectively) and the most strikeouts (260 and 170, respectively) in their leagues, thereby earning the pitching Triple Crown. Bruno also turned in excellent stats as a batter, with a .332/.434/.563 slash line and 18 homers. He finished fourth in batting average (.332 vs. .351), second in on base percentage (.434 vs. .459), and first in slugging average (.563); he also came in second in homers (18 vs. 22). Tunnison turned in a more-than-adequate batting record, batting .272 with eight homers while playing first base and the outfield.

2. Top Batters Among Day-In/Day-Out Double-Duty Diamondeers

There were four day-in-day-out double-duty diamondeers who compiled the highest batting average in their respective leagues. Each of the four batting champions—Myril Hoag (1947), Roy Sanner (1948), Fred Campbell (1948), and Joe Roseberry (1949)—played for a Class D minor league. Hoag's PA% (89) was just a notch below the specified 90%, but according to the unofficial rules in effect prior to 1950—i.e., appearance in at least 100 games—Hoag was the official batting champ, having played in 102 of Gainesville's 137 games.

Moreover, adding 6 imaginary hitless at bats to Hoag's actual 377 PA (thereby giving him the requisite minimum 383 PA and affording him a 90 PA%) reduced his batting average to a hypothetical .343, a value still far greater than runner-up Al Pirtle's .316 batting average.

Only two day-in/day-out double-duty diamondeers topped their circuits in home runs—Roy Sanner of the 1948 Houma Indians of the Class D Evangeline League clouted 34 round-trippers, and Lou Bevil of the 1949 Daytona Beach Islanders of the Class D Florida State League smacked 18. Three double-duty men emerged as RBI leaders in their leagues—Roy Sanner (126 in 1948), Fred Campbell (105 in 1948), and Bama Rowell (127 in 1953). Thus, in 1948 Sanner won the prestigious Triple Crown in batting. While Sanner's record as a batsman was outstanding, his pitching was superb, leading the league in winning average (.913) thanks to a 21–2 record, and only one win behind the league leader's 22. Similarly, his 2.58 ERA was runner-up to the league leader's 2.37, and his 251 strikeouts were the second-most to 259. Thus, Sanner finished a close second in all three pitching Triple Crown categories.[4]

Only two day-in/day-out double-duty diamondeers emerged as the stolen base leader in their circuits— Wilbur Caldwell (58 in the Georgia State League) and John Bohna (44 in the Kitty League), each in 1952.

3. A Composite All-Star Lineup of Day-In/Day-Out Double-Duty Diamondeers

Taking into consideration the single-season performances of all 59 players who were Day-In/Day-Out Double-Duty Diamondeers during the 1946–60 period, Table 3A presents a composite All-Star lineup (irrespective of year or league). Table 3B (see p 92) provides the batting and pitching statistics for each of the All-Stars.

Six of the Table 3A All-Stars were selected for their league's All-Star team, as given in *The Encyclopedia of Minor League Baseball* (Second Edition, 1997)—Paul Bruno (first base), Bama Rowell (second base), Jesse Cade (third base), Myril Hoag (outfield), James Warren (outfield), and Lee Tunnison (pitcher). With regard to the other Table 3A players, some pertinent information follows on page 96.

Table 3A. Composite All–Star Lineup of Day–In/Day–Out Double–Duty Diamondeers (1946–60)

Player	Year	Team	League (Level)	IP%/PA%	P (G) [F% (rank)]
▲ Paul Bruno	1947	Hammond	Evangeline (D)	100/100	1B (89) [.987 (2)]
▲ Bama Rowell	1953	Cocoa	Florida State (D)	93/100	2B (113) [.952 (2)]
▲ Jesse Cade	1953	DeLand	Florida State (D)	100/100	3B (105) [.912 (3)]
• Fred Campbell	1948	Griffin	Georgia–Alabama (D)	97/100	SS (96) [.905 (7)]
▲ Myril Hoag	1947	Gainesville	Florida State (D)	100/89	OF (64) [.947 (17)]
Lou Bevil	1949	Daytona Beach	Florida State (D)	100/100	OF (95) [.964 (5)]
▲ James Warren	1954	Statesboro	Georgia State (D)	100/99	OF (80) [.887 (13)]
▲ Hack Miller	1947	Tyler	Lone Star (C)	100/100	C (110) [.990 (1)]
▲ Lee Tunnison	1951	Centralia	Mississippi–Ohio Valley (D)	100/100	RHP (33) [.968 (9)]
• Roy Sanner	1948	Houma	Evangeline (D)	100/100	LHP (23) [.983 (5)]

NOTES: 1) Players who were chosen for his league's All-Star team are indicated by ▲ (as given in reference 3)
2) Players whose league apparently did not name an All-Star team are indicated by •

Table 3B. Batting and Pitching Statistics for the Players on the Composite All–Star Lineup

Player	AB	R	H	RBI	HR	BA	OBA	SLG	IP	W–L (Avg)	SO	BB	ERA
P. Bruno	389	86	129	91	18	.332	.434	*.563*	253	*25*–5 (.833)	*260*	45	*1.96*
B. Rowell	498	104	172	*127*	12	.345	.426	.490	128	11–8 (.579)	52	45	2.95
J. Cade	501	118	176	82	4	.351	.454	.483	131	10–3 (.769)	65	45	2.68
F. Campbell	471	98	168	*105*	3	*.357*	.435	.473	122	8–5 (.615)	99	70	3.69
M. Hoag	323	72	113	75	4	*.350*	.437	.474	173	17–3 (*.850*)	115	51	*1.82*
L. Bevil	430	93	125	86	*18*	.291	.423	.493	251	19–11 (633)	180	84	2.39
J. Warren	371	70	123	99	30	.332	.376	*.620*	178	15–7 (.682)	169	66	3.19
H. Miller	455	88	129	87	6	.284	.384	.411	145	10–4 (.714)	48	33	3.79
L. Tunnison	357	59	97	60	8	.272	.318	.429	205	*20*–8 (.714)	*170*	121	*3.12*
R. Sanner	492	99	190	*126*	34	*.386*	.454	*.669*	199	21–2 (.913)	251	96	2.58

NOTE: Players with league-leading stats are shown in boldface and their league-leading stats are shown in boldface italics.

- **Roy Sanner** – The Evangeline League apparently did not name an All-Star team for the 1948 season. However, it seems reasonable to speculate that, if there had been a 1948 Evangeline League All-Star team, Roy Sanner would have been included, at least as an outfielder, and perhaps also as a pitcher.

- **Fred Campbell** – The Georgia-Alabama League did not name an All-Star team for the 1948 season, but Fred Campbell could have been chosen as the loop's All-Star shortstop. For comparison, Appendix Two provides the relevant statistics for the principal shortstops of the 1948 Georgia-Alabama League. The Tobacco State League did choose an All-Star team in 1948, naming double-duty diamondeer Robert Keane, but my preference for inclusion in Table 3A is Fred Campbell.

- **Lou Bevil** – Appendix Two presents the batting statistics for each of the three players selected as outfielders for the 1949 Florida State League All-Star team—Herb McLeod, Manuel Rivera, and Al Pirtle. However, since none of them pitched in any games, none of them were eligible for the composite All-Star lineup. While Roy Sinquefield (Andalusia—Alabama-Florida League, 1953) was deservedly chosen as an All-Star for his league, Lou Bevil is my preference for the Table 3A composite All-Star lineup.

- **Hack Miller** – The 1947 Lone Star League's All-Star catcher was Joe Kracher of the Kilgore Drillers;

his batting slash line (.333/.424/.505) was quite a bit better than Miller's .284/.384/.411. However, since Kracher did not pitch in any games, he was not eligible for the composite day-in/day-out double-duty diamondeer All-Star lineup. Miller's batting and pitching records were superior to those achieved by John Farkas (1948) and Sam Lamitina (1952), the only other day-in/day-out double-duty diamondeers whose principal non-pitching position was catcher.

As can be seen (in Table 3B?), nine of the ten players comprising the composite All-Star lineup were league leaders in various batting and pitching categories—RBIs (3), home runs (2), batting average (3), slugging average (3), wins (2), winning average (2), strikeouts (2), and earned run average (3). Finally, note that Bama Rowell was also chosen as his league's All-Star manager.

4. Player-Managers—Triple-Duty Diamondeers

Table 4 presents a list of day-in/day-out double-duty diamondeers who were also full-time player-managers. Each of them can be justifiably regarded as a Triple-Duty Diamondeer! Two of them guided their teams to their league's pennant—George Washburn (1949 Evangeline League) and Sam Lamitina (1952 Kitty League). Two of the Triple-Duty Diamondeers piloted their clubs to their league championship in the end-of-the-season playoffs—Paul Bruno (1947 Evangeline League) and Myril Hoag (1947 Florida State League). Bruno was not meant to be Hammond's manager for

Table 4. Player–Managers—Triple–Duty Diamondeers (1946–60)

Player Manager	Year	Team	League (Level) [Clubs]	IP%/PA%	W–L (Avg) Place
Herb Moore	1946	Albany	Georgia–Florida (D) [8]	100/100	54–71 (.432) 6
Paul Bruno	1947	Hammond	Evangeline (D) [8]	100/100	*73–60 (.549) 4*
	1948			100/94	79–58 (.577) 2
Woody Wheaton	1947	Moline	Central Assn. (C) [6]	100/92	27–35 (.435) 5
		Martinsville	Carolina (C) [8]		22–37 (.373) 8
	1948	Welch	Appalachian (D) [8]	100/100	70–53 (.569) 2
Al Barillari	1947	Port Chester	Colonial (B) [6]	98/91	51–71 (.418) 5
Hack Miller	1947	Tyler	Lone Star (C) [8]	100/100	76–64 (.543) 4
Bob Benish	1947	Troy	Alabama State (D) [8]	100/100	58–80 (.420) 7
Myril Hoag	1947	Gainesville	Florida State (D) [8]	100/89	*80–57 (.584) 2*
George Washburn	1947	Houma	Evangeline (D) [8]	100/90	57–62 (.479) 5
	1949		Evangeline (C) [8]	98/100	81–58 (.586) 1
Al Gardella	1949	Peekskill	North Atlantic (D) [8]	97/100	64–75 (.460) 4
Sam Lamitina	1952	Fulton	Kitty (D) [8]	100/100	82–37 (.689) 1
Bama Rowell	1953	Cocoa	Florida State (D) [8]	93/100	78–59 (.569) 3

NOTES: (1) In the "League (Level) [Clubs]" column, the entry in brackets gives the number of clubs in the league. (2) In the "W–L (Pct.) Place" column, an entry bracketed with * asterisks * indicates that the team won the end–of–the–season Playoff Championship. (3) See text for detailed explanations of the unusual managerial records achieved by Wheaton and Washburn for the 1947 season.

1947; Babe Benning was. As it turned out, however, Benning "resigned from the pilot's job at Hammond just before the season opened."[5] Bruno entered the picture at this point and became Hammond's manager for all of 1947.

Only three of the Table 4 player-managers were repeat day-in/day-out triple-duty diamondeers—Paul Bruno and Woody Wheaton in 1947 and 1948, George Washburn in 1947 and 1949.

Wheaton and Washburn each had unusual triple-duty seasons in 1947:

- Wheaton began the 1947 season with the Moline Athletics (Philadelphia's farm club in the Class C Central Association). With him as manager, the team compiled a 27–35 W-L record, good for fifth in the standings. On July 11, he joined the Martinsville Athletics (Philadelphia's farm club in the Class C Carolina League) when Martinsville's W-L record was 31–51 and they were in eighth (last) place. For the remainder of the season, Wheaton piloted them with a 22–37 W-L record; overall, Martinsville finished with a 53–88 W-L record.

- Washburn began the 1947 season with New Orleans (AA Southern Association), where Fred Walters was the manager. Two weeks after playing in his one-and-only game for the Pelicans (a complete-game 8–5 triumph over Memphis on April 21), his contract was purchased by Houma to replace player-manager Copeland Goss, who departed with a 6–14 W-L record. Washburn made his Houma debut as player-manager on May 8. Under his guidance, the Berries went 57–62, thereby giving Houma a final W-L record of 63–76, which placed them fifth in the standings.

5. Players with Multiple Day-In/Day-Out Double-Duty Seasons

Close inspection of Table 2 reveals that twelve players were day-in/day-out double-duty diamondeers for more than one season. Eight players met our criteria for two seasons:

- Paul Bruno (1947, 1948)
- Woody Wheaton (1947, 1948)
- George Washburn (1947, 1949)
- Edward Bowles (1948, 1949)
- Eddie Carnett (1950, 1952)
- Perry Roberts (1950, 1952)
- James Warren (1952, 1954)
- Juan Izaguirre (1954,1955))

Four players were three-time day-in/day-out double-duty diamondeers:

- Robert McGimsey (1949, 1950, 1952)
- Roy Parker (1949, 1951, 1953)
- Wilbur Caldwell (1952, 1953, 1955)
- John Karpinski (1952, 1953, 1954)

There were no players with four or more day-in/day-out double-duty seasons during the 1946–60 period. An interesting item which may be gleaned from Table 2 is that five of these dozen players played in the Evangeline League—Bruno, Washburn, Bowles, Karpinski, and Izaguirre.

6. Minor League Day-In/Day-Out Double-Duty Diamondeers Who Played in the Major Leagues

As previously noted, no day-in/day-out double-duty diamondeers have played in the major leagues since 1919. But since we have identified 59 in the minor leagues, it follows that we consider two questions: (1) "Which, if any, of the 59 minor league day-in/day-out double-duty diamondeers progressed to the major leagues as pitcher or as a field-position player?" (2) "How did they perform when they got there?" As it turns out, 16 of the minor league double-duty diamondeers from the 1946–60 period did make the Show. However, there are two distinct groups of players within the 16, those who made their major league debut *before* 1946, and those *after* 1946. Tables 6A and 6B (next page) provide pertinent information for these two groups.

Table 5A (page 98) reveals that most of these players had their big-league careers during World War II. None of the six players who toed the rubber accumulated a career total of even 77 innings pitched (the equivalent of a half-season for a pitcher). Only two of the ten players accumulated more than 1000 big-league plate appearances—Myril Hoag and Bama Rowell.

Hoag (.271/.328/.364) was in the bigs 13 of the 15 seasons from 1931 through 1945 (except 1933 and 1943), and after that he continued his professional baseball career in the minors. Interestingly, he was a teammate of Babe Ruth (1931, 1932, and 1934) and was on the New York Yankees World Series championship teams of 1932, 1936, 1937, and 1938. Rowell (.275/.316/.382) played six major-league seasons (1939–41 and 1946–48).

A Table 6A player with an exceptional (but brief) big league career (seven games) was Hack Miller. Beginning in perhaps the best way possible, Miller hit a home run in his first at bat—on April 23, 1944 (second game) off Cleveland's Al Smith. He concluded his time in the bigs with the 1945 World Champion Detroit Tigers as a backup catcher (although he did not appear in any of the Fall Classic games).

The Table 6A player who came the closest to being a double-duty diamondeer in the majors was Woody Wheaton, who played two seasons (1943, 1944) for the Philadelphia Athletics. He appeared in 11 games on the mound (all in 1944) and came away with an 0–1 W–L record with an earned run average of 3.55. He was utilized as a relief pitcher except once, when he hurled a complete game against the St. Louis Browns on July 6, 1944, losing 5–0. Wheaton also played center field in 15 games—seven in 1943 and eight in 1944— and was also employed as a pinch hitter in twelve games. For his entire major-league career he turned in a .191 batting average (17 hits in 89 at bats).

Tommy Warren, playing for the Brooklyn Dodgers for one season (1944), was the Table 6A player who appeared in the most games as a pitcher—22. He compiled a W–L record of 1–4 with an ERA of 4.98. Warren's only other major-league action was as a pinch hitter or pinch runner (21 games).

Turning now to Table 5B and the double-duty diamondeers with post-1946 major-league debuts, only one player accumulated more than 1000 plate appearances—Bob Borkowski. Borkowski had a single season as a minor league double-duty diamondeer, 1946, and zero mound appearances in the majors. Primarily an outfielder during his six seasons with the Cubs, Red Legs, and Dodgers, Borkowski put together a career slash line of .252/.298/.346 with 16 home runs.

Among the Table 5B players, Dick Hall—who won the ERA crown as a double-duty diamondeer in the Western League in 1955—carved out the most impressive record in the majors. While he debuted with the Pittsburgh Pirates as an outfielder (14 games in 1952, 102 in 1954), Hall switched his emphasis to the mound in 1955 and by 1957 had become exclusively a pitcher. After limited mound time with Pittsburgh (44 games with 23 starting assignments, 1955–59), Hall's mound work accelerated with the Kansas City Athletics (29 games with 28 starts in 1960) and he flourished as a fireman with the Baltimore Orioles (1961–66, 1969–71) and Philadelphia Phillies (1967–68)—79–49 W–L (.617) with an ERA of 2.92 and 69 saves. Hall was on the O's World Series Championship teams of 1966 and 1970. With regard to Hall's performance with the bat as a big leaguer, he manufactured a slash line of .210/.271/.259 with 4 homers.

The other four Table 5B players—Paul Pettit, Bob Trice, Red Murff, and Von McDaniel—had rather brief careers in the majors. The latter three at least gained the honor of appearing on a Topps baseball card.

Paul Pettit is perhaps most-remembered as the first recipient of a six-figure signing bonus in major-league history—$100,000 from the Pittsburgh Pirates on January 30, 1950. Unfortunately, Pettit encountered arm problems and lost the zip on his fastball. His career

Table 5A. Minor League Double–Duty Players (1946–60) Who Made the Majors _Before_ 1946

Player	ML Years	GP (IP)	TG (PA)	Other Field Positions (G)
Myril Hoag	1931–45	3 (4.0)	1020 (3462)	OF (877); IF (3); PH/PR (179)
Bama Rowell	1939–48	–	574 (2042)	2B (246); OF (238); 3B (24); PH/PR (91)
Eddie Carnett	1941–45	6 (5.1)	158 (568)	OF (104); 1B (25); PH (25)
George Washburn	1941	1 (2.0)	1 (1)	–
Stan Goletz	1941	–	5 (5)	PH (5)
Lou Bevil	1942	4 (9.2)	4 (3)	–
Woody Wheaton	1943–44	11 (38.0)	37 (99)	OF (15); PH (12)
Tommy Warren	1944	22 (68.2)	41 (45)	PH/PR (21)
Hack Miller	1944–45	–	7 (11)	C (7); PH (1)
Al Gardella	1945	–	16 (33)	1B (8); OF (1); PH/PR (9)

Table 5B. Minor League Double–Duty Players (1946–60) Who Made the Majors _After_ 1946

Player	ML Years	GP (IP)	TG (PA)	Other Field Positions (G)
Bob Borkowski	1950–55	–	470 (1262)	OF (316); 1B (12); PH/PR (163)
Paul Pettit	1951–53	12 (30.2)	13 (12)	PH (1)
Dick Hall	1952–71	495 (1259.2)	669 (821)	OF (119); IF (13); PH/PR (55)
Bob Trice	1953–55	26 (152.0)	27 (59)	PR (1)
Red Murff	1956–57	26 (50.1)	26 (12)	–
Von McDaniel	1957–58	19 (88.2)	19 (28)	–

W–L record was 1–2 with a 7.34 ERA. Nonetheless, Pettit continued to try to make it in the minors for a few years (1953–56) and in 1954, with the Salinas Packers of the Class C California League, accomplished a day-in/day-out double-duty season with the following stats: batting .324/.488/.573 with 20 homers in 361 at bats (488 plate appearances); pitching numbers— 8–7 W–L (.533), 68 SO, 51 BB, 3.61 ERA in 132 innings pitched. Pettit's .488 on base average and .573 slugging average each ranked second in the loop.

Bob Trice is remembered as being the first African American to play for the Philadelphia Athletics. He debuted on September 13, 1953, following a late-season call-up from Ottawa, the A's Triple-A farm club in the International League. At Ottawa, Trice had netted the IL "Pitcher of the Year" with a sterling slab record— 21–10 W–L (.677) with a 3.10 ERA. The previous season, with St. Hyacinthe (the A's farm club in the Class C Provincial League), Trice had put together his only double-duty campaign—16–3 W–L (.842) with a 3.49 ERA in 152 innings from the pitcher's box and a .297/.399/.383 slash line with 1 home run in 300 at bats (351 plate appearances) from the batter's box. He led the league in wins (16) and winning average (.842). In his only full major-league season (1954) Trice turned in a 7–8 W–L (.467) with a 5.60 ERA in 119 innings pitched. But among all full-time pitchers in the AL, Trice compiled the highest batting average (.286), on base average (.348), slugging average (.429), and OPS (.776). For his career, Trice compiled a 9–9 record with a 5.80 ERA in 152 innings pitched. Trice appeared in one game as a pinch runner and produced a very solid .288/.351/.423 slash line with one homer in 52 at bats (59 plate appearances).

Red Murff was *The Sporting News* Minor League Player of the Year in 1955, having turned in a superb 27–11 W–L ledger (.711) with a 1.99 ERA in 303 innings pitched for the Dallas Eagles, the New York Giants' farm team in the AA Texas League; he was exclusively a pitcher. His only season as a day-in/day-out double-duty player was in 1950 with the Baton Rouge Red Sticks (Class C Evangeline League) He compiled .332/.371/.423 with 3 homers in 404 at bats (429 PA) as a bat swinger and 17–4 W–L (.810) with a 2.97 ERA as a ball slinger. As a major leaguer (exclusively as a pitcher) Murff ended up with a 2–2 W–L (.500) with a 4.65 ERA in 50.1 innings pitched for the Milwaukee Braves (1956 and 1957).

Von McDaniel began his major-league career with the St. Louis Cardinals right after graduating from high school. In his Cardinals debut (June 13, 1957) he relieved Herm Wehmeier and tossed four shutout innings

of one-hit ball against the Phillies. In his next outing, against the Dodgers at Ebbets Field, he again tossed four scoreless relief innings of one-hit ball, picking up his first big-league victory in the process. His next mound task was a starting assignment against the Dodgers at Busch Stadium in St. Louis; he finished with a two-hit, complete-game whitewash. McDaniels's next game was another home-start, this time against Philadelphia. He extended his string of career-beginning scoreless innings to 19 when he kept the Phillies from crossing the plate in the first two frames.[6] McDaniel was relieved after 7.1 innings, but was credited with the win. A little later in the season he tossed a one-hit masterpiece against the Pirates, facing just 28 batters. For the season he ended up with a 7–5 W–L ledger (.583) and a 3.22 ERA. However, he was winless in his last three starts and pounded harshly in his last 3.1 innings—24 batters, 6 walks, 8 hits (including 2 homers), 7 runs (all earned). That disastrous performance was a harbinger of the difficulty he would encounter in his next season. McDaniel's 1958 season was bleak and short: after just two appearances—2.0 innings, 16 batters, 5 walks, 5 hits, 3 runs (all earned)— he was sent down to the minors, thereby finishing his major league career less than a year after his debut. He kept at it in the minors and in 1959 produced his only day-in/day-out double-duty season. With the Daytona Beach Islanders (the Los Angeles Dodgers farm club in the Class D Florida State League) he produced a .313/.361/.442 slash line with 10 homers in 342 at bats (375 plate appearances) and a 13–5 W–L (.722) with a 3.49 ERA in 147 innings pitched. Significantly, he was selected for the Florida State League's All-Star team as a utility player, having played first base (22 games), shortstop (19 games), and the outfield (16 games) in addition to pitching (20 games).

DISCUSSION

In transitioning from being an elite full-time pitcher (1915–17) to an elite full-time batsman (1920–35), Babe Ruth established an exemplary standard of performance for a day-in/day-out double-duty diamondeer during the 1918 and 1919 seasons, particularly from the batter's box, as indicated by his league-leading stats, shown in bold in Table 6 (page 100).

In the AL in 1918, Ruth's W-L percentage and ERA ranked second and ninth, respectively; his corresponding rankings in 1919 were 10th and 22nd. (Note: The qualifier that I used is having an IP% ≥ 90 and a PA% ≥ 90, since in those times, there were no official rules about qualifying for the ERA or win percentage crowns. The unofficial rule was, as I understand it from Pete Palmer, 10 complete games.) Swinging the bat, the emerging Bambino topped the AL in slugging percentage both years and in on base average in 1919. He was also the home run champion in each campaign and led in runs scored and runs batted in for the 1919 season. With that background, the following question can be asked: "Which of the 59 day-in/day-out double-duty diamondeers from the 1946–60 period can be mentioned in the same breath with Ruth?"

Among the 59 day-in/day-out double-duty diamondeers from the 1946–60 period, only two emerge with at least one blue ribbon in each of two different seasons. The first one was Paul Bruno of the 1947–48 Hammond Berries of the Class D Evangeline League. As shown in Table 7, in the 1947 campaign he won the pitching Triple Crown and also captured the slugging average crown as a hitter. Then, in 1948 he again claimed the leadership position in pitching victories.

The only other day-in/day-out double-duty diamondeer with a pair of trophy-winning campaigns was Roy Parker. Playing with the Pampa Oilers in the West Texas-New Mexico League (Class C), he topped the loop in wins and strikeouts in 1949. Then while playing for the Clovis Pioneers in 1953, he led the circuit in runs scored. Table 8 provides the relevant details for Parker's pitching and batting accomplishments. Also included is Parker's performance line for 1951, during which he played for the Sherman-Denison Twins in the Class B Big State League.

Focusing on just one season of outstanding day-in/day-out double-duty performance, the player with the best pitching and batting record was Roy Sanner.

As mentioned previously, in 1948 with Houma of the Class D Evangeline League, Sanner won the batting Triple Crown and finished a close second in each of the pitching Triple Crown departments.

While Bruno, Parker, and Sanner did have superb day-in/day-out double-duty seasons, there is a major caveat—each of their glowing double-duty campaigns was accomplished in the low minors (Class D or Class C). None of them was able to transfer those pitching and/or batting performances to the upper minors and none of them ever made it to the Big Show.

CONCLUDING REMARKS

The primary objective of this research project was to ascertain which players (if any) were day-in/day-out double-duty diamondeers in the minor leagues during the fifteen seasons between 1946 and 1960. As presented in the Results and Discussion sections, the principal research objective was achieved. As shown in Table 2, 59 players achieved a total of 75 day-in/day-out double-duty seasons. Moreover, consideration of all the information gathered in this research effort reveals four additional items that merit comment.

1. The number of day-in/day-out double-duty diamondeers pretty-much paralleled the decline in the number of minor leagues from 1952 through 1960, as summarized in Figure 1.

2. Of the 75 day-in/day-out double-duty seasons produced in the 1946–60 period, 45 were accomplished in Class D, 26 in Class C, 3 in Class B, and just 1 in Class A.

Table 6. Babe Ruth's Pitching and Batting Record for 1918 and 1919

Year	IP	W–L (%)	SO	BB	ERA	PA	BA/OBA/SLG	R	HR	RBI
1918	166.1	13–7 (.650)	40	49	2.22	382	.300/.411/**.555**	50	11	61
1919	133.1	9–5 (.643)	30	58	2.97	543	.322/**.456/.657**	**103**	**29**	113

Table 7. Paul Bruno's Pitching and Batting Record for 1947 and 1948 with the Hammond Berries

Year	IP	W–L (%)	SO	BB	ERA	PA	BA/OBA/SLG	R	HR	RBI
1947	253	**25**–5 (.833)	**260**	45	**1.96**	459	.332/.434/**.563**	86	18	91
1948	248	**22**–5 (.815)	228	55	2.87	404	.337/.479/.546	67	16	77

Table 8. Roy Parker's Pitching and Batting Record for 1949, 1951, and 1953

Year	IP	W–L (%)	SO	BB	ERA	PA	BA/OBA/SLG	R	HR	RBI
1949	263	**23**–10 (.697)	**235**	117	4.86	453	.296/.396/.582	96	24	91
1951	156	11–10 (.524)	110	125	4.55	532	.345/.408/.559	100	18	92
1953	182	12–11 (.522)	102	112	4.94	651	.353/.451/.690	**177**	41	160

Figure 1. Year-By-Year Number of Minor Leagues (All Classes) and Day-In/Day-Out Double-Duty Seasons

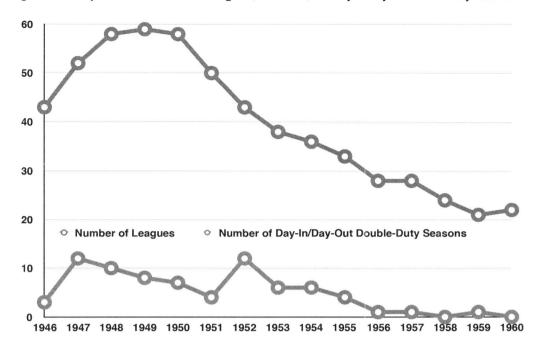

3. The league that produced the most day-in/day-out double-duty seasons was the Evangeline League, with a total of 13—5 when it was a Class D league (1946–48) and 8 when it was a Class C league (1949–57). The runners-up were the Class D Florida State League (10), the Class C West Texas-New Mexico League (7) and the Class D Georgia State League (7)

4. The distribution of principal fielding positions is Outfield (45), First Base (16), Second Base (1), Third Base (7), Shortstop (3), and Catcher (3).

Based on the dearth of day-in/day-out double-duty diamondeers during the 1956–60 period, it would not be surprising if during the ensuing six decades (through the 2019 season) there were very few. However, that situation may be about to change. The encouraging double-duty performance achieved by Shohei Ohtani in 2018 (although an injury to his pitching arm limited him to just ten games and 52 innings on the slab) and his continued success from the batter's box as a DH in 2019 could provide inspiration and motivation for others to pursue double-duty activity. ■

ACKNOWLEDGMENTS

Many thanks to Baseball-Reference for its comprehensive presentation of performance statistics—both minor league and major league—for all of the several hundred players I researched in detail for this project. While all of the minor league statistical information presented in this article was obtained from the relevant editions of the *Official Baseball Guide and Record Book* (published by *The Sporting News*), the Baseball-Reference website was particularly helpful for additional information and perspective for the players. Finally, I appreciatively thank my good friend Gary Stone for his superb reviewing of the first and last drafts of this manuscript.

DEDICATION

With enormous gratitude I dedicate this article to all of the Retrosheet volunteers whose outstanding contributions over more than 30 years have resulted in the invaluable Retrosheet website—each of them is truly a baseball research enabler! I especially wish to dedicate this article to four Retrosheeters who have been particularly helpful to me many, many times over the years—respectfully, to the memories of the late Clem Comly and the late David Vincent, and to Dave Smith and Tom Ruane.

NOTES

1. Jay Jaffe, "Shohei Ohtani and Beyond: A History of Double-Duty Players," *FanGraphs*, April 6, 2018.
2. The "Official Baseball Rules, 2019 Edition" as provided on MLB.com (the official website of Major League Baseball) have the following rule: 9.22 Minimum Standards for Individual Championships ... "To assure uniformity in establishing the batting, pitching and fielding championships of professional leagues, such champions shall meet the following minimum performance standards: (a) The individual batting, slugging or on-base percentage champion shall be the player with the highest batting average, slugging percentage or on-base percentage, as the case may be, provided the player is credited with as many or more total appearances at the plate in league championship games as the number of games scheduled for each Club in his Club's league that season, multiplied by 3.1 in the case of a Major League player and by 2.7 in the

case of a National Association player. Total appearances at the plate shall include official times at bat, plus bases on balls, times hit by pitcher, sacrifice hits, sacrifice flies and times awarded first base because of interference or obstruction. Notwithstanding the foregoing requirement of minimum appearances at the plate, any player with fewer than the required number of plate appearances whose average would be the highest, if he were charged with the required number of plate appearances shall be awarded the batting, slugging or on-base percentage championship, as the case may be. (b) The individual pitching champion in a Major League shall be the pitcher with the lowest earned-run average, provided that the pitcher has pitched at least as many innings in league championship games as the number of games scheduled for each Club in his Club's league that season. The individual pitching champion in a National Association league shall be the pitcher with the lowest earned-run average provided that the pitcher has pitched at least as many innings in league championship season games as 80% of the number of games scheduled for each Club in the pitcher's league."

3. Lloyd Johnson and Miles Wolff, Editors, *The Encyclopedia of Minor League Baseball*, 2nd Edition , (Durham, NC: Baseball America, Inc., 1977). See also Neil J. Sullivan, *The Minors*, (New York: St. Martins Press, 1990), Part Two.

4. Shortly after hurling a two-hitter in Houma's 4–0 triumph over Abbeville on August 29, Sanner bolted from the Houma Indians because of a financial disagreement, thereby freezing his Evangeline League statistics. One can only speculate what Sanner might have accomplished in Houma's remaining eleven games—he might have even emerged with the pitching Triple Crown! On August 10, Houma had sold his contract to the Dallas Rebels of the Class AA Texas League for the 1949 season. An agreement was subsequently worked out and Sanner ultimately ended up finishing the 1948 campaign with Dallas, playing in seven games, producing a .364 batting average (8 hits in 22 at bats) and a 1–1 W–L record with a 4.76 ERA.

5. Ray Lee, "Once Over Lightly," *The Town Talk* (Alexandria, Louisiana), May 10, 1947, 10.

6. McDaniel's career-starting 19 scoreless innings streak was the longest consecutive innings scoreless streak by a pitcher from the start of his career since Al Worthington had hurled a string of (also) 19 in 1953 with the New York Giants. Von's career-starting 19 shutout innings streak was six innings short of the then major-league record of 25 innings accomplished by George McQuillan in 1907 with the Philadelphia Phillies. The current record is 39 consecutive scoreless innings by Brad Ziegler of the 2008 Oakland Athletics; McQuillan's 25 consecutive scoreless innings streak is still the National League record.

7. Some of the results described in this article were presented at the virtual SABR-50 meeting—Herm Krabbenhoft, "Day-In/Day-Out Double-Duty Diamondeers, Full-Time Two-Way Players (1946–60)," SABR Virtual: Day 4 (July 12, 2020)—YouTube [1:29:23].

APPENDIX ONE – Chronological Summary of Official Rules for Batting Average and Earned Run Average Titles (1946–60)

BATTING AVERAGE

- **For the seasons prior to 1950**, there were no official rules defining the minimum requirements for determining the batting champion. The customary practice was to award the championship to the player with the highest batting average provided he played in at least 100 games.

- **For the 1950 and 1951 seasons**, the official rules stated the following: "Batting championships, how determined, 10.18"

"**BATTING CHAMPIONSHIPS 10.18** To be eligible for the individual batting championship of any minor league, a player must have appeared in at least two-thirds of the games played by his team. Thus, if a team plays 154 games, a player must appear in 102 games. If his team plays 150 games, he must appear in 100. If his team plays 140 games, he must appear in 93, etc.

(a) To be eligible for the individual batting championship of a major league a player must be credited with at least 400 official 'times at bat.'"

- **For the 1952–56 seasons**, the official rules stated the following: "Batting championships, how determined, 10.18 (a)"

"**CHAMPIONSHIPS 10.18** (a) The individual batting championship of any league shall be the player with the highest batting average, if—he is credited with as many or more times at bat as the number of games scheduled for one club in his league during the season, multiplied by 2.6. However, if there is any player in the league with fewer than the required number of times at bat whose average would be the highest if he were charged with this at-bat total, then that player shall be awarded the batting championship. **Example**: The major leagues and many others schedule 154 games. 154 times 2.6 equals 400. If a player shall have, say, 390 times at bat and, by adding 10 imaginary hitless times at bat to his total, he would still have the highest batting average in his league, he shall be the champion batter."

- **For the 1957–60 seasons**, the official rules stated the following: "Championships, how determined, 10.22"

"**10.22** To assure uniformity in establishing the batting, pitching, and fielding championship of professional leagues, such champions shall meet the following minimum performance standards:

(a) The individual batting champion shall be the player with the highest batting average, provided he is credited with as many or more total appearances at the plate in league championship games scheduled for each club in his league that season, multiplied by 3.1. **Example**: The major leagues schedule 154 games for each club. 154 times 3.1 equals 477. Some minor leagues schedule 140 games. 140 times 3.1 equals 434.

Total appearances at the plate shall include official times at bat, plus bases on balls, times hit by pitcher, sacrifice hits, sacrifice flies, and times awarded first base because of interference or obstruction."

EARNED RUN AVERAGE

- **For the seasons prior to 1951**, there were no official rules defining the minimum requirements for determining the ERA champion. The customary practice was to award the championship to the pitcher with the lowest ERA provided he pitched at least 10 complete games.

- **For the 1951–53 seasons**, the official rules stated the following:

"**CHAMPIONSHIPS 10.18** (b) To be designated as the leader in his league's pitchers in the minimum averaged number of earned runs allowed a pitcher is required to pitch at least as many innings as the number of games scheduled for each team in his league. (This would be 154 innings in a major league.)"

- **For the 1954 season**, the official rules were exactly the same as for the 1951–53 seasons except that the rule number was "**10.17** (b)"

- **For the 1955–56** seasons, the official rules were exactly the same as for the 1951–53 seasons except that the rule number was "**10.19** (b)"

- **For the 1957–60 seasons**, the official rules were exactly the same as for the 1951–53 seasons except that the rule number was "**10.22** (b)"

APPENDIX TWO – Comparative Statistics for Selected Day-In/Day-Out Double-Duty Diamondeers

The following chart provides the pertinent statistics for Campbell, Keane, and the principal shortstops for the teams in the Georgia-Alabama League (1948).

Player	Team League (Level)	IP (%)	W–L (AVE)	SO	ERA	PA (%)	BA/OBA/SLG	HR	POS (G)	F AVE
*Fred Campbell	Griffin Georgia-Alabama (D)	122 (97)	8–5 (.615)	99	3.69	540	**.357**/.435/.473	3	SS (96)	.905
Robert Keane	Sanford Tobacco State (D)	128 (94)	7–8 (.467)	78	4.99	571	.303/.385/.364	1	SS (99)	.914
John Millard	Newnan Georgia-Alabama (D)	–	–	–	–	535	.263/.364/.401	4	SS (126)	.934
Ray Clark	Valley Georgia-Alabama (D)	–	–	–	–	453	.235/.305/.286	0	SS (112)	.913
Eugene Monarchi	Carrollton Georgia-Alabama (D)	–	–	–	–	420	.236/.406/.264	0	SS (110)	.905
Luther Gunnells	Opelika/Alexander City Georgia-Alabama (D)	–	–	–	–	461	.323/.453/.493	13	SS (106)	.911
Frank Monaco	Tallassee Georgia-Alabama (D)	–	–	–	–	422	.223/.369/.276	2	SS (92)	.900
Bobby Adams	LaGrange Georgia-Alabama (D)	–	–	–	–	545	.231/.382/.307	2	SS (88)	.931
Benjamin Catchings	Alexander City Georgia-Alabama (D)	–	–	–	–	391	.208/.375/.254	0	SS (73)	.915

The following chart provides the pertinent information for Bevil (1949), Sinquefield (1953), McLeod (1949), Rivera (1949), and Pirtle (1949).

Player	Team League (Level)	IP (%)	W–L (AVE)	SO	ERA	PA (%)	BA/OBA/SLG	HR	POS (G)	F AVE
*Louis Bevil	Daytona Beach Florida State (D)	251	19–11 (.633)	180	2.39	529	.291/.423/.493	**18**	LF (95)	.964
Roy Sinquefield	Andalusia Alabama-Florida (D)	152	14–4 (.778)	121	1.89	386	.346/.426/.512	11	OF (74)	.961
Herb McLeod	Palatka Florida State (D)		–	–	–	582	.349/.408/.471	3	OF (128)	.958
Manuel Rivera	Gainesville Florida State (D)	–	–	–	–	594	.335/.405/.537	13	CF (137)	**.983**
Al Pirtle	Gainesville Florida State (D)	–	–	–	–	571	**.383**/.471/.543	9	RF (132)	.966

Miami Hustlers

Magic City's First Officially Sanctioned Minor League Team

Sam Zygner

Major league baseball arrived in South Florida on April 5, 1993, when the Florida Marlins took to the field against the Los Angeles Dodgers at Joe Robbie Stadium. Prior to this momentous day, there existed a long and largely forgotten history of minor league baseball in Miami.

On April 6, 1927, Florida State League president J.B. Asher extended an invitation to a group of community leaders headed by Louis K. MacReynolds to join the Class D league. Asher's goal was to expand his league to the south and replace failed teams in Bradenton, Fort Myers, and Lakeland, Florida. Asher took advantage of the city's rapidly growing population in order to increase attendance in his financially strapped league.[1]

MacReynolds, and other representatives from Miami, were quick to accept the offer to join the FSL. As part of the arrangement, the floundering Bradenton Growers would transfer to Miami to play their home games at Miami Field (formerly Tatum Park/Field).[2]

On April 11 MacReynolds made a formal announcement declaring that the Magic City would have its first officially recognized minor league team approved by the National Association, the governing body of minor league baseball. Under the direction of president W.B. Kirby, the team would begin play during the 1927 season featuring a split-season format with the first and second half leaders meeting in a best-of-seven series for the championship.[3]

In short order, the team received the moniker "Hustlers" and named new player-manager William "Bill" Holloway to lead the club. A first baseman by trade, Holloway previously played with Bloomington (1922) and Rockford (1923) of the Class-B III-League before moving to Florida and catching on with an independent team that moved from Daytona Beach to Clearwater.[4]

Tryouts to fill the 14-man roster began in earnest with the opener set for April 21. The late start posed several problems—including the late arrival of equipment and uniforms as well as the hastily built roster—which the team paid dearly for during the first half of the scheduled split season.[5]

An overflow, standing-room-only crowd of 5,000 greeted the Hustlers for opening day at Miami Field (capacity 3,400). Pre-game ceremonies included a parade through town led by the Fireman's Band, putting many of the locals in quite the festive mood.[6] Miami city manager Frank Wharton, with his customary cigar clenched firmly between his teeth, threw out the first ball to a chorus of cheers.[7] Unfortunately for the hometown supporters, the Hustlers were not up to the task against the visiting Sarasota Tarpons. Miami starting pitcher Joe Domingo was chased early leaving Holloway to call on Dick Peel to finish the game. The Tarpons prevailed, 7–5, the beneficiaries of four Miami errors, two by shortstop Rip Turner.[8]

Early season results continued to be disappointing after the Hustlers dropped 16 of their first 22 games. Before closing out the first half, Miami experienced an 18-game losing skein and fell deeply into last place.

Table 1. First Half Standings

	W	L	GB
Orlando Colts	38	26	–
Sarasota Tarpons	36	29	2.5
Tampa Smokers	35	29	3
Sanford Celeryfeds	33	30	4.5
St. Petersburg Saints	32	30	5
Miami Hustlers	18	48	21

Wholesale changes were in order based on the disastrous first-half results. W.B. Kirby resigned as team president and Holloway stepped aside as manager. Taking over control of the club was Smiley Tatum, a prominent land developer and entrepreneur, who was the driving force in constructing Miami Field. With the intention of turning his club around, Tatum immediately recruited and named Henry "Cotton" Knaupp as his new manager.[9] The 38-year old, flaxen-haired former mid-infielder brought with him a wealth of experience. He began his professional career as a player in 1910 with the Victoria Rosebuds of the Southwest Texas League. So impressive was the

20-year-old that the Cleveland Indians signed him to serve as their reserve shortstop. After a pair of campaigns with the Tribe, he returned to the minors for 17 more seasons, twelve with the New Orleans Pelicans of the Southern Association, where he became a local diamond legend.[10,11]

Knaupp brought immediate discipline to the club and dispelled the negative attitudes that had festered previously. He began by completely rebuilding the roster. One of his first moves was signing an upstart pitcher from the West Coast, "Lefty" Wetsell (sometimes spelled Wetzel). He followed by releasing infielders Eddie Dean and C.E. Vincent, pitcher Heinie Hymel, and outfielder J.W. Richards, and inked Benjamin Keyes from the Cotton States League, as well as pitcher "Hy" Meyer (sometimes spelled as "Hi" and Myers). He also shifted former Cincinnati Reds prospect Walter "Babe" Bennin from behind the plate to the outfield.[12]

Throughout the summer, Knaupp tinkered with the roster and made all the right moves. He accepted the resignation of Holloway, who had stayed on to play first base, and released infielder Mike Maloney. He recruited new blood, including shortstop Clint Bingham, first baseman Cotton Tatum, and Matt Hinkle.[13]

Bingham and Tatum shored up the shaky infield defense, while pasture worker Fausto "Cas" Casares, one of the few to survive the changes, continued to drive the offense as their leading home-run hitter. At the same time, Miami developed the league's top pitching staff, consisting of Chad "Georgia" Davis, Meyer, Dick Peel, and Wetsell.

The improved Hustlers played with newfound enthusiasm, engaging in a tight pennant race with the Sanford Celeryfeds (the colorful nickname referencing the city as the celery capital of the world) during the second half. Miami received a temporary setback on July 26 when Peel, the only pitcher remaining from the opening day roster, went down with a leg injury during a pre-game warmup. Knaupp moved quickly and replaced the injured hurler with pitcher Buster "Lefty" Brown.[14] Later he would add Pryor "Chief" McBee, who had appeared briefly with the Chicago White Sox in 1926. The latter arrived from Jacksonville of the Class-B Southeastern League.[15]

On August 17, the Hustlers passed Sanford in the standings, pasting St. Petersburg, 7–2, while Tampa pummeled the Celeryfeds, 10–4. Bennin led Miami's offense with a trio of base knocks while Davis earned another "W" with help from Meyer to close out the game and seal the deal.[16]

Miami finished the season strong, winning 16 of their final 20 games, putting three games between them and Sanford. Knaupp did not rest on his laurels and continued to fortify his club in order to compete for a championship by acquiring two St. Petersburg stars, pitcher Jose "Joe" Hernández, and Saints hitter Bill Brazier, a minor league veteran.[17]

On September 4, Hernandez tossed a 5–0 shutout at Miami Field, clinching the second half championship for the Hustlers. The "Knauppmen" recorded only five hits. They made the most of their opportunities, plating all of their runs in the sixth inning, highlighted by Hernández helping his own cause with a triple. Miami had gone from the basement to the penthouse in the biggest turnaround in the short history of the FSL (established in 1919).[18]

Sanford, the previous year's champions that fell short of qualifying for postseason play, felt slighted by Miami's roster moves. The Celeryfeds lodged a complaint with the league's offices pointing out that Miami broke a league rule that stated, "Only up to three players with higher level professional experience are allowed per team." Wetsell, accused of being the fourth player with said experience, made Miami ineligible to compete for the FSL championship. Upon further review by league officials, the Sanford protest was overturned and Miami was able to meet Orlando to determine the league champion.[19]

Table 2. Second Half Standings

	W	L	GB
Miami Hustlers	39	20	–
Sanford Celeryfeds	35	23	3.5
Orlando Colts	33	26	6
Sarasota Tarpons	26	33	13
Tampa Smokers	22	36	16.5
St. Petersburg Saints	20	37	18

On September 7, the championship series began under a canopy of dark clouds, as rain battered the opener at Orlando's Tinker Field, leading to a postponement. The series resumed the next day under clearer skies, but with tempers running high between the two clubs. McBee, who joined Miami late in the season, squared off against the Colts' best starter, "Red" Sweeney. The game featured several arguments and questionable calls by the umpires. The first of two major brouhahas came in the third inning on a tag up play, when Orlando's Paul Kirby left second base too early and was called out. Manager Phil Wells (who also served as the team's catcher) erupted at what he perceived as an obvious slight and engaged in a heated exchange with the umpiring crew. By the time the fur stopped flying, the angry skipper found himself ejected from the game.[20]

In the seventh inning, a second disturbance began. Fisticuffs ensued when Rollie Tinker (son of Hall of Famer Joe Tinker) received the benefit of a call on a close play. Miami's Clem Foss blew a gasket, leading to another heated disagreement with umpire Fredericks. The pair soon traded punches that led to Foss getting the heave-ho. The exchanges on the field were so violent that police arrived to quell the disturbance. After the game, Foss received a 90-day suspension rendering him unable to play the remainder of the series.[21]

Orlando took the second game, 1–0, after a day off due to the previous day's rainout.[22] Miami bounced back to win game three. The Hustlers plated a run in the fifth on a Colts error, and an insurance run in the sixth, courtesy of a Tatum RBI single. Davis kept Orlando in check, twirling a one-hitter for the 2–0 win.[23]

The fourth game of the series found the Colts back in the driver's seat. The contest turned into another pitchers' duel between Wetsell and Sweeney. A Bingham error in the tenth inning proved costly as Orlando edged Miami, 1–0. The Colts held a commanding 3–1 edge and were poised to take the championship trophy home.[24]

After a day off, and some much-needed rest, The Hustlers offense came to life in game five, knocking around three Colts pitchers. Orlando absorbed their worst defeat of the year against the Hustlers, 12–4, at Miami Field.[25] The Hustlers had their eyes on the next game to even the series.

The sixth game resulted in one of the most bizarre outcomes ever played out in the FSL. Going into the bottom of the ninth inning, with the Hustlers trailing, 1–0, the Colts looked poised to celebrate the championship. With one out, Casares took a lead off third. Keyes then hit a low line drive to second baseman Tinker. It appeared he had snagged it just inches above the infield dirt. Tinker was so confident that he had made the catch that he failed to make the customary throw to first, while Keyes raced down the line. To Tinker's astonishment, the umpire ruled that the ball was trapped and Keyes was safe. A hysterical Wells bolted from the dugout. When his protestations with arbiters failed to change the call, he refused to let his team return to the field. Miami was rewarded the win by forfeit, thus forcing a deciding seventh game.[26]

What followed should have been the climax to the season, but instead it turned out to be a let-down. Orlando cruised to an easy 12–1 victory, taking the league crown on Miami Field. The *Miami News and Metropolis* called the Hustlers' performance the poorest of the year. McBee turned in his worst start of the year, while the Colts immersed themselves in sweet celebration.[27]

Miami looked forward to play in 1928, but the season came to an early halt as the league ceased operations before finishing the schedule. The economy in Florida had been on a downturn since 1926 and the Great Depression loomed, bringing with it hard economic times.

Baseball did not return to the Magic City until 1940 when the Florida East Coast League was established. The Miami Wahoos and Miami Beach Flamingos joined the league. Miami would not experience a championship team until 1950 when the Sun Sox, led by their colorful skipper Pepper Martin, would capture their first Florida International League title.[28] ■

NOTES

1. "Miami Offered League Berth," *Miami Daily News and Metropolis*, April 7, 1927, 11.
2. "Fifty Players Seeking Berths in Miami Team," *Miami Daily News and Metropolis*, April 13, 1927, 11.
3. "State League Team For City Will Be Urged," *Miami Daily News and Metropolis*, April 11, 1927, 12.
4. Baseball-Reference.com.
5. "120 Game Play Opening Is Set For April 21," *Miami Daily News and Metropolis*, April 12, 1927, 11.
6. "Street Parade Will Precede Opening Game," *Miami Daily News and Metropolis*, April 21, 1927, 12.
7. "Opening Game Offered Fans Run For Money," *Miami Daily News and Metropolis*, April 22, 1927, 11.
8. "Opening Game Offered Fans Run For Money".
9. "S.M. Tatum Is New President Of The Miami Baseball Club," *Miami Daily News and Metropolis*, June 16, 1927, 10.
10. Milb.com. New Orleans Baseball History.
11. Baseball-Reference.com.
12. "Sanford Plays Here Saturday With Hustlers," *Miami Daily News and Metropolis*, June 25, 1927, 9.
13. "Hustlers Play Tampa Thursday At Miami Field," *Miami Daily News and Metropolis*, July 7, 1927, 7.
14. "Visitors Have Another Field Day In Battle," *Miami Daily News and Metropolis*, July 27, 1927, 9.
15. Baseball-Reference.com.
16. "Sanford Loses To Tampa 10–4; Miami On Top," *Miami Daily News and Metropolis*, August 18, 1927, 9.
17. "Saints Release Cuban Hurler," *Evening Independent* (St. Petersburg, Florida), July 8, 1927, 2.
18. "Double Header Monday Closes League Series," *Miami Daily News and Metropolis*, September 5, 1927, 5.
19. "League Moguls Find Against Sanford's Club," *Evening Independent* (St. Petersburg, Florida), August 7, 1927, 8.
20. "Orlando Wins Series Opener," *Sarasota Herald-Tribune*, September 9, 1927, 3.
21. "Orlando Wins Series Opener."
22. "Hustlers Need Victory Badly In Flag Race," *Miami Daily News and Metropolis*, September 10, 1927, 10.
23. "Davis Pitches One Hit Game For Knauppmen," *Miami Daily News and Metropolis*, September 12, 1927, 6.
24. "Bingham Lets Orlando Score In The Tenth," *Miami Daily News and Metropolis*, September 13, 1927, 15.
25. "Orlando Loses Hectic 12 To 4 Tilt Wednesday," *Miami Daily News and Metropolis*, September 15, 1927, 16.
26. "Colts Forfeit Thursday Game In The Ninth," *Miami Daily News and Metropolis*, September 16, 1927, 16.
27. "Hustlers Lose Final Contest Of The Series," *Miami Daily News and Metropolis*, September 17, 1927, 10.
28. Baseball-Reference.com.

Andy Oyler's Two-Foot Home Run

Is It Okay to Destroy a Legend?

Stew Thornley

Minneapolis Millers shortstop Andy Oyler topped a pitch into the mud in front of home plate at Nicollet Park. Before the visiting team could find the ball, Oyler raced around the bases for what may be the shortest home run in history.

This story has been around for over 100 years. For more than half that time, I have tried to find documentation of it. I learned of the tale in a 1966 article about Nicollet Park by Dave Mona in the *Minneapolis Tribune*, one that had a lasting effect on me.[1] Through its anecdotes, the article sparked an interest in Nicollet Park that fit with my fascination for old ballparks. It created an obsession with the Minneapolis Millers, which led to hundreds of hours at microfilm machines to document every game played by the Millers. The result was my first book, *On to Nicollet: The Glory and Fame of the Minneapolis Millers*, as well as the revelation that no home run of this type ever happened at Nicollet Park.[2]

During my research on the Millers, I paid particular attention to 1903–10—when Oyler played for Minneapolis—and looked closely for any event approaching this story. Nothing emerged. Oyler hit only one home run for the Millers. It came in an 8–6 loss at Milwaukee on August 2, 1904, and the newspapers made no mention of anything special, something that would have been noted had the ball traveled only a few feet.

That didn't keep the story from being told—and retold. It appeared the year after Oyler's career with Minneapolis ended.[3] The earliest mention found was April 20, 1911, in a Buffalo, New York, newspaper; hundreds of other papers—generally in small towns across the United States—picked up the story through telegraph services and repeated it. The story says the home run was a game-ender against the rival St. Paul Saints, replete with colorful descriptions such as, "Oyler rounded third like Casey Jones in his six-eight wheeler, making connections with the Santa Fe, and pulled up at home plate, scoring the winning run."[4]

Oyler's muddy home run has turned up in *Catholic Digest* in 1953 and, more than once, in *Baseball Digest*, including a 1958 article by Bill Bryson, a longtime sportswriter in Iowa. Bryson's son, Michael G. Bryson, used it as the title story in a 1990 book, *The Twenty-Four Inch Home Run and Other Outlandish, Incredible but True Events in Baseball History*. Bryson embellished his version with a description of Oyler ducking an inside pitch with the ball striking his bat and landing in the mud in front of home plate.[5]

Good researchers know that sometimes the essence of a story may be true even if details of it get mangled over time. Could it have been a triple into the mud that, in multiple retellings, grew into a home run? Or even a single? The closest resemblance found came during a June 28, 1904, game. A reporter for the *Minneapolis Journal* wrote a whimsical account of a sixth-inning run by the Millers, driven in by Oyler when he "attempted to duck a wild throw, inadvertently hit it and it rolled fair." The *Minneapolis Tribune* reported that rain threatened the game in the early innings but held off, and the field was dry in the sixth when Oyler topped the pitch in front of the plate. Nothing more happened than Oyler reaching base while driving home a runner from third.[6]

In 2005 I heard from Bob Kotanchik, a boyhood friend of John Oyler, Andy's grandson. Kotanchik had read of the feat on the back of a baseball card in the mid-1950s and asked his friend about it.[7] I also talked to John, who said he and Bob later got a first-hand account of the story from Andy.[8]

In January 2020, Oyler's alleged ball turned up on *Antiques Roadshow*. Ted Oyler told appraiser Leila Dunbar that his grandfather sent the muddy ball to his family—scrawling an address on it, affixing a stamp, and putting it in the mail. "And then he followed it with a letter, explaining what it was," said Ted. "We have a letter, I don't have it on me, but there is a letter and it's been rolling around in a desk drawer for a hundred years."[9]

I tracked down that branch of the Oylers. As for the letter that was supposed to have explained everything, a family member acknowledged no such letter existed and attributed Ted Oyler's claim of it as "ancestral elaboration."[10]

I had a couple of phone conversations with Fred Oyler, Andy's son and Ted's dad, who lives in Carlisle in central Pennsylvania, an area where Andy lived most of his life. Fred is the owner of the ball and lent it to his son for *Antiques Roadshow*. Fred confirmed there was no letter that followed the ball and freely stated that the story may be "folklore or fact."[11]

The *Antiques Roadshow* appearance sent me back to the archives of the SABR-L listserv, a longtime resource for me on this and other topics, and I found this gem of a response from 1999: "Sabermetric research has gone too far! Somebody stop Stew Thornley before he proves without a doubt that Oyler's HR never happened. The story is far too beautiful to be potentially sullied by cold-hearted Truth."[12]

Was this a tongue-in-cheek comment? I interpreted it as such although in ensuing years I've encountered serious opinions from people who don't want their legends destroyed and who claim people like me have a "fetish" for accuracy. Anyone familiar with the movie *The Man Who Shot Liberty Valance* knows the sentiment: "When the legend becomes fact, print the legend."

Before the Society for American Baseball Research—an organization founded in 1971 with establishing "an accurate historical account of baseball through the years" as one of its objectives—frivolous yarns ruled. Alfred H. Spink's 1911 book, *The National Game*, includes a wild tale of a St. Paul pitcher losing a game to Minneapolis when a batted ball stuck on a nail high up on the outfield fence, allowing three runs to score before his teammates could get a ladder.[13]

Mac Davis in his 1958 book, *Sports Shorts: Astonishing Strange but True*, has equally implausible stories, including one of a dead man winning a game for a Benson, Minnesota, team "around the turn of the century." According to the county historical society, "The story was a figment of the imagination of a railroad man here who got together with an umpire and concocted the story, sending it out on the telegraph wire." Most stories emanating from thin air can't be traced back to a source, if, indeed, the historical society version isn't apocryphal itself.[14]

Hugh Fullerton, a writer deeply connected with the 1919 White Sox intentionally losing the World Series (itself the subject of widespread myths that have been debunked by SABR's Black Sox Scandal Research Committee), had a reputation for whoppers. In his 2016 book, *The Betrayal: The 1919 World Series and the Birth of Modern Baseball*, Charles Fountain wrote that when accused of sacrificing accuracy for the sake of a good story, Fullerton replied, "You would sacrifice a good story for the sake of accuracy."[15]

Perhaps no one got more mileage from fanciful anecdotes than Bill Stern, the sportscaster renowned for hyperbole and outright fabrications on his weekly radio show. Stern bristled at criticism of his myth-making and, in his 1959 autobiography, wrote that his sports program was "strictly entertainment and being such was one in which I was entitled to unlimited dramatic license."[16]

Entertainment allowing for dramatic license even when the stories are presented as fact? This question became central to a captivating SABR-L thread in 1995–96 about Ken Burns's *Baseball*.

An innocuous inquiry on the listserv led to a discussion of the accuracy of *Baseball* and eventually to questions of whether Burns had intentionally misrepresented information for the sake of the story. The topic came down to the primary question: "*If* Burns took such liberties, was it proper?"

A consultant on the Burns project, former Hall of Fame librarian Tom Heitz, responded with a post, "In defense of Ken Burns," in which he wrote, "The art of myth-making in baseball journalism has unfortunately been largely lost by the current generation of broadcasters and scribes who have been subjected to 'training' in journalistic accuracy, etc."[17]

Spirited debate followed from SABR stalwarts Larry Gerlach, John Pastier, Tom Wark, John Thorn, Marvin Bittinger, and Stewart Wolpin until Nancy Jo Leachman cut to the core with the question, "WHY, WHY, WHY is this a debate about choosing between historical accuracy and folkloric awe and wonder?"[18]

Over time, I have learned the value of colorful tales, even dubious ones, and that they can be told with a buyer-beware disclaimer. Dave Mona's 1966 article on Nicollet Park sent me on a life-long journey of baseball research, fueled by stories that may or may not be true. Mona produced the "folkloric awe and wonder" that Nancy Jo Leachman wrote of while also noting, "Part of Nicollet's lore exists in the realm of 'hard to believe and verify' anecdotes."[19]

Matt Tavares, then a SABR member, contacted me in 2004 as he worked on a children's book about the home run, *Mudball*. Tavares knew the story was suspect and acknowledged it in the book's afterword: "...[M]any baseball historians believe that Andy Oyler's muddy home run never happened. Over the years, the legend of Andy Oyler has grown. With each retelling, details have been added and altered. And what has emerged is a classic American folktale... Even though these stories might not be true, they endure because they give us heroes we can emulate and Everymen with whom we can identify."[20]

On the other hand, Michael G. Bryson, who included "True" in the title of his book and referred to "professional baseball's shortest *bona fide* homer," presented no such disclaimer or caveat.

Skepticism is an essential quality in a researcher. So is sensitivity.

I learned a lesson in 1984 when I told Joe Hauser that 50 of his 69 homers in 1933 came at cozy Nicollet Park, ruining his recollection that he had hit at least half on the road. Researchers can be sensitive with the subjects of stories but remain true to facts they disseminate. Although I felt bad for the clumsy manner in which I diminished Hauser's achievement in his mind, I didn't doctor the details when I listed his home runs in *On to Nicollet*.

As I've been in touch with Oyler family members, I have avoided talking in terms of debunking the story. Instead, I focused on trying to get information to nail down the date of the event. Perhaps something of the sort happened sometime—when Oyler played baseball at Washington & Jefferson College or on an amateur team in Chambersburg or Newville in Pennsylvania—and the story morphed into a home run in professional baseball.[21]

My initial conversations with Fred Oyler, Andy's son, in March 2020 indicated his own skepticism about the story. Three-and-a-half months later, Fred called me. In his dad's trunk, Fred discovered an article by me with the news that the only home run Oyler hit with the Millers was definitely not a mud ball.[22] "You answered the question," he said. "It is definitely [just] a legend."

Fred also recalled a Harrisburg, Pennsylvania, newspaper talking to his dad and printing the legend. Fred asked his dad if the story was real. "He demurred. He didn't deny it. He didn't say it was true. He was a pretty straight-laced guy. He would have told me if it was true."

True or not, the legend has been interesting for the Oylers and others. Fred worked in Japan for five-and-a-half years and told his dad's story to a co-worker who was a baseball fan. Thanks to the co-worker's connections, Fred ended up on a Japanese version of the television show *I've Got a Secret*.

Far from upset about the truth, Fred is at peace with it. He plans to donate the ball to the Cumberland County Historical Society. I told him when we were past the COVID-19 pandemic that R.J. Lesch, a SABR member who lives in Carlisle, was going to invite him to a SABR meeting. When I said I would come out there for such a meeting, Fred told me he would pay for my plane ticket (a kind offer that I declined).

The experience has been another lesson—the pursuit of facts doesn't mean the end of a legend. It may even enhance it. After all, what baseball myth is more memorable than Abner Doubleday being the game's creator? And the story behind it is even greater: a committee created not to learn the true origins of baseball, only that it was American in its roots, and its reliance on a 1905 letter written by a most unreliable source, Abner Graves.[23]

Andy Oyler's alleged mudball has also taken on a life of its own, one more interesting than the original tale.

"I think we'll put the story to bed…finally," Fred Oyler concluded. "It will be in the historical society for people to enjoy that way."[24] ◼

Acknowledgments

Thanks to members and friends of the Oyler family—Fred (Andy's son), John (Andy's grandson), Bob Kotanchik (boyhood friend of John Oyler), and Steve Ruetter (Andy's grandson-in-law)—as well as SABR members Ev Cope (who alerted me to the segment on *Antiques Roadshow*), David McDonald, Dave Mona, Rich Arpi, Tim Herlich, F.X. Flinn, Paul Ember, Cary Smith, Wayne McElreavy, Jim Wohlenhaus, Matt Tavares, Ed Morton, Bob LeMoine, Rod Nelson, and Curt Smith. For more on Minnesota Sports Myths and the phenomenon of how myths can happen, see https://milkeespress.com/minnesotamyths.html.

Notes

1. "Nicollet Park: A Colorful Page in Baseball History" by Dave Mona, *Minneapolis Tribune*, November 6, 1966: 2, Home and Recreation.
2. Stew Thornley, *On to Nicollet: The Glory and Fame of the Minneapolis Millers*, Minneapolis: Nodin Press: 1988 and 2000.
3. Oyler had been beaned in 1909 and, unable to regain his former skills, retired in 1910. He did try a comeback with Kansas City in the American Association in 1912 but lasted only four games.
4. "Made a Home Run on a Bunt," *Buffalo* (New York) *Enquirer*, April 20, 1911: 9.
5. "There Was Joy in Mudville," *Catholic Digest*, Volume 17, June 1953: 12; "Inch-hit Homer!" by Jocko Maxwell, *Baseball Digest*, April 1953: 29–30; "The World's Shortest Home Runs" by Bill Bryson, *Baseball Digest*, October-November 1958: 67–68; Michael G. Bryson, *The Twenty-Four-Inch Home Run and Other Outlandish, Incredible But True Events in Baseball History*, Chicago: Contemporary Books, 1990: 21–23.
6. O'Loughlin, "Kansas City Not in the Running," *Minneapolis Journal*, June 29, 1904: 14; "Second Victory for the Millers," *Minneapolis Tribune*, June 29, 1904: 9.
7. 1955 Topps card, number 114, of Lou Ortiz.
8. Email correspondence and telephone conversations with Bob Kotanchik and John Oyler, 2005.
9. *Antiques Roadshow*, aired on PBS, January 20, 2020.
10. The term "ancestral elaboration" was used by Steven Reutter, the husband of one of Andy Oyler's granddaughters. Emails with Steve Reutter, March 3, 4, and 24, 2020.
11. Telephone conversations with Fred Oyler, March 5–6, 2020.
12. Tod Powell on SABR-L, December 25, 1999. My sense that Tod's comment was tongue-in-cheek is buttressed by his other sentence that follows: "Plugging my ears and singing 'Pinball Wizard' until it's safe to unplug and shut up, I am Tod Powell, inventor, KARMA LEAGUE BASEBALL."

13. Alfred H. Spink, *The National Game*, St. Louis: National Game Publishing Company, 1911 (Reprinted by Carbondale, Illinois: Southern Illinois University Press, 2000), 367. The pitcher who lost this game was Frank Isbell. Not surprisingly, nothing like this happened when Isbell pitched for St. Paul in the 19th century.

14. Mac Davis, *Sports Shorts: Astonishing Strange but True*, New York: Bantam Books, 1958: 143; "Sports of the County" by Lefty Ranweiler, *Centennial History of Kandiyohi County*, 1970: 323.

15. Charles Fountain, *The Betrayal: The 1919 World Series and the Birth of Modern Baseball*, New York: Oxford University Press, 2016: 114.

16. Bill Stern with Oscar Fraley, *The Taste of Ashes: A Famous Broadcaster's Courageous Comeback for Addiction and Disaster*, New York: Henry Holt and Company, 1959: 111.

17. Tom Heitz on SABR-L, December 23, 1995.

18. Nancy Jo Leachman on SABR-L, January 5, 1996.

19. Mona.

20. Matt Tavares, *Mudball*, Somerville, Massachusetts: Candlewick Press, 2005. Email correspondence with Tavares, 2004.

21. I found nothing resembling a hit into the mud in any college or amateur/semi-pro games Oyler played in.

22. Andy Oyler died in 1970, well before I wrote anything about the home run. Fred said the trunk was with his son for many years and then with his sister, who died in 2004. Likely a family member got this article/monograph at some time and put it in the trunk.

23. Graves's 1905 letter claimed Doubleday had invented the game in Cooperstown in around 1939. Graves's stories varied over time—from hearing of the creation second hand, to actually having witnessed Doubleday laying out a diamond, to even playing in the first game of baseball, as a student at Cooperstown's Green College in 1840 (even though Graves would have been only six years old at the time). Many of the newspapers, like the commission, loved his stories and didn't bother to check his claims, no matter how outlandish. Graves had twice been institutionalized before coming up with the stories about Doubleday and again in 1924, after murdering his wife in a fit of paranoia. More on Graves is available in "Mr. Abner Graves: Colorado's Connection to the Doubleday Myth," by David Block, *Above the Fruited Plain: Baseball in the Rocky Mountain West*, edited by Thomas L. Altherr, Souvenir publication of the 2003 Society for American Baseball Research national convention, Denver, Colorado: 9–12.

24. Telephone conversation with Fred Oyler, June 20, 2020.

Dismantling Fenway Park Before the 1920 Baseball Season?

Bill Nowlin

We know it didn't come to pass, but when Fenway Park was less than 10 years old, there was discussion of disposing of it. The park was opened in 1912 and at the time had hosted the world champion Boston Red Sox in four of its eight years—1912, 1915, 1916, and 1918. But in October 1919, respected sports journalist I.E. Sanborn wrote in the *Chicago Tribune* that "according to the most authentic information obtainable" there was a plan that—by a "process of amalgamation"—"two, and possibly three, major league base ball plants will be dismantled next season."[1]

In New York, the Polo Grounds was shared by the National League Giants and the American League Yankees.[2] Sanborn declared that other such sharing arrangements were imminent: "Before another season opens it is more than probable the St. Louis National league [sic] club will be sharing the plant of the St. Louis Browns and the Philadelphia Nationals will be under contract to play in Shibe Park, the home of the Athletics. It is within the scope of the possible that the Red Sox will amalgamate with the Braves, so as to cut down the overhead by occupying one plant jointly."

In both St. Louis and Philadelphia, the two competing ballparks were fairly near each other and in each instance there were compelling reasons to dispose of one in favor of sharing a facility. This came to pass in St. Louis, where the Cardinals did start playing in Sportsman's Park in 1920, leaving Robison Field. From 1920 through 1953, the Cardinals and Browns shared Sportsman's Park. In 1953, the park's name was changed to Busch Stadium. After the 1953 season, the Browns departed to Baltimore and became the Orioles. The Cardinals continued to play games at the newly-named Busch, into 1966 when they started to play games in Busch Stadium II.

The Phillies and Athletics ultimately did share Shibe Park, but it wasn't for nearly two decades after Sanborn's assertion.[3] In 1938, the Phillies began to play home games at Shibe and did so through the 1970 season, long after the Athletics had departed for Kansas City, following the 1954 campaign.[4]

Returning to look at the situation in Boston, both parks were fairly new and both were sizable. Fenway Park's capacity was 24,000—though they managed to shoehorn in more than 34,000 fans for both Games Three and Five of the 1912 World Series. Several blocks away, Braves Field opened in August 1915 with a much larger capacity of 43,250.[5] The two clubs had shared facilities at times in the past. The Braves, for instance, played the 1914 World Series against the Philadelphia Athletics with Fenway Park as their home park, because it was a larger venue than the South End Grounds. They had played a number of regular season games at Fenway, too, before Braves Field itself opened in 1915.[6] (Fenway also hosted boxing matches and both high school and college football in the fall of 1918 and 1919.) And the Red Sox played their home World Series games in the larger Braves Field both in 1915 against the Phillies and in 1916 against Brooklyn. In later years, the Red Sox would also play a number of Sunday games at Braves Field, because of a local ordinance that prevented them playing at Fenway due to its closer proximity to a house of worship.[7]

Let us see what Sanborn said about Boston on October 20, 1919:

A ticklish situation exists in Boston, where both National and American league [sic] clubs are struggling to lift heavy overhead charges, due to the cost of their plants. The American league club, having built its plant several years ago, probably is in better condition as to its bonds than the National league is. Moreover, its grounds are better situated for commercial purposes, being in the heart of "automobile row," but the American league park is better adapted to baseball because it is more compact than the plant occupied by the Braves.

The latter, with a seating capacity of 42,000 all on the ground level, is the biggest baseball plant in America, but it smothers the average crowd and stifles enthusiasm. It would be the rational solution, however, for the two Boston clubs to combine on the rental of the Braves' park and dispose of the Red Sox grounds.[8]

On October 31, the *Boston Post* further reported that Red Sox owner Harry Frazee, Red Sox manager Ed Barrow, and James E. Gaffney of the Braves met in conference at Braves Field and "gave the place a thorough overlooking." Fenway Park was "growing enormously valuable," the *Post* declared. "In fact it has become far too hefty a real estate proposition to be used merely as a plant for baseball."[9] Combining under one roof was not a new idea. Melville E. Webb had published an article almost exactly a year earlier in the *Post* entitled "One-Park Baseball Likely to Come." He declared the idea a good one.[10] That same day, James C. O'Leary

wrote in the *Boston Globe* that "The Fenway Park property is rapidly increasing in value and in time may be regarded as too valuable to be applied to its present use."[11]

The day after the *Post*'s report of his visit to Braves Field, Frazee claimed the meeting was a coincidence, that he'd encountered Gaffney at a restaurant—never having met him before—and that it was the first time he'd ever seen Braves Field. He had no immediate intention of selling Fenway Park at the time; it would be at least two or three years, he thought, before he could realize enough to make it worth selling.[12] Apparently Gaffney had proposed the two teams both play at Braves Field, but Barrow said Frazee was not going to accept the offer and that the Red Sox "will use Fenway two years more, anyway."[13]

Interior of Fenway Park, 1914, seen from seats in right field.

Exterior of Fenway Park, 1914.

But Fenway changed hands early in 1920, with Frazee cutting a deal with a perhaps surprising source. In November 1916, when then Red Sox owner Joseph Lannin had sold the team to Frazee and Hugh Ward, he had taken a note for $262,000, which was secured by the capital stock of the Fenway Realty Trust, the company that owned Fenway Park. The note had come due on November 1, 1919, and had not been paid. Accordingly, Lannin was prepared to sell the stock at auction.[14] Paul H. Shannon of the *Boston Post* wrote that Frazee "has always considered Fenway Park the chief asset of the Boston club, and many a time he has intimated that this land, increasing yearly in value, was the bulwark of the Red Sox assets."[15]

That said, Lannin was owed the money. A number of court actions followed and Massachusetts Superior Court ruled that Fenway Park would be put up for sale via auction to secure payment to Lannin. The court ruling prompted Frazee to sell a mortgage on Fenway Park to Jacob Ruppert, owner of the New York Yankees, as part of the Babe Ruth deal.[16] On March 5, 1920, a settlement was agreed upon. Jacob Ruppert, Inc. held a $300,000 mortgage on Fenway Park itself, not to be paid off until years later, after Tom Yawkey became owner of the Sox.[17]

The amalgamation Sanborn anticipated never came to pass and seems to have not attracted further comment or speculation in the Boston press. There was a brief note in the *Denver Post*, however, that said if the Red Sox team were sold "it is likely the new owners will abandon the Fenway park now used by the club. The grounds would be sold for other purposes."[18]

The Braves and Red Sox played each in their own parks for the next 30-plus years. And 100 years later, Fenway Park still hosts Red Sox games. ∎

Notes

1. I.E. Sanborn, "Major Leagues Plan to Cut Expense for Parks; Only One Field for Two Teams in Same Cities," *Chicago Tribune*, October 20, 1919: 18. Irving Ellis "Sy" Sanborn" had been one of the founders of the Baseball Writers' Association of America in 1908. Before working nearly 20 years at the *Tribune*, he spent a dozen years in Massachusetts writing for the *Springfield Union*.
2. The Giants held the lease on the Polo Grounds, and the Yankees were a tenant; there was some form of paperwork in place to prevent the Giants from summarily evicting them. In February 1921, Yankees ownership purchased land in The Bronx and Yankee Stadium would open on the site in 1923.
3. There had been occasional sharing, to accommodate circumstances. As Bob Davids noted, "When part of the Baker Bowl stands collapsed in a minor accident on May 14, 1927, the Phillies played a few home games at the Athletics' field." L. Robert Davids, "Baker Bowl," *Baseball Research Journal*, 1982. See https://sabr.org/journal/article/baker-bowl.
4. Shibe Park was renamed to Connie Mack Stadium in 1953.
5. Capacities are as noted in Philip J. Lowry, ed., *Green Cathedrals*, 5th edition (Phoenix: SABR, 2019), 47, 50. The Boston Braves did not own Braves Field. When James E. Gaffney sold the ballclub in early 1916, he retained ownership of the park. It was only in 1950 that then Braves owner Lou Perini purchased Braves Field from the Gaffney estate.
6. For a detailed listing, see Bill Nowlin, "The Time(s) the Braves Played Home Games at Fenway Park," in Bill Nowlin, ed., *The Miracle Braves of 1914* (Phoenix: SABR, 2014), 320–27.
7. The Red Sox played Sunday home games at Braves Field from April 28, 1929 through May 29, 1932, as well as the occasional holiday separate-admission doubleheader, such as Patriots Day in 1930 and 1932. After a May 8, 1926, fire destroyed a good part of Fenway's third-base seats, the Red Sox were offered use of Braves Field. They expressed their thanks but declined. James C. O'Leary, "Sox at Fenway Despite Fire," *Boston Globe*, May 10, 1926: 8. Attendance for Red Sox games in the 1920 was sparse enough they didn't need the extra capacity.
8. Sanborn. As to whether or not Sanborn was confused as to the location of "Automobile Row," SABR member Bob Brady, president of the Boston Braves Historical Association, explained, "Automobile row extended from Kenmore Square down Commonwealth Ave. Probably both team's homes would be logistically in close enough proximity to be so categorized." Email to author July 20, 2020. See also Patricia L. Kennedy, "A Trip Down Automobile Row," *BU Today*, October 20, 2011, at http://www.bu.edu/articles/2011/a-trip-down-automobile-row.
9. "Shift of Red Sox In Sight," *Boston Post*, October 31, 1919: 9 15. The shift in question was from Fenway Park to sharing the facility at Braves Field.
10. Melville E. Webb, "One-Park Baseball Likely to Come," *Boston Post*, October 31, 1918: 7. The notion of the Red Sox departing Fenway Park was probably not pure fancy, given the stories by both Sanborn and Webb which were published just over a year apart. Webb was, like Sanborn, well-connected and a charter member of the BBWAA. See Charlie Bevis, "Melville Webb," SABR.org, at https://sabr.org/bioproj/person/melville-webb/
11. James C. O'Leary, "Red Sox May Join in Use of Braves Field," *Boston Globe*, October 31, 1918: 4. See Bob Ruzzo's Fall 2012 *Baseball Research Journal* article on the history of Braves Field at https://sabr.org/journal/article/braves-field-an-imperfect-history-of-the-perfect-ballpark/
12. Paul H. Shannon, "Frazee Denies Moving," *Boston Post*, November 1, 1918: 19. He said, "Braves Field is certainly one vast plant but I don't think it would ever be the popular resort that Fenway Park has become."
13. "Sportsman," "Live Tips and Topics," *Boston Evening Globe*, November 8, 1918: 7.
14. "Seeks Settlement By Red Sox Owners," *Boston Globe*, February 11, 1920: 7.
15. Paul H. Shannon, "Stop Frazee from Selling Red Sox," *Boston Post*, February 11, 1920: 11.
16. "Court Enjoins Frazee," *The New York Times*, February 17, 1920: 10. One can find a public notice regarding the sale of Fenway Realty Trust shares at auction in the February 21, 1920, issue of *The Sun and New York Herald* on page 15.
17. For a contemporary explanation of the mortgage, and how it was not that the New York Yankees held a mortgage on Fenway Park, see "Here's Version of Red Sox Lawyer on Ruppert Mortgage," *Chicago Tribune*, December 2, 1920: 18, and "No Connection with Club," *The New York Times*, December 2, 1920: 18. On the Yawkey purchase of the mortgage, see Bill Nowlin, *Tom Yawkey: Patriarch of the Boston Red Sox* (Lincoln: University of Nebraska Press, 2018), 7–10. In 1923, ownership of the Red Sox changed hands from Frazee to a group headed by Robert Quinn. See Rory Costello, "Bob Quinn," SABR.org, at https://sabr.org/bioproj/person/bob-quinn.
18. "Boston Red Sox May Have New Park," *Denver Post*, November 14, 1919: 30. See also "Ball Park May Be Given Up," *Oregonian* (Portland, Oregon), November 24, 1919: 11. Why the possibility was being discussed in Chicago and cities further west, but there appeared to have not been more speculation in the *Boston Globe* is a little difficult to understand.

The First Baseball War

The American Association and the National League

Richard Hershberger

Organized baseball is, among other things, a business structure: an ordered way of operating for the benefit of its member organizations. It follows that it is not established for the benefit of any outside organization. Should such an outside organization attempt to seize these benefits, either exclusively or (more often) alongside the existing establishment, a baseball war results.

Five great baseball wars have been waged by outside organizations: the American Association in 1882, the Union Association in 1884, the Players League in 1890, the American League in 1901–02, and the Federal League in 1914–15. We could, should we wish to complicate matters, add various skirmishes between established major leagues, principally the American Association and the National League in 1891. And if we were to add abortive attempts to establish a challenger that never played any games, the list would be considerably longer. So too if we add "outlaw" minor leagues, acting within a limited scope and only challenging the system inasmuch as it claimed authority over them. But the five great wars stand out.

The American Association (AA) war was modest compared with its later counterparts. It should not be discounted because of this. The AA war of 1882 set the pattern for future wars, and the settlement bringing it to a conclusion set the pattern for how major league baseball would be organized in the twentieth century.

OBJECTIVES AND WEAPONS

A baseball "war" is, of course, a metaphor. How does the war metaphor translate to baseball? Combatants go to war seeking to attain objectives, and use weapons to achieve these goals. What, in a baseball war, are the participants' objectives, and what weapons do they use?

Organized baseball in its mature form is a collection of leagues arranged hierarchically, with procedures regulating their interactions, principally control of geographical markets and movement of players. The leagues higher in the hierarchy claim exclusive control of more desirable markets, and mechanisms are enacted to move better players up the hierarchy. The top of the pyramid is occupied by one or more leagues, defined as "major," while the various tiers below the top were occupied by leagues defined as "minor." In this developed form, the wartime goal of an upstart league is to force its way to the top tier.[1]

This system did not yet exist in 1882. The top tier existed in the form of the National League (NL), founded in 1876, but the lower tiers were as yet inchoate. Professional clubs had always existed outside the NL, but the manners in which they organized among themselves and interacted with the NL had not yet evolved to their later forms. The issues in dispute in 1882 were similar to those of later wars, but where the later hierarchical structure bundled the areas of dispute into a package, in 1882 these were distinct. They fell into four categories: (1) territories, (2) exhibition games, (3) player discipline, and (4) player contracts.

Territories would play only a minor role in 1882, unlike the later baseball wars, but the issue was not entirely absent. There was, as will be seen below, some maneuvering with regard to New York and Philadelphia. The results would be important in the long term, but in the short term the fight was not yet over territory.

Exhibition games between NL and outside clubs were more important. These were a substantial source of revenue for both sides. The NL Boston Club, for example, had revenues of about $30,000 in 1877, with over $7,500 of that from games with non-League clubs.[2] The League was only too happy to use its strength to demand favorable terms. It regulated when and where League teams would play exhibitions. The rules varied from year to year, but a typical rule was to ban exhibition games on NL fields, so as to avoid watering down the attraction of championship (i.e. regular season) games. This was a break from the tradition of "home and home" series where the two sides would play a game on each field. The result was to exclude the non-League teams from access to the larger populations of most NL cities. The most onerous requirement was that for a guaranteed payment, even if the game was rained out. The playing of exhibition games with the NL on equal terms would be one goal of the AA.

Player discipline was a major issue in this era. The infractions covered a wide range of seriousness. The most extreme were players throwing games at the behest of gamblers. Four members of the 1877 NL Louisville club were found to have thrown games and were banned permanently. The League held the moral high ground with the Louisville four, but it could not resist the temptation to expel players for lesser offenses, ranging from drunkenness and insubordination to poor play. The League had a point. The drunkenness of ballplayers was legendary, and poor play sometimes was the result of a player receiving a better offer and "playing for his release." On the other hand, poor play was more often the result of a lingering injury or simply a slump. A heavy-handed club management could rapidly make the situation intolerable for the players.

Expulsions were issued by individual clubs for specific offenses. The NL in 1881 expanded the disciplinary regime with the instigation of the "black list" for "dissipation and general insubordination." The process consisted of club officers at a special meeting of the League sitting down together and drawing up a list of names, unencumbered by any pretense of due process.[3]

These disciplinary measures would be ineffective if the player could simply go elsewhere. The League extended its reach to non-League clubs by refusing to play any club that included an expelled player. This would entail the sacrifice of gate receipts from these exhibition games, but the League clubs were better able to sustain this loss than were the clubs subject to the ban. The League further extended this regime beginning with the 1879 season, forbidding play with any club that had played a club that included an expelled (and later black-listed) player.[4] Non-League clubs complained about the League presuming upon them, but the measure had the desired effect of driving most expelled players out of professional baseball.

There was a right of appeal, but this was largely theoretical. In practice, players were only reinstated in extraordinary circumstances after being expelled or black-listed, with these extraordinary circumstances having more to do with NL interests than any sense of equity. A notable example was Edward "The Only" Nolan, expelled in 1878 for insubordination. He went to California, the only locale with professional baseball beyond the League's reach. This became a problem for the League in 1879, when the Chicago club made a post-season tour of California. Nolan's play rendered the entire California League ineligible for games with the Chicago club, so the League hurriedly reinstated

him. The hypocrisy was not lost on the rest of the baseball community.[5]

While the Nolan case showed the system to be arbitrary and self-serving, Charley Jones was the exemplar for League abuse of the system. Jones played for the Boston club in 1880. On September 3, while the team was in Cleveland, he demanded $378 in overdue pay, and refused to play when it was not given him. He was fined and suspended, and then expelled for insubordination. The club's argument was that while his contract called for him to be paid on the first of the month, standard practice was to delay payment while on the road, and that he would have been paid upon the team's return to Boston. The club further claimed that he was using this as an excuse to be released so that he could return to his home in Cincinnati and play there. In legal terms the club was claiming that while it was in technical breach of contract, the breach was not material. Later litigation, however, brought out that his monthly salary was $250, making it clear that his pay was in arrears more than merely the two days the club acknowledged.[6] It is entirely plausible that, given the state of the Boston club's finances, they were indeed behind in their payroll. He sued in Ohio, and a protracted legal battle followed, featuring a seizure and subsequent release of the club's baggage while in Cleveland, garnishment of its share of the gate receipts, and eventually a final judgment against the club.[7] Jones's legal victory established his position as a victim of League abuse and called into question the entire system of expulsions and black listing.

While the NL demanded that other organizations respect and enforce its disciplinary measures, it refused to similarly recognize theirs. This was a source of complaint, but there was nothing other organizations could do about it.[8] The AA did not have any principled objection to the system of discipline, whatever critiques it might have of specific instances, but it demanded equal standing.

As important as the other disagreements were, disputes over player contracts were by far the largest. Clubs and players routinely entered into contracts intended to be legally binding, but in actual practice rarely turned to the civil courts. This was partly due to the expense of litigation and partly due to uncertainty—which proved entirely justified—over whether the contracts were in fact legally enforceable. (The legal issues will be explored further below.) Owners instead developed a parallel "baseball law."

Baseball law went back to the 1860s, when the National Association of Base Ball Players created a

William Hulbert, President of the National League until his death in April 1882. His illness gave the AA the opening it needed.

BASEBALL 1876–81

The dominant fact about professional baseball in the second half of the 1870s was that the national economy had fallen into a depression following the Panic of 1873. The baseball economy was affected by 1875 and would not see serious recovery until 1881. Nearly every development of organized baseball in this era was a response to economic stress. This reaches even to the founding of the National League in 1876. The predecessor National Association had structural weaknesses that were no longer sustainable, the most important being that it was an open organization. Any club could declare itself professional and join, without regard to its competitive or financial strength. The eight most financially sound clubs reorganized themselves into the National League.

The NL in its early years had constant turnover. League clubs were financially sound only compared with non-League clubs. The years 1876–80 saw a series of club failures, usually following the end of the season but in a few cases during it. Only two of the original members survived to 1880: Chicago and Boston (respectively the modern Cubs and Braves). The rest of the League lineup had to be replaced from one year to the next.

This had geographic implications that would be important during the AA war. The original lineup of clubs had a geographical footprint that formed a rough quadrilateral with the corners at Boston, Philadelphia, St. Louis, and Chicago, similar to that of the major leagues in the first half of the twentieth century. As clubs dropped out over the next five years, the replacements were selected with an eye to minimizing travel expenses. By 1881 the League's footprint was a line stretching from Chicago to Boston. Of the other six clubs, two were in modern major league cities (Detroit and Cleveland), two were in cities that were at least plausible (Buffalo and Providence—then the twentieth largest city in the country) while two were in cities obviously too small (Troy, New York, and Worcester, Massachusetts). This lineup would present the AA with the opening to form a more southerly circuit controlling larger markets.

Salaries were by far the largest expense for League clubs. They undertook various measures to reduce salaries. They repeatedly vowed to refuse to pay "fancy" salaries—a resolution that lasted only until a star player had multiple clubs bidding for his services. Various ideas were floated such as coming up with a system to rate each player's ability and set a standardized pay schedule by position and skill class, or more simply to establish a salary cap for each

judiciary committee. The National League considered itself the keeper of baseball law, while using it to advance its own interests. This manifested itself immediately in 1876. The League freely poached players from non-League clubs without regard to any existing contracts. Examples include outfielder Dan Collins, who abandoned the St. Louis Red Stockings for the NL Louisvilles, and pitcher Dale Williams who left Indianapolis for the NL Cincinnati club on the pretext of visiting his parents.[9] At the League's December 1876 meeting, the member clubs committed to respect non-League contracts beginning March 15, 1877.[10] The implication was lost on nobody that the League considered itself free to disregard outside contracts until then. Nor was this a genuine commitment to respect contracts after that. The League created the "League Alliance" in the hope of including all non-League clubs. Members of the League Alliance ceded dispute resolution to the League in return for a promise by the League to honor Alliance club player contracts, implying that the NL still felt free to disregard contracts between players and non-Alliance clubs.[11] The League through the 1870s never acknowledged any general obligation to respect contracts, and player contracts would always be the principal dispute in any baseball war. That the NL respect the AA player contracts was the AA's highest priority.

These were the objectives in the baseball war. The weapons used might be direct threats against these objectives. An upstart league might, for example, be willing to take in players expelled by the older league, thereby threatening player discipline. The most important weapon was brute financial muscle: the ability to offer players in the competing league higher salaries. Ultimately, every baseball war came down to financial wherewithal.

position.[12] Such schemes were never enacted, and in any case would have been unenforceable. The incentive to cheat on the salary cap would be too great.

Finally they arrived at the idea of the reserve system. (Today this is habitually called the "reserve clause," but it was not yet a part of the player contract during the period in question, so it is here called the "reserve system" or simply the "reserve.") Under this system the various NL clubs agreed not to negotiate with one another's reserved players, forcing those players to sign only with the club that reserved them, negotiating salary from a weak position. The system started out modestly. It was limited to only five players per team, and no one claimed that this restriction prevented outside clubs from signing reserved players.

The reserve system was immediately criticized:

> The plan said to be adopted by the League to prevent competition between the several clubs for the others' players is open to criticism, as by it a League club could force a player who has been under contract with it the past season to either play at a reduced salary or play with no League club the coming year.[13]

Players understood exactly that the purpose of the reserve system was to suppress salaries, and they were not happy about it. The most prominent was George Wright, reserved by Providence. He refused to sign with Providence. Whether this was due to personal conflicts or merely money depends on whose version one believes. Either way, he became baseball's first holdout.[14]

The reserve system would prove to be the foundation upon which organized baseball would be built, but that was in the future. Through 1882 it was a minor element of conflict. The NL's reserved players were signed shortly after the close of the 1881 season, and were not pursued by the AA.

The National League clubs were comparatively well prepared to ride out the economic depression of the late 1870s. Non-League clubs had a harder time of it. This is not immediately apparent. The NA closed the 1875 season with eight active clubs. Six of these, along with two new organizations, formed the National League the following year, while the other two clubs also opened the season, for a total of ten openly professional clubs in 1876. The season of 1877 saw some forty or fifty.[15] Superficially, this looks like a new golden age for professional baseball. The reality was different. Most of these were old clubs, which had been only nominally amateur. The NA had claimed to comprise all professional clubs, with all professional clubs competing for the national championship. Any club, therefore, that chose not to join the NA was by definition classified as amateur, regardless of the reality of paying players. The NL, being a closed organization, made no claim to comprise all professional clubs. This opened up the possibility of unaffiliated professional clubs. Developments in 1876 occurred too fast for clubs to take advantage of this, but going into the 1877 season clubs felt free to drop the pretense of amateurism.

This raised the question of how non-NL clubs would be organized, if at all. L.C. Waite, secretary of the Red Stocking club of St. Louis, circulated a letter dated September 23, 1876, to the various "non-League baseball clubs" to form an association.[16] This would result in the International Association (IA—the "International" part reflecting its two Canadian members). Its main purpose was to prevent its members from poaching players under contract to another member. It also organized a championship, but with the key difference from either the old NA or the NL that participation in the pennant race was optional. A club could join the IA to protect its player contracts without incurring the expense of long-distance travel.

The mere existence of the IA presented a potential threat to NL hegemony. Exactly what form of threat requires skeptical scrutiny. Modern writers often present it as a direct challenger to major league status, like the upstart major leagues of later decades. They frequently point to IA clubs' success against NL clubs in exhibition games. This misses the point. Later baseball history is filled with examples of major league clubs losing exhibition games to semi-pro teams. This doesn't tell us those semi-pro teams were better, but that the major league clubs weren't trying, often playing backups, particularly in the pitcher's position. The

George Wright became baseball's first holdout when he was reserved by Providence and refused to sign.

HERITAGE AUCTIONS

major league club had nothing to lose. A victory would give the semi-pro club, on the other hand, collective prestige, and in the era before scouts these games served as tryouts for the individual players. Under such circumstances it is not surprising that the lesser club might win the game.

This was no mystery at the time, but the IA victories were publicized by Henry Chadwick, the foremost baseball reporter of the day. This mostly reflects Chadwick's priorities. He had been cut out from the information loop when the NL formed. It took him a few years to get over the slight, and in the meantime used his bully pulpit to criticize the NL at every chance. Modern writers have taken Chadwick's peeving at face value and concluded that the IA was a direct challenger to the NL. In reality its clubs mostly occupied second- and third-tier cities. Its best clubs often were tapped to fill vacancies in the NL, and almost always turned out to be tail-enders.[17]

The NL saw the IA as a threat, not to the NL's superiority on the field, but to the NL's hegemony. Were it to prove able to act collectively, it might be able to protect its player contracts against NL incursions and demand better terms for exhibition games.

The NL's first response was to organize a competing organization, the League Alliance (LA). It promised the same protections as did the IA, with the added benefit of the NL's promise to respect LA clubs' player contracts, as well as the more questionable "benefit" of authorizing the NL to resolve any disputes. It also included a pennant race, but with the twist that it was determined strictly by wins in games between LA clubs, with no schedule. The individual clubs arranged as many or as few games as they saw fit.[18] This gambit was partially successful, attracting most of the western clubs, while the IA was largely an eastern organization.

The LA in this form lasted only the season of 1877. The economy hit the LA clubs hard. Many folded, and those that survived did not bother to rejoin for 1878. The IA was also hit by the economy, but continued with fewer clubs. The NL devised a new gambit to play against the IA: divide and conquer. It imposed onerous conditions for exhibition games, then offered more favorable terms to select clubs. These terms were eagerly accepted, the IA lacking the cohesion to act for the common good.[19] It was further reduced in 1879, and no longer having any Canadian clubs was renamed the National Association. 1880 was its last season, down to just two clubs by season's end, the Rochester Club and the Nationals of Washington.

Midsummer of 1880 was the nadir of professional baseball. That August the Rochesters and Nationals played a series of games in Brooklyn. This was an act of desperation. Professional baseball was known to be thoroughly dead in the metropolis, killed off by a combination of the economy and the corrupt baseball establishment of earlier years. It was a surprise when respectable paying crowds turned out for the games. This led to the hurried formation of new clubs, formed by old players who had been laid off.

The most important of these was styled the Metropolitans. It was backed by John B. Day, a local cigar manufacturer who had been involved in amateur baseball. It was managed by James Mutrie, who had been kicking around minor clubs for several years. Day sublet a playing ground from the Manhattan Polo Association. The first game on the Polo Grounds, and in fact the first professional game played on the island of Manhattan, took place September 29, 1880, between the Metropolitans and the Nationals.[20]

The success of these late-season games led to a burst of baseball activity in 1881. The Eastern Championship Association formed with clubs from Washington to Albany, the Metropolitans taking the pennant easily, with only a reformed Athletic Club of Philadelphia as serious competition. Independent clubs played in the west, the most important in Cincinnati and St. Louis. This was the setting for the creation of the American Association in the fall.

THE COMING OF THE AMERICAN ASSOCIATION

The idea of a new association was in the air: not merely a regional association, but one of national scope. This association would be a true rival to the NL. Early canvassing started in August, when Horace Phillips and Charles Mason of the Athletics of Philadelphia journeyed west "on business appertaining to the club both for this and next season."[21] A report in September listed the prospective members as St. Louis, Louisville, Philadelphia, Baltimore, Washington, Cincinnati, Pittsburgh, and New York.[22] New York and Washington would not, in the end, be in the new league, but the list would prove otherwise accurate. These early efforts culminated in a preliminary meeting in Pittsburgh on October 10 with John Day of the Metropolitans elected president.[23]

The American Association was formally organized at a meeting in Cincinnati held over two days, November 2 and 3, 1881. Delegates were present from Cincinnati, St. Louis, Louisville, Pittsburgh, Philadelphia, Boston, Brooklyn, and New York. Two developments beyond the act of organizing would prove critical.

The AA considered the question of eligibility of players expelled by the NL. They finally adopted a resolution

A.G. SPALDING COLLECTION, NEW YORK PUBLIC LIBRARY

Charley Jones. His expulsion by the Boston Club was the prime example of the National League's abuse of power.

that "they would always refuse to hire players expelled by the League for drunkenness, dishonesty or any venal offense, and believed that that body should similarly act toward their black sheep..." This language was crafted to allow for the Cincinnati club to sign local favorite Charley Jones, which it promptly did.[24]

The second development was the inaction of the New York delegation, represented by James Mutrie, manager of the Metropolitans, and W.S. Appleton, one of the club's financial backers. They encouraged the new organization, but declined to join it at that time. Immediately after the meeting they took a train to Chicago and conferred with NL President William Hulbert. Hulbert told them that the Jones matter would prevent harmonious relations between the two organizations. The Metropolitans had made a lot of money the previous season playing games with NL clubs. This would not be possible if they joined the AA. In light of later events, we can also read between the lines and speculate that Hulbert promised a NL franchise when one next came available. In any event, the Metropolitans announced that they were not joining the new AA after all.[25]

In the event, the AA ended up backing off its policy on NL expelled players. It voted at its meeting in March to prohibit the hiring of any player blacklisted by the NL, forcing Cincinnati to default on the Jones contract. This allowed for spring exhibition games between the two leagues, cynics entirely reasonably suspecting this to be the reason for the change of heart.[26] At the same time Baltimore replaced Brooklyn, where the financing had failed to materialize. Nothing had ever come of the Boston membership, resulting in a six-team circuit: St. Louis, Louisville, Cincinnati, Pittsburgh, Philadelphia, and Baltimore.

The spring exhibition games proved a mixed blessing to the AA. While the revenue was important, the new league was embarrassed by an unbroken string of defeats at the hands of the senior circuit. While exhibition games generally are not a good indicator of relative strength, this applies more to a weaker side defeating a stronger one, the question being how hard the stronger side was trying. An unbroken string of victories by the presumed stronger league is especially embarrassing, suggesting that the stronger won effortlessly.

BASEBALL CONTRACTS AND THE LAW

The AA had made concessions about signing players on the NL blacklist. The NL did not return the favor. Its clubs poached several players already signed by AA clubs. The NL took the position of reserving the right to simply refuse to recognize the existence of the AA clubs. This was an expression of "baseball law," unencumbered by the niceties of civil law. NL President Hulbert made this explicit in correspondence with Denny McKnight, the AA president, regarding the case of John "Dasher" Troy. Troy had signed with the AA Athletics before accepting a higher offer from the NL Detroit club. When McKnight protested, Hulbert responded:

> For years the League has proffered the use of its machinery for the recording and enforcement of players' contract to any and all Ball Clubs that chose to avail themselves of the conditions offered. Annually we have published in our book the form of agreement to be signed by Clubs that desired to avail themselves of the privilege. Not the slightest trouble has ever arisen between any League Club and League Alliance Club. ... John Troy, by all our laws, is a player under contract with the Detroit Club, and no Club on earth can inflict any penalty on John Troy that the Chicago or any other Club in the League will recognize except it be inflicted by the Detroit Club or by the League.[27]

The AA, rather than endangering the spring exhibition season by expelling these players, determined instead to attempt to enforce the AA contracts through the civil courts, taking as their test case Sam Wise, originally signed by AA Cincinnati and then by NL Boston. This would be the first of a series of such cases stretching into the twentieth century. It would, like most of its successors, fail.

The legal point is that a court, under English and American law, cannot force someone to fulfill a contract. In legal language, this is "specific performance." There are some exceptions to this principle, but contracts for personal service, such as to play baseball, clearly are not among them. The club need not pay the non-performing player, of course, but the court cannot force the player to play against his will.

This principle was well established and widely understood. The hope for the AA was not to force Wise to return to Cincinnati, but to prevent him from playing for Boston. There was an English case from 1852 in which a singer jumped a contract to sing at one theater after receiving a better offer from another. The court could not force her to sing at the first theater, but it issued an injunction restraining her from singing at the second.[28]

This hope proved futile, though the precise reason is unclear. The first round was in federal court, the court ultimately ruling in May that it lacked jurisdiction on technical grounds and this was a state matter. The matter was then moved to Massachusetts state court. A hearing was scheduled for June 5, but it never took place. Furthermore, the baseball press—after having followed the case closely—quietly dropped the matter. The usual explanation for litigation being quietly dropped before a hearing is that the parties have settled. This clearly was not what happened here. Rather, the Cincinnati Club expelled Wise two months later.[29] What happened in the meantime? This is not reported. Perhaps the AA balked at the growing legal expenses. Perhaps it received legal advice that it would probably lose the case (as indeed it almost certainly would have, judging from the outcomes of later cases making similar arguments).

There was a second go-round in the fall, the player in question this time being Charlie Bennett. He had played the 1882 season for NL Detroit, then in August agreed to sign a contract for 1883 with the AA Pittsburgh Allegheny Club, receiving $100 in advance money. Before signing the formal contract he jumped back to Detroit. The Allegheny Club sued him in federal court and lost on multiple grounds.[30]

The Wise and Bennett cases wouldn't completely discourage clubs from turning to the courts to enforce player contracts. While these cases didn't establish a precedent in the legal sense of the word, they set the pattern. Only rarely would the legal strategy prove effective.

THE AA AND NL SEASON OF 1882

The AA's actions in August, one of expelling Wise and the second of signing Bennett, constituted a declaration of war with the NL. The only alternative for the AA would have been to accept an inferior status, with whatever protection of player contracts the NL was willing to grant it. This was really no choice at all, so long as the AA had the ability to fight.

The AA was indeed able to fight, because the 1882 season had succeeded beyond all expectation. This is not merely an expression, but the literal truth. This is shown by the Cincinnati Club ownership question. A syndicate had been formed the previous summer to revive the sport in Cincinnati. Its documentation was, from a legal draftsmanship perspective, slapdash to the point of incoherence. This is not the act of businessmen expecting to turn a profit. Indeed, a cynic might suspect that they expected to lose money, and were entirely satisfied by vague personal responsibility for any debts. This changed when it became apparent that the club was going to turn a profit worth fighting over. It took two lawsuits for the courts to sort out the mess.[31]

The AA did very well. Exactly how well is hard to say. One report claimed profits ranging from $25,000 for St. Louis (saying that most of it was in beer sales) down to $5,000 in Baltimore. These numbers probably should not be taken too seriously.[32] By way of comparison, and more likely to be accurate, the NL Worcester Club is said to have been slightly in the red, Boston about $4,000 in the black, and an actual financial statement from the Buffalo Club showed a profit of just under $4,000.[33]

While these numbers, especially the claims for AA profits, should not be taken as reliable, it is difficult to do better. On the revenue side, there are estimated attendance numbers, but they are even less reliable than their modern counterparts, and are difficult to convert to revenue. The NL charged fifty cents for general admission, while the AA charged only twenty-five cents. This does not mean, however, than the AA only got half per person. Both leagues charged an extra twenty-five cents for seating in the grandstand. Even with reliable attendance numbers, we don't know how many fans paid for premium seating.[34] Furthermore, the AA sold alcohol at games—the source of the "Beer and Whiskey League" nickname beloved of modern writers—while the NL did not, giving the AA an additional revenue source.[35]

On the NL side, finances were not quite so rosy. The rising tide of the economy lifted all boats, but the NL was not designed to receive the full benefit. It was laid out to minimize travel expenses, not to maximize revenue. The irony was that the improving economy of 1881 allowed Troy and Worcester, the NL's weak sisters, to survive to play in 1882. This was the first time in the NL's history that it fielded the same teams from one year to the next. Ordinarily one would take this as a sign of fiscal health, but here it meant that a quarter of the league wasn't carrying its weight.

On the expenditure side, the AA again came out ahead. The previous year most of its players had been working day jobs while perhaps bringing in a bit on the side playing semi-pro ball. They were thrilled to be playing ball full time, and didn't quibble over salaries. AA owners in later years looked back wistfully at the payrolls of 1882. But that was later. In 1882, the AA clubs benefitted from low salaries. The NL had the better players—players who had been negotiating their salaries upward for several years.

The upshot is that while we don't know the true state of league finances, the AA did well enough that by August the AA owners found themselves in a position to fight. The Wise expulsion meant that postseason exhibition games were off the table. The Cincinnati Club, upon winning the AA pennant, arranged a series with NL clubs under the pretense that the club had actually disbanded and the players had been hired by an unnamed local businessman. Only four games were played, two with Cleveland and two with Chicago, splitting the results with each. The Cincinnati victories were the only games that year where an AA club defeated an NL club. The rest of the AA was unimpressed, and told the Cincinnati Club to end the games or be expelled.[36]

The NL realized that Troy and Worcester were no longer sustainable as league members, at least to the rest of the league. The league took the straightforward action of expelling both in a special meeting held September 22, adopting a resolution by a vote of 6 to 2 "declaring it the sense of the meeting that these clubs be not represented in the association next season." This was in spite of neither club having violated any NL rule. Both complained, murmuring about taking legal action, but the writing was on the wall and both ended up submitting their resignations at the NL annual meeting on December 6.[37]

The NL now had two openings, which it used to good effect. New York and Philadelphia were the obvious locations to fill the slots. John Day's Metropolitans filled the New York need. Alfred Reach, a former player turned sporting goods manufacturer who had fielded a Phillies team in 1882, took the second slot. Applications from both were received at the December meeting and promptly accepted.[38]

John Day of the Metropolitans then managed the neat trick of obtaining an AA franchise to go along with his NL franchise (the AA expanding to eight clubs, also adding Columbus, Ohio). Both leagues needed to enter the New York market. Day's was by far the most established organization there, so both leagues wanted

him. This put Day in the position to accept both offers. This, however, meant that he had two franchises with only one team. His solution was to sign the Troy players *en masse*, throwing all his players into one pool, and divvying them up again between his two franchises, the AA franchise ending up with the Metropolitan name. This is the source of the modern claim that the NL New York Club (eventually known as the Giants) was a transfer from Troy, and by the process of elimination the Phillies from Worcester. This would imply some compensation for the Troy and Worcester owners. They in fact received no such consideration.

THE PEACE SETTLEMENT

The AA's newfound bellicosity, and their obvious ability to back it up, forced the NL to take them seriously. At the same time, the interests of both sides were for peace, especially with the potentially awkward New York situation, with its dual franchises under one ownership. Into this budding potential for peace stepped the newly formed Northwestern League. It had no desire to get involved in a fight with anybody, and so invited both leagues to meet with it to negotiate an agreement. The presence of an outside party might have had a calming influence. In any case, the NL made the overture, proposing a peace conference, which the AA accepted after much discussion—in the end only St. Louis voting for war.[39]

There were three major points of dispute: the sanctity of player contracts, the NL's blacklist, and the reserve system. With everyone wanting peace, these proved susceptible to amicable resolution. The result was the first National Agreement, often called the Tripartite Agreement with the inclusion of the Northwestern League. This was the first of a series of such agreements that continue to today. Each party to the agreement agreed to respect the others' player contracts. The NL reinstated the players on its blacklist except for those who had thrown games. The reserve was not only expanded to all three leagues, but expanded from five to eleven players per club—nearly the entire roster. This was a sticking point for the AA, as it would preserve the NL's superiority on the playing field, but it was non-negotiable for the NL and the AA eventually came around. It also guaranteed member clubs exclusive territorial rights, apart from the fait accompli of shared territory in New York and Philadelphia. And so the first baseball war was over.[40]

ERRORS AND OMISSIONS

No war is perfectly fought. Both the American Association and the National League made missteps. New

York was the biggest prize. Either side might have had it to themselves, had they played their hand better.

On the AA side, they wavered over signing players on the NL's blacklist, and Charley Jones in particular. It is entirely possible that New York would have joined the AA for 1882, had it not been scared off by the prospect of losing lucrative games with NL clubs. Had the AA early on declared the NL's blacklisted players off limits, there would have been no barrier to these games. That they later reversed themselves showed indecision. Had the Metropolitans joined the AA for 1882 they likely would have done very well and taken a leadership role against the NL, blocking it from the New York market and possibly resulting in a very different later history of baseball.

On the NL side, they too could have had New York in 1882, and possibly Philadelphia as well. The Troy and Worcester problem was readily apparent in the fall of 1881. The correct move would have been to expel them then and invite Day and Reach to join the NL for 1882. This was before the AA was yet a fact, and the NL was the established and prestigious organization. Both Day and Reach would almost certainly have taken the opportunity. This would have blocked the AA entirely from New York, and even if it did not discourage the AA Athletics from even trying, it would have given the NL Philadelphia club a head start. (In the event, the Athletics would win the 1883 AA pennant, while the NL Phillies finished in eighth place, 46 games behind Boston. The net result was to firm up the Athletics' fan base.)

Why didn't the National League do this? There are two explanations frequently given. The first, which seems to be modern, is that William Hulbert, president of both the NL and the Chicago Club, had a grudge against the cities of New York and Philadelphia going back to 1876, when their respective clubs failed to complete the season. This explanation is highly unlikely. It makes Hulbert out to be petty and vindictive, and prepared to let these outweigh good business sense. He was cutthroat and ethically challenged, but not petty, and certainly not a bad businessman.

The second explanation has the benefit of coming from Hulbert himself. He gave an interview in July 1881 to a reporter about the prospects for 1882. The question of expelling Troy and Worcester in favor of New York and Philadelphia was discussed:

As one member of the League, he would never consent to any course toward any member of the body, no matter how weak, looking to securing its withdrawal, in order to let in any other organization, however strong, or however much it may promise in the way of patronage of the game. The present members, who had helped to build up and make the League the success that it is, had rights in it, and, as long as they did not see fit to withdraw from it, he would vote to retain them to the exclusion of all others. Whether all the eight would elect to remain in next year he did not know. If one of them, or two of them, should drop out, there would be so many places to be filled from the most available materials at hand; if not, he did not see any chance for outside applications.[41]

The problem with this explanation is that it is obvious nonsense. The NL under Hulbert had a history of kicking out member clubs to improve the circuit, and had never had any qualms about niceties such as its own rules, much less the club's wishes. The most egregious was the Milwaukee Club after the 1878 season. The NL constitution at that time included a provision requiring a club to pay its players or be subject to expulsion. The Milwaukee Club ended the season with outstanding debts to some of its vendors, but its players were paid in full. Hulbert simply ignored the actual rule, pretending it said something it did not. Then following the 1880 season the NL made a new rule against liquor sales and expelled the Cincinnati Club (ignoring the procedures for this in the NL constitution) when it refused to agree. The idea that Hulbert and the other NL owners were so committed to high ideals as to sacrifice their own interests for the benefit of one of their members is simply untenable. Indeed, it would have been trivially easy to expel Troy and Worcester. The NL constitution required member clubs to be in cities of not less than 75,000 population, except by unanimous vote. Troy and Worcester were both well below that limit. The NL could simply have discovered a newfound commitment to that rule.

Why didn't they? Hulbert was ill, and would die in April of 1882. This suggests the likely explanation is that he was off his game, and the rest of the NL followed along. Had he full command of his powers he would have foreseen what needed to be done and would have done it without hesitation. As it was, he had a moment of inattention and the moment passed.

CONCLUSION: WHAT IS A MAJOR LEAGUE?

Why did the American Association succeed? Of course it didn't, in the long run, but in 1882 it was a resounding success. To explain this we turn to an apparently unrelated question: What is a major league? Most people would answer this with something along the lines that a major league is one playing at the highest competitive level. A league is major because it is good. This presents a paradox. The AA was a major league. It forced the NL to treat it as an equal. It is recognized as a major league by modern Major League Baseball, and this assessment rarely arouses controversy. Yet the AA in 1882 manifestly was not playing at the highest level. The humiliating exhibition games with the NL show this. The NL's superiority is unsurprising. The NL, after all, had already picked its players before the AA starting hiring. NL managers were every bit as capable as AA managers at spotting talent. It is to be expected that the NL had the cream of the crop. The AA got better over the course of the decade, but this doesn't answer how we justify classifying it as major in 1882. One fallback is that its major status is backdated from when it was actually good. The problem with this is that the American League of 1900 and the Federal League of 1913 are both classified as minor, then the following year as major. Why is the American Association not treated the same way?

We should instead regard major and minor status from a structural perspective. Organized baseball is a hierarchy of leagues, with one or more major leagues at the top and a descending ladder of minor leagues. Players move up the ladder according to their abilities, the best making their way to the majors. Why do the minor leagues allow their best players to leave? It is easy to take this for granted in the modern farm system, with major and minor league teams formally affiliating and with the major affiliate having complete control of all the players. But the movement of players is older than the farm system. So why were minor league teams willing to give up their best players?

The answer is brute financial force. Player contracts were not, as we have seen, legally enforceable. A major league team could simply offer the player more money. The minor leagues therefore took the best deal they could get, which the major leagues offered so as to maintain the flock of sheep to be fleeced. The majors could offer players more money because, in turn, they were located in larger markets and therefore had more revenue. A major league is one controlling major markets. This is why they have fiercely defended their territorial rights throughout the history of organized baseball.[42] In other words, a league is not major because it is good. It is good because it is major. The system guarantees this. A league is major because it has the finances to act as a major league. This forces

other leagues to respond to it, whether in peace or war, as a major league.

The system of major and minor leagues was not yet formed in 1882. The Tripartite Agreement is the founding document of the system, and also demonstrates its undeveloped state. The Northwestern League's minor status is implied in the enactment of the reserve rule, which included a minimum salary for reserved players. This was not out of concern for the player's wallet, but to prevent a team from stockpiling players it wasn't actually paying. The AA and NL minimum was $1,000, while the Northwestern League minimum was $750. It was understood that the minor league would pay lower salaries. At the same time, the Northwestern League was a full signatory to the agreement and enjoyed full protections, as if it were of equal stature. This was not out of any great respect for the Northwestern League but rather a sign that the logic of the system had not yet been worked out, and in any case the AA and NL were not, in 1883, in direct competition with the Northwestern League for rising players. In any event, the national agreement would be renegotiated three years later, by which time the Northwestern League was defunct and the newer minor leagues were excluded.

This brings us to the explanation for the American Association's success, and spectacular success at that. The NL had abandoned the southern tier of major cities. This gave the nascent AA the opening to move in unopposed. Its control of major-league cities gave it the financial wherewithal to demand equal status with the National League. This was a nearly unique moment in baseball history. The only time like it would be 1900, after the NL reduced from twelve to eight clubs, abandoning both markets and players for the American League to snap up. It is no coincidence that the American League would become the only other successful new major league.

The AA would last ten years. The two major leagues merged following the 1891 season, with the AA the decidedly junior partner. This gives the AA the stench of failure. Why this came about is a topic for another day. In the meantime, we should not let later events obscure the triumph of the American Association of 1882 in the first baseball war. ■

Notes

1. The exception was the Players League of 1890, which sought to overturn the system entirely. Other challengers often used similar rhetoric, particularly with regard to the reserve clause, but showed little sign of meaning this seriously.
2. "Ball Talk," *New York Clipper*, January 19, 1878.
3. "The League Meeting," *Cincinnati Enquirer*, October 1, 1881.

4. "The League Convention of 1878," *New York Clipper*, December 14, 1878.

5. "Expelling Players," *New York Clipper*, August 24, 1878; "The League Meeting" October 11, 1879.

6. "The Jones Case," *New York Clipper*, September 18, 1880; "Jones Sues the Boston Club," Boston Herald, May 15, 1881.

7. "Baseball," *New York Clipper*, June 4, 1881, July 2, 1881; "Base Ball Notes," *Boston Journal*, October 11, 1881.

8. "The International Association forbids the engagement of any player who has been expelled from any association, while the League declines to recognize any other association, and allows any of its clubs to engage a player who has been expelled from the Internationals, or any other association." "Notes and Gossip," *New York Sunday Mercury*, March 10, 1878.

9. "A St. Louis Revolver," *New York Clipper*, August 19, 1876; "Expulsion of a Player" August 26, 1876.

10. "The Professional Arena," *New York Sunday Mercury*, January 7, 1877.

11. "Mr. Spalding's Plan," *Chicago Tribune*, January 21, 1877.

12. "Grading Professional Salaries," *New York Clipper*, April 20, 1878; " Meeting of the National League at Providence Yesterday," *New York Sunday Mercury*, August 11, 1878.

13. "Baseball Notes," *New York Clipper*, October 18, 1879

14. "George Wright's Wrongs," *Cincinnati Enquirer*, March 28, 1880; "The Wright Case," *Chicago Tribune*, April 4, 1880. Some modern writers repeat a claim that players considered being reserved an honor, reflecting praise upon their skill. This was a piece of League propaganda, repeated today by the credulous.

15. The exact number is somewhat arbitrary, as the line between fully professional and semi-professional clubs was loosely defined. *Spalding's Base Ball Guide* for 1878, pages 33–39, lists 33 professional clubs, plus the six in the NL and an additional 14 clubs "employing part of all of their players."

16. "A New Movement Out West," *New York Clipper*, October 21, 1876.

17. See, for example, Harold Seymour, *Baseball: The Early Years* (New York, Oxford University Press, 1960) in which chapter 9, on the IA, is titled "The First Outside Threat." The exception to IA clubs doing poorly in the NL is the 1878 IA Buffalo club, which went 46-32 to place third in the NL in 1879.

18. The 1877 LA pennant winner was the Red Caps of St. Paul. This raises an intriguing possible explanation for the widespread but entirely baseless claim that the Boston club was known as the Red Caps. Boston won the 1877 NL pennant. Perhaps some later writer confused the LA and NL pennants and mistakenly attributed "Red Caps" to Boston.

19. "The National League at Buffalo," *New York Sunday Mercury*, April 7, 1878; "The Buffalo Conference," *New York Clipper*, April 13, 1878.

20. "September 29, 1880: Metropolitan club opens new Polo Grounds with a win" https://sabr.org/gamesproj/game/september-29-1880-metropolitan-club-opens-new-polo-grounds-win.

21. "Defeated by the Trojans," *Philadelphia Times*, August 12, 1881.

22. "A New Association," *Cincinnati Enquirer*, September 12, 1881.

23. There is a widely told amusing story that when few clubs turned up for an initial meeting, Horace Phillips sent telegrams to the others reporting the meeting a huge success, with everyone present except the telegram's recipient and offering the chance to correct this omission at the next meeting. Some version of this story might be true, but it is significant that its earliest known publication is from 1884, and in this version it is Justus Thorner of Cincinnati who sent the telegrams, with Phillips not present at all. "The American Association: Who Was the Originator?— A Bit of History," *Sporting Life*, June 25, 1884.

24. "The First 24 Run," *Cincinnati Enquirer*, November 4, 1881.

25. "Sporting Events," *Chicago Tribune*, November 6, 1881.

26. "Sporting Matters," *Cincinnati Enquirer*, March 14, 1882.

27. "Hulbert's Hobby," *Cincinnati Enquirer*, January 1, 1882. The claimed perfect relations with League Alliance clubs is disingenuous. The NL expelled the Nationals of Washington from the LA after the 1880 season, and divided the desirable players among the NL clubs.

28. Lumley v. Wagner, 42 Eng.Rep. 687 (1852). It was unremarkable for American courts to look to English precedents.

29. "Crushed Again," *Cincinnati Commercial*, May 13, 1882; "Heavy Hitting," *Boston Herald*, May 17,1882; "Base Ball," *Cincinnati Commercial*, June 4, 1882; "Base Ball," *Cincinnati Commercial*, August 5, 1882.

30. Allegheny Base-Ball Club v. Bennett 14 F. 257 (C.C.W.D.Pa. 1882). This case is more widely known than the Wise case, with a hearing resulting in an opinion on the substance, reported in legal reports. It is nonetheless widely misunderstood, with many modern writers, including many who should know better, confusing its issues with the unrelated reserve clause. See, for example, Richard L. Irwin, "A Historical Review of Litigation in Baseball." Marquette Sports Law Review 1, no. 2 (1991): 283–300. Irwin describes the case as "The earliest litigation regarding the reserve clause..."

31. For the initial formation, see "Clapps Detective Agency," *Cincinnati Enquirer*, June 16, 1881; and "Base Ball," *Cincinnati Enquirer*, June 24, 1881. For the lawsuits, see "John R. Mclean vs. O. P. Caylor" *Cincinnati Gazette* July 15, 1882; "Base Ballists at Outs," *Cincinnati Commercial*, September 28, 1882; "Honors Easy," *Cincinnati Commercial*, October 8, 1882; "The Courts," *Cincinnati Commercial*, December 3, 1882: and "Base Ball," *Cincinnati Commercial*, December 31, 1882.

32. "Battles at the Bats," *Philadelphia Times*, September 3, 1882.

33. "Base Ball," *New York Clipper*, October 7, 1882; "The Boston Club," *New York Clipper*, December 30, 1882; "Base Ball," *Cincinnati Enquirer*, December 24, 1882.

34. Scattered reports over the 1880s stating the number of people in the grandstand suggest that a reasonable approximation of average gate receipts per fan in the AA was about 5/8 that in the NL.

35. The NL Cincinnati Club prior to the 1880 season s 35 old the refreshment "privilege" (i.e. concession) for $2,000. "Base Ball," *Cincinnati Enquirer*, January 25, 1880. How much this would be, were alcohol not included, is unknown. So too is the profit the concessionaire made, though presumably it was enough to be worth his while. It is reasonable to estimate that alcohol sales to the larger crowds of 1882 resulted in several thousand dollars of profit per club, some clubs splitting this with a concessionaire and some selling alcohol directly.

36. "It Ended Well," *Cincinnati Commercial*, September 24, 1882; "Base Ball," *New York Clipper*, October 7, 1882.

37. "The Late League Meeting," *New York Clipper*, September 30, 1882; National League minutes for the special meeting held September 22, 1882, and the annual meeting held December 6, 1882: *Constitution and Playing Rules of the National League of Professional Base Ball Clubs*. Chicago, 1882. The minutes for the special meeting do not include the resolution, suggesting that it was unofficial, but no less effective for it.

38. National League minutes for the annual meeting held December 6, 1882: *Constitution and Playing Rules of the National League of Professional Base Ball Clubs*. Chicago, 1882. A letter from Day dated September 22, 1882, applying for membership was sold at auction by Christies in 2016. Persistent reports claim that Reach was less eager to join the NL, preferring to field an independent team, but was persuaded that an NL franchise was going to be placed in Philadelphia with or without him, for which see "Seven Straights," *Cincinnati Enquirer*, September 28, 1882.

39. "The American Association Convention," *New York Clipper*, December 16, 1882; "The League Convention," *New York Clipper*, December 16, 1882; Cincinnati Commercial December 17, 1882.

40. "The Work of the Conference," *New York Clipper*, February 24, 1883.

41. "League Figures," *Cincinnati Enquirer*, July 11, 1881.

42. Compare this with the English system pioneered by the Football Association, which lacks territorial rights and includes promotion and relegation of clubs. The combination of territorial and league franchise rights is inherent in the American system.

Contributors

RON BACKER is an attorney who is an avid fan of both movies and baseball. He has written five books on film, his most recent being *Baseball Goes to the Movies*, published in 2017 by Applause Theatre & Cinema Books. A long-suffering Pirates fan, Backer lives in Pittsburgh, Pennsylvania. Feedback is welcome at: rbacker332@aol.com.

ALAN COHEN has been a SABR member since 2010, and his first *Baseball Research Journal* article appeared in 2013. He serves as Vice President-Treasurer of the Connecticut Smoky Joe Wood Chapter and is datacaster (MiLB First Pitch stringer) for the Hartford Yard Goats, the Double-A affiliate of the Colorado Rockies. His biographies, game stories and essays have appeared in more than 40 SABR publications. Alan has contributed stories on Black baseball to several SABR books and has continued to expand his research into the Hearst Sandlot Classic (1946–65) from which 88 players advanced to the major leagues. He has four children and eight grandchildren and resides in Connecticut with wife Frances, their cats Morty, Ava, and Zoe, and their dog Buddy.

EVAN L. FREDERICK, PH.D., is an Associate Professor of Sport Administration at the University of Louisville. His research interest is the intersection of sport and social media. He currently serves as the Vice-Chair for the Association for Communication and Sport.

DR. DAVID J. GORDON is a retired NIH epidemiologist, who specialized in the conduct and analysis of cardiovascular clinical trials. Since his retirement in 2016, he has pivoted to his longtime love of baseball, writing articles for the *Baseball Research Journal* on the Deadball era, racial parity in the Hall of Fame, and the impact of free agency on competitive balance and a soon-to-be-published book called *Baseball Generations*. Dr. Gordon is currently working on a book, based on his NIH experience, analyzing the causes of the 80% decline in heart attack deaths in the US since the 1960s.

RICHARD HERSHBERGER is a paralegal in Maryland and the author of the book *Strike Four: The Evolution of Baseball*. He has written numerous articles on early baseball, concentrating on its origins and its organizational history. He is a member of the SABR Nineteenth Century and Origins committees. Reach him at rrhersh@yahoo.com.

MARY A. HUMS, PH.D. is a Professor of Sport Administration at the University of Louisville. A North American Society for Sport Management Ziegler Lecturer and Diversity Award recipient, her research interest is policy development in sport organizations, especially regarding inclusion of people with disabilities and also sport and human rights. Email: mary.hums@louisville.edu Twitter: @mahums

HERM KRABBENHOFT, a SABR member since 1981, began the research described in his "Double-Duty Diamondeers" article more than 60 years ago—in 1957 for a sixth-grade term paper addressing a claim that minor league pitchers were better hitters than major league pitchers. At that time, he wrote to Commissioner Ford Frick asking for some relevant information. Mr. Frick kindly sent him a complimentary copy of the 1956 edition of the TSN *Baseball Guide*, which Herm still has and uses.

WILL MELVILLE joined SABR in March of 2020. He was an applied and computational mathematics undergraduate student at Brigham Young University when this paper was being written. He graduated in April 2020 and is now pursuing a career in baseball R&D as an intern with the Tampa Bay Rays.

IRWIN NAHINSKY is professor emeritus at the University of Louisville, where he taught cognitive psychology and advanced statistics until his retirement in 1993. His prior effort in SABRmetrics was an article in Perceptual and Motor Skills in 1994 demonstrating a significant tendency for teams to bounce back after a loss in the World Series. He holds a Bachelor of Arts degree and a Ph.D. degree, both in psychology, from the University of Minnesota. He has been a SABR member since 2010. He lives in Louisville but remains a loyal Twins fan.

BILL NOWLIN still lives in the same Cambridge, Massachusetts house he was in when he joined SABR in the last century. He's been active both in the Boston Chapter and nationally, a member of the Board of Directors since 2004 (a good year for Red Sox fans). He has written several hundred bios and game accounts, and helped edit a good number of SABR's books.

ANN PEGORARO, PH.D. is the Lang Chair in Sport Management at the University of Guelph and the co-director of the EAlliance— a National Network for Gender Equity in Canadian Sport. Her recent research in digital media focuses on gender and diversity.

CHARLIE PAVITT has been a SABR member since 1983 and contributing to the Statistical Analysis Research Committee since then. His retirement after 31 years as a professor allows him more time to spend on sabermetric research. The completed chapters of his book reviewing the sabermetric literature can be found at https://charliepavitt.home.blog/; the rest of the book is in progress. He is happy to be contacted at chazzq@udel.edu.

RANDY S. ROBBINS is a Philadelphia-area native who grew up a Big Red Machine fan before eventually converting to the hometown nine. He is obsessive about the game though he doesn't much care for the recent turns baseball has taken. He worked as an editor in the medical and pharmaceutical fields for nearly 30 years and his own articles and op-eds (both sports- and non-sports-related, humorous and serious) have been published in numerous newspapers, magazines, and websites over the years. Despite once having driven Henry Aaron in his car, he considers his greatest moment in baseball to be the time a 60-something, Brooklyn-born umpire in a men's league game, while observing him scooping low throws at first base between innings, told him he was reminded of Gil Hodges.

NINA SIEGFRIED is a University Fellow and Ph.D. student in the Sport Administration Program at the University of Louisville where she previously completed her M.S. on a Fulbright Scholarship. Her main research areas focus on establishing and maintaining sport partnerships in parasports and also developing successful adaptive sports programs.

STEW THORNLEY has been researching Minnesota baseball history for more than 40 years. His first book, *On to Nicollet: The Glory and Fame of the Minneapolis Millers*, covered the history of baseball in Minneapolis. He has been a SABR member since 1979. Stew is an official scorer for Major League Baseball and is a member of the MLB Official Scoring Advisory Committee.

THEO TOBEL is a sophomore at Santa Monica High School, where he pitches and plays middle infield on the baseball team. In his spare time, Theo enjoys watching Dodger baseball and collecting baseball cards. He combines his love for baseball and mathematics by studying baseball analytics. Theo can be reached at theotobel@yahoo.com.

HOWARD M. WASSERMAN is Professor of Law and Associate Dean for Research and Faculty Development at FIU College of Law, where he has taught since 2003. His research focuses on civil rights litigation, freedom of speech, and baseball rules. His baseball writing includes *Infield Fly Rule Is in Effect: The History and Strategy of Baseball's Most (In)Famous Rule* (Durham: McFarland Press 2019); "Against Stealing First Base," *NINE: Journal of Baseball History and Culture* (forthcoming 2020); "Sport and Expression, Sport as Expression," *FIU Law Review* (forthcoming 2020); "When They Were Kings: Greenberg and Koufax Sit on Yom Kippur," *Tablet Magazine* (2016); and "If You Build it, They Will Speak: Public Stadiums, Public Forums, and Free Speech," 14 *NINE: Journal of Baseball History and Culture* 15 (2006).

ELI A. WOLFF directs the Power of Sport Lab, and co-founded Disability in Sport International and Athletes for Human Rights. His work highlights the intersection of research, education and advocacy in and through sport, with a focus on sport and social justice, diversity, disability and inclusion.

BRINLEY ZABRISKIE, Ph.D., is an assistant professor in the Department of Statistics at Brigham Young University. She received a doctorate in statistics from Utah State University. She specializes in developing statistical methods to better analyze data with small sample sizes or rare events, with her current focus on meta-analysis data.

SAM ZYGNER has been a member of the Society for American Baseball Research (SABR) since 1997, and has served as the Chairperson for the South Florida Chapter of SABR since 2007. Zygner has written for the *Baseball Research Journal*, *The National Pastime*, and was previously a sports columnist for *La Prensa de Miami*. He is the author of the books *Baseball Under the Palms* and *The Forgotten Marlins*.

Friends of SABR

You can become a Friend of SABR by giving as little as $10 per month or by making a one-time gift of $1,000 or more. When you do so, you will be inducted into a community of passionate baseball fans dedicated to supporting SABR's work.

Friends of SABR receive the following benefits:
- ✓ Recognition in This Week in SABR, SABR.org, and the SABR Annual Report
- ✓ Access to the SABR Annual Convention VIP donor event
- ✓ Invitations to exclusive Friends of SABR events

SABR On-Deck Circle - $10/month, $30/month, $50/month

Get in the SABR On-Deck Circle, and help SABR become the essential community for the world of baseball. Your support will build capacity around all things SABR, including publications, website content, podcast development, and community growth.

A monthly gift is deducted from your bank account or charged to a credit card until you tell us to stop. No more email, mail, or phone reminders.

Josh Gibson

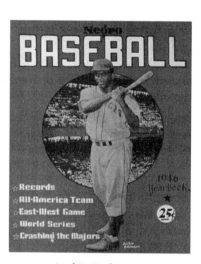
Jackie Robinson

Cool Papa Bell

Join the SABR On-Deck Circle

Payment Info: __Visa __Mastercard __ Discover

Name on Card: _____

Card #: _____

Exp. Date: _____ Security Code: _____

Signature: _____

○ $10/month

○ $30/month

○ $50/month

○ Other amount _____

Go to sabr.org/donate to make your gift online